Luxury Marketing, Sust and Technology

Luxury Marketing, Sustainability and Technology explores how new technologies, sustainability, and relationship marketing impact and change the future of luxury brand management. Whilst the luxury industry is experiencing exponential growth, further research is vital to improve knowledge and understand how luxury management operates in the new age of marketing.

Through a range of empirical and theoretical contributions, this book offers clear insights into relationship marketing and luxury management. It examines the growth of luxury, marketing strategies for luxury brands, advertising and communication of luxury brands, AI and disruptive technology in luxury marketing, and sustainability and pro-environmental luxury. All the chapters close with practical summaries and recommendations for businesses practice.

This book is a useful reference for scholars and postgraduate researchers across luxury management and marketing, including those interested in international marketing, social media marketing, and fashion management, as well as innovation management and sustainability.

Park Thaichon is the Australian most published author (marketing) by SciVal Scholarly Output in Australia over the period 2017 to >2022 and 2019 to >2022. Park's research, teaching, and consulting focus are on digital marketing, technology, relationship marketing, and consumer behaviour. He is open to research collaboration, consulting projects, and commercial research. He has been working with organizations such as Australia-ASEAN Council, the Commonwealth Scientific and Industrial Research Organisation (CSIRO), AGL Energy Ltd, True Corporation Ltd, Nhon Trach New Industry City Ltd, among others.

Sara Quach has been recognized as the Rising Star in the Marketing Discipline 2020 by *The Australian*. Sara has published over 40 A-ranked journal articles since 2015 (ABDC). Her research has been published in leading marketing journals including but not limited to the *Journal of the Academy of Marketing Science*, *Industrial Marketing Management*, the *European Journal of Marketing*, the *Journal of Business Research*, the *Journal of Retailing and Consumer Services*, the *Journal of Business and Industrial Marketing*, the *Journal of Strategic Marketing*, and *Marketing Intelligence and Planning*.

Routledge Studies in Luxury Management

This series explores the luxury industry through an interdisciplinary lens, bringing together cutting-edge research to define and advance this growing field. Contributions to the series present original research from established and emerging scholars across the globe, offering a diverse range of empirical and critical perspectives on the luxury industry. Topics include, but are not limited to, marketing, brand management, sustainability, and supply chain management.

The Rise of Positive Luxury
Transformative Research Agenda for Well-being, Social Impact, and Sustainable Growth
Edited by Wided Batat

Made in Italy and the Luxury Market
Heritage, Sustainability and Innovation
Edited by Serena Rovai and Manuela De Carlo

Luxury Marketing, Sustainability and Technology
The Future of Luxury Management
Edited by Park Thaichon and Sara Quach

For more information about this series, please visit: www.routledge.com/ Routledge-Studies-in-Luxury-Management/book-series/RSLM

Luxury Marketing, Sustainability and Technology

The Future of Luxury Management

Edited by
Park Thaichon and Sara Quach

Routledge
Taylor & Francis Group

LONDON AND NEW YORK

First published 2023
by Routledge
4 Park Square, Milton Park, Abingdon, Oxon OX14 4RN

and by Routledge
605 Third Avenue, New York, NY 10158

Routledge is an imprint of the Taylor & Francis Group, an informa business

British Library Cataloguing-in-Publication Data
A catalogue record for this book is available from the British Library

ISBN: 978-1-032-34291-7 (hbk)
ISBN: 978-1-032-34292-4 (pbk)
ISBN: 978-1-003-32137-8 (ebk)

DOI: 10.4324/9781003321378

Typeset in Bembo
by codeMantra

Contents

Contributors

Md. Abdul Alim is a PhD student in the Department of Marketing at Griffith University Gold Coast campus, Australia. He is also holding a faculty member position in the Department of Marketing at the University of Rajshahi in Bangladesh. His research interest mainly addresses digital marketing, influencer marketing, consumer behaviour, technology in tourism, and small and medium tourism enterprises (SMTEs). The mixed-method approach includes partial least squares-based structural equation modeling (PLS-SEM), which is the main focus of his research. Mr. Alim has published a number of research papers in different referred journals including the *Asia-pacific Journal of Business Administration*, the *International Journal of Agile Systems and Management*, the *International Journal of Business and Society*, the *Asian Journal of Business and Accounting*, the *Malaysian Journal of Consumer and Family Economics*, and so on.

Monica Chaudhary is currently working as Associate Professor of Marketing with S P Jain School of Global Management, Sydney, Australia. She is a postgraduate in Economics and holds an MBA and a PhD in Marketing with more than 15 years of experience in Academics, Research, and Consulting. She is an active researcher and has authored several refereed research papers in reputed research journals with academic citations. Her research area is Consumer Behaviour, Social Media, and Digital Marketing.

Isaac Cheah is a prolific scholar in the fields of consumer behaviour, advertising, branding, and marketing, with a focus on consumer decision-making across different domains, including conspicuous, affiliative, prosocial, and sustainable behaviours. He has consulted with companies, including Independent Grocers of Australia (IGA), StudyPerth, and the Department of Primary Industries and Regional Development's Buy West Eat Best program. Associate Professor Cheah currently serves as Editor of the *Journal of Global Scholars of Marketing Science* and Associate Editor of the *International Journal of Advertising*.

Narayanage Jayantha Dewasiri is a professor attached to the Department of Accountancy and Finance, Sabaragamuwa University of Sri Lanka. He also serves as the Honorary Secretary/Chairman – Education and Research at the Sri Lanka Institute of Marketing. He is currently serving as the co-editors-in-chief of the *South Asian Journal of Marketing* published by Emerald Publishing, senior associate editor of the *FIIB Business Review* published by SAGE Publishing, and managing editor of the *South Asian Journal of Tourism and Hospitality* published by the Faculty of Management Studies. Recently, he has been accredited as a fellow chartered manager (FCMI CMgr) by the Chartered Institute of Management, UK. Considering his valuable contribution to research and academia, Emerald Publishing, UK has appointed him as the Brand Ambassador for its South Asian region.

Lars-Erik Casper Ferm is a current PhD student at the University of Queensland Business School. His research focuses on value cocreation, digital marketing, privacy, and AI. He has had his research published in leading marketing journals such as the *Journal of Retailing and Consumer Services* and the *Journal of Global Scholars of Marketing Science*.

Tusher Ghosh is a promising young researcher. He received significant experience as a research assistant in various research projects in Bangladesh. He has published a number of scientific articles in different referred journals.

Nicolas Hamelin is an associate professor and director of SPJAIN neuroscience lab in Sydney and a research associate in the Department of Journalism and Mass Communication at the American University in Cairo. He holds a PhD in Physics from Sussex University in the UK, an MSc in Environmental Management from Ulster University, and a PhD in Business at the Royal Docks Business School, University of East London. In Hong Kong, he worked as a photojournalist for Window, Elle, and Virgin. He later trained as a TV news reporter at INA, Paris, and worked for TV-Grenoble as a local news reporter. Previously, he was a research fellow for the City University of Hong Kong, the Foundation for Fundamental Research on Matter, and the Energy Center of the Netherlands. Hamelin served as an assistant professor in the School of Business at Al Akhawayn University in Ifrane, Morocco, and Franklin University in Switzerland. He is the director of the SPJAIN neuroscience lab in Sydney. His main research interests are in the fields of Social Marketing, Social Media, Neuromarketing, PR, and environmental management.

Reyhane Hooshmand is a research assistant (RA) and teaching assistant (TA) in marketing. She has expertise in conducting marketing and consumer sustainable behaviour research.

Nirma Sadamali Jayawardena is an assistant professor in O P Jindal Global University, India. She completed her Graduate Diploma of Business Research and PhD in Marketing from Griffith University, Australia. Further, she completed her BSc in Business Management (first-class honours) from NSBM Green University, Sri Lanka and MBA in International Business from the University of Colombo, Sri Lanka. Her research interests include consumer psychology, consumer social cognition, digital video advertising, and experimental research. She has published her research in leading journals such as *Industrial Marketing Management*, the *Journal of Business Research*, *Technological Forecasting and Social Change*, the *Journal of Global Information Management*, the *Journal of Strategic Marketing*, the *Asia Pacific Journal of Marketing and Logistics*, *Production Planning and Control*, *Young Consumers*, the *International Journal of Educational Management*, and the *Journal of Electronic Commerce in Organizations*.

Ting Jin has worked in the education industry for a few years. She received her PhD in marketing degree from Griffith University in 2021. She is currently a marketing and business trainer and a learning resource developer at Entrepreneur Education. Her principal research interests lie in the broader fields of consumer behaviour, consumer psychology, luxury marketing, experiential marketing, and brand management.

Joo Hee Kim is a current student in a Graduate Research Diploma in Business Research Methods in the Marketing discipline at The University of Queensland (UQ). She completed a Bachelor's degree in Business Management at UQ in 2019 and a Master's degree in Marketing Management from Australian National University (ANU) in 2021.

Cecilia Lindh, PhD, is Associate Professor in Marketing and lectures mainly in business research methods, marketing, and international business. Her research concerns the digital transformation of business relationships within industrial, or B2B markets, as well as consumer-orientated markets. Current research topics involve (1) changing interaction patterns and business creation as a consequence of increased digitalization use within B2B relationships, and (2) influencers in marketing and online purchasing.

Nadezhda Lisichkova is a freelance marketing and IT consultant. Her research and consulting focus on digital and relationship marketing, with an emphasis on influencer marketing and technology. Other research areas include female entrepreneurship and networking.

Udgam Mishra is currently working as Assistant Professor at Tribhuvan University. He has completed his MPhil and currently pursuing PhD in Marketing.

Charitha Harshani Perera is a lecturer in Marketing at the Department of Marketing, Operations, and Systems at the Northumbria University, United Kingdom. She obtained her PhD in Business specializing in Marketing Communication with recognition for outstanding work from RMIT University, Australia. Prior to joining academia, she held a marketing management role, and she has built a broad area of expertise across the marketing discipline. She has been accredited as an associate member (ACIM) by the Charted Institute of Marketing, United Kingdom. Her research has been published in several journals such as the *Journal of Marketing Communication* and the *Journal of Marketing for Higher Education*, and she has published a book with a reputed publisher, Springer. She attended a range of international conferences in several countries and held positions such as conference co-chair, session chair, and scientific committee member. She is serving as a reviewer of reputed journals in the area of marketing. She is collaborating with several international universities and working with many researchers on several different projects.

Felix Septianto is a marketing scholar who primarily investigates the influence of feelings and emotions on consumer decision-making across different domains, including ethical, prosocial, and sustainable behaviours. He currently holds a senior lecturer position at The University of Queensland (UQ) and a research fellowship from the Australian Research Council (ARC DECRA). Felix has (co-)authored more than 90 journal articles, which are published in outlets ranked A* or A (highest and second highest) by the Australian Business Deans Council (ABDC).

Wei Shao is a lecturer in Marketing at Griffith University, Gold Coast, Australia. Her research interests include branding, social media marketing, and corporate apology. She is published in journals such as *Journal of Retailing and Consumer Services* and *European Journal of Marketing*.

Sara Shawky is Lecturer and Research Fellow at Griffith University. Her research interests focus on digital media, behaviour change, and relationship marketing. Her work is published in leading peer-reviewed journals, including the *Journal of Business Research*, the *International Journal of Market Research*, the *Australasian Journal of Environmental Management*, the *Journal of Social Marketing*, and *Health Marketing Quarterly*. She endeavours to leverage her industry experience in leading the development of communication campaigns for FMCGs (e.g., Nestle and Kraft foods), investment banking, and real estate, and working for companies including Ogilvy and Mather company, EFG Hermes, LJ Hooker, and Harcourts to offer theoretical knowledge that would serve practical application.

Anwar Sadat Shimul, PhD, is a senior lecturer at the School of Management and Marketing, Curtin University, Australia. His research interests include luxury branding, consumer behaviour and consumer-brand relationship. His research work got published in the *Journal of Brand Management, Psychology & Marketing*, the *Journal of Strategic Marketing, Appetite,*

Marketing Intelligence & Planning, and several other ABDC-ranked journals. Shimul is serving as the associate editor for the *Asia Pacific Journal of Marketing and Logistics* (APJML) and the *Journal of the Global Scholar of Marketing Scholars* (JGSMS).

Billy Sung is an award-winning Associate Professor at the School of Management and Marketing, Curtin University. He specializes in consumer research, neuromarketing, and consumer biometrics, consulting for many local, international, and multinational industry partners. His research to date has been based on the study of emotion and the application of psychophysiological methodologies in multiple disciplines including psychology, marketing, health, nursing, and robotics.

Kevin Teah is an early-career researcher. His research interests are in Corporate Social Responsibility in luxury brands and financial services, psychophysiological methods, advertising appeals, consumer behaviour and psychology, and food consumption. His previous professional experience spans the following sectors: Banking and Commerce, IT, Hospitality, and Marketing.

Scott Weaven is a professor and head of the Department of Marketing at the Griffith Business School. He has a PhD on asymmetric marketing exchange relationships and firm performance, and has active research interests in relationship marketing, 'big data', and behavioural aspects of consumers and sellers in offline and online contexts. His research has been published in various national and international journals including the *Journal of the Academy of Marketing Science*, the *Journal of Retailing*, the *European Journal of Marketing*, the *Journal of Small Business Management*, the *Journal of International Marketing,* and the *International Small Business Journal*. Professor Weaven's recent research has focused on examining digital, relational, and hybridized methods of international market entry, e-commerce and encroachment issues in franchise systems, hybrid sales structures, online relationship marketing, and consumer sentiment analysis and market segmentation in a variety of business contexts.

1 Luxury Marketing and Sustainability in the South Asian Context

Nirma Sadamali Jayawardena, Sara Quach, Charitha Harshani Perera, Park Thaichon, and Narayanage Jayantha Dewasiri

1.1 Introduction

There has been an increasing amount of criticism directed at luxury brands for their lack of transparency in their supply chains, as well as accusations that they exploit animals and workers (Dekhili & Achabou, 2016; Athwal et al., 2019; Kapferer, 2017), creating growing tensions among luxury brands. Therefore, the luxury industry is slowly recognizing its responsibilities and opportunities in sourcing, manufacturing, and marketing sustainable products (Wells et al., 2021). Due to the widespread reach of luxury goods consideration of social issues is particularly important in this sector (Athwal et al., 2019), for example, fashion, vehicles, tourism, food, liquor, and fine arts (D'Arpizio & Levato, 2017; Donvito et al., 2020).

A luxury item, when compared to a non-luxury item, indicates superior quality, uniqueness, and a degree of sophistication (Dekhili & Achabou, 2016). In recent years, consumer activists have criticized luxury brands for not being transparent with sustainable business practices by accusing them of exploiting both animal and human rights while operating within the industry (Dekhili & Achabou, 2016; Kapferer & Michaut-Denizeau, 2020). Some examples include the usage of animal testing for cosmetics, the usage of exotic animal hair for clothing, forced labor, and unfair working practices in the Apparel Sector (Kapferer & Michaut-Denizeau, 2017).

Sustainability in consumption is defined as "meeting basic needs without jeopardizing future generations' needs" (Bossink, 2002). The luxury sector has seen an increase in interest in sustainability among brand managers, scholars, policymakers, journalists, and academics (Ghosh & Varshney, 2013; Dekhili & Achabou, 2016).

In South Asian culture, luxury is used to refer to a trademark, expensive product, or higher-end foreign brands (Jain, 2022). When considering luxury retail brands, prior to the pandemic almost 30% of the luxury marketing was located outside the home countries of the consumers in South Asia (Achille & Zipser, 2020). The local population did not consume many luxury goods (Ghosh & Varshney, 2013; Dekhili & Achabou, 2016). This led to

DOI: 10.4324/9781003321378-1

many companies catering to tourists rather than to locals (Prokopec, 2022). COVID-19 is causing marketers to focus on how to cater to local consumers who can spend more money because they are unable to travel (Prokopec, 2022). A luxury marketer must consider how to motivate local clientele to spend locally rather than plan their purchases for travel (Prokopec, 2022).

In terms of the second shift, it is about how luxury brands are engaging with their wealthy customers through digital channels (Ranfagni & Ozuem, 2022). It was identified that Western counterparts are slow in moving at the same pace as their eastern counterparts with regard to digital savvy (Prokopec, 2022). Singapore became a regional hub in the third shift (Prokopec, 2022) even though Japan used to be the first luxury market in the last decade (Isozaki & Donzé, 2022). Most luxury companies have their headquarters in Hong Kong, but after that, China became one of their most important markets to compete in (Isozaki & Donzé, 2022; Henninger et al., 2017). It has become evident, however, that Southeast Asia has become increasingly important, especially with the growth of markets such as Indonesia, Thailand, Vietnam, and most recently the Philippines (Prokopec, 2022). There are a growing number of luxury brands opening stores there and tapping into that niche market which historically has been the domain of affluent consumers who travel and also a change in behavior in those markets that are experiencing more local consumption and growth (Prokopec, 2022). One such example is the relocation of L'Oreal's headquarters from Hong Kong to Singapore.

The remaining sections are structured as follows. Section 1.2 provides the importance of luxury marketing and sustainability-related research by categorizing existing studies. Considering how significant the luxury industry is globally, sustainable luxury is gaining more power among luxury firms and academic research institutions as a concept that has a lot of potential (Ranfagni & Ozuem, 2022). In addition to skill, quality, and endurance, luxury is also environmentally friendly. Luxury has recently been mass-marketed (Kapferer & Michaut-Denizeau, 2017), possibly weakening its compatibility with sustainability in the South Asian Context. Section 1.3 explicates the implementations of luxury marketing and sustainability practices in the South Asian context by considering the existing research work.

1.2 Overview of the Luxury Marketing and Sustainability-Related Practices in the South Asian Context

Scholars in South Asia have focused more attention on corporate social responsibility (CSR) and sustainable activities mainly due to the reasons of climate change, declining natural diversity, and scarcity of natural resources (Dhaliwal et al., 2020). Several published literature reviews have addressed topics as diverse as the association between corporate social and sustainable engagement and financial performance to structure and foster this emerging research field on luxury brand marketing and sustainability (Sun et al., 2021; Testa et al., 2021). It has been reported that several literature reviews were published on topics such as the relationship between CSR and financial performance (Margolis & Walsh, 2003), while more focus on consumer engagement and the impact of CSR by highlighting the responsibilities of the employees in different levels of the organization (Gond et al., 2017).

Recently, scholars have begun to investigate CSR and sustainability in the luxury sector after focusing mostly on commodity products in South Asia (Amatulli et al., 2017). Further, this change was incorporated due to a growing public interest in issues such as climate change, animal testing, forced labor, and unfair labor practices (Haunschild et al., 2019) leading luxury producers to make their business processes more sustainable. Further, existing research revealed that a result of fast-moving economies such as China do have growing luxury brand marketing and it also implies that the luxury industry is facing a shortage of resources, showing the need for the conservation of these resources (Kale & Öztürk, 2016). Finally, luxury products and brands are often considered industry models in many industries (e.g., Choi, 2014). In mass markets, companies copy luxury product-related innovations, thereby influencing societal trends.

1.2.1 Sustainability and Sustainability Consumption

Sustainable development is defined as "progress that meets the needs of the present without impairing the ability of future generations to meet their own needs". The stages of behavioral adoption of sustainable development include knowledge, influence, conclusion, implementation, and affirmation. Sustainability varies according to context as follows (Figure 1.1) (Parris & Kates, 2003; Sharma & Rani, 2014).

Modern consumption not only meets private needs but also considers social justice and the environment (Sharma & Rani, 2014). From individuals to governments and multinational corporations, sustainable consumption

Brundtland (1987)	Pearce, Makandia & Barbier (1989)	Pearce (1989)
• As a concept, sustainable development is development which is designed to meet the present needs without compromising the future needs of future generations	• A sustainable development agenda enhances real income, raises educational standards, improves health, and improves quality of life for everyone.	• A sustainable society is one that tries to compensate future generations for the costs of development

Figure 1.1 Evolution of the most prominent definitions of sustainability
Note: Adapted from Sharma and Rani (2014)

Table 1.1 Recent research studies which describe the factors contributing to environmental sustainability both internally and externally

Source	Internal Factors	External Factors	Context	Findings
Fischer et al. (2021)	Behavior change and self-empowerment	Sustainable consumption communication	Consumer behavior	The existing studies focus on incremental changes in individual consumer behavior with less focus on communication science and theory
Sharma and Rani (2014)	Sustainable attitude	Economic, social, and environmental dimensions	Consumer behavior	Educating children about childhood sustainable consumption will change the future sustainable consumption behavior
Laukkanen et al. (2022)	Self-empowerment	Virtual technologies	Consumer attitudes	Consumer attitudes toward sustainable consumption can potentially be influenced by virtual technologies
Weber et al. (2021)	Sustainable products and lifestyles	International food supply	Consumer behavior	Experiential marketing tools foster sustainable consumption behavior by connecting consumers to producers
Haider et al. (2022)	Sustainable attitude	Infrastructure on developing the sustainable attitudes	Consumer attitudes	Consumption with a mindful mindset involves educating consumers and providing them with the infrastructure for doing so
Kilian et al. (2022)	Personal benefits of green consumption	Nongreen counterparts	Marketing strategies	Many recent studies focus on approaches that emphasize individual benefits (e.g., healthier, more energy efficient) as well as green consumption alternatives
Sun et al. (2021)	High-end products	Effective marketing strategies	Marketing strategies	High-end consumers exhibit more sustainable behavior when purchasing high-end goods, owning them for longer periods of time and disposing of them in an environmentally friendly manner

targets everyone, across all sectors and nations (Amatulli et al., 2017). People can be motivated to consume sustainably by a variety of factors as per a recent literature review conducted by Jain et al. (2022). These four main strategies that could motivate consumers to make sustainable consumption choices are regulations by the government, organizational-level incentives, changing attitudes through education, and management of small groups/communities and moral appeals (Sharma & Rani, 2014). Table 1.1 further presents the research studies which describe the factors contributing to environmental sustainability both internally and externally.

Many scholars suggested that the current research on sustainable consumption focuses on incremental changes in individual consumer behavior with less focus on communication science and theory (Sharma & Rani, 2014; Fischer et al., 2021; Haider et al., 2022). Further, Consumer attitudes toward sustainable consumption can potentially be influenced by virtual technologies (Laukkanen et al., 2022); experiential marketing tools which foster sustainable consumption behavior by connecting consumers to producers (Weber et al., 2021; Kilian et al., 2022) and the fact that high-end consumers exhibit more sustainable behavior when purchasing high-end goods, owning them for longer periods and disposing of them in an environmentally friendly manner (Sun et al., 2021). The attitude-behavior gap in the existing studies shows the challenges faced by consumers when adopting to consumer sustainable product alternatives.

Key Takeaways

- The term sustainable development refers to progress that meets the needs of the present without impairing the ability of future generations to meet their own needs.
- Sustainable development involves knowledge, influence, conclusion, implementation, and affirmation.
- Consumers can be motivated to make sustainable consumption choices by four main strategies: concern, rewards, and moral appeals.
- Recent studies examining the factors contributing to environmental sustainability, both internally and externally, indicate the need for research with communication theory and science, usage of virtual technologies, experiential marketing tools, and the importance of high-end consumers in sustainable consumption.

1.2.2 Engaging with South Asian Luxury Consumers While Maintaining Sustainability

Before the COVID-19 pandemic period, it was reported that 30% of luxury products were happening beyond the home country of the consumer (Prokopec, 2022). For example, many luxury brands were targeting foreign consumers rather than local consumers (Prokopec, 2022). Following the

COVID-19 pandemic, marketers have had to adapt their marketing strategies to attract local consumers with extra money to spend due to their inability to travel, resulting in discounts on luxury brands even though they are not often used in luxury marketing. This also provided an opportunity for South Asia and Singapore to turn into a hub for the Asian region (Amatulli et al., 2017; Ghosh & Varshney, 2013; Jain, 2022).

Most luxury companies had their headquarters in Hong Kong until China became a giant and crucial market for them (Ghosh & Varshney, 2013; Jain, 2022). Gradually, with time, this changed into Southeast Asia becoming much more important with rapidly developing countries such as Indonesia, Thailand, Vietnam, and recently, the Philippines marketing luxury products to consumers who were among the top group of travelers in previous times (Prokopec, 2022). Markets with a greater degree of local consumption and growth are experiencing a change in behavior such as the growth of the hub of Singapore. For example, L'Oréal, for instance, shifted its headquarters to Singapore from Hong Kong (Prokopec, 2022).

While Non-Asian context-based research has focused on sustainable supply chain practices, it has not fully explored how luxury firms manage and design sustainable supply chains within the South Asian context (Sharma & Rani, 2014; Fischer et al., 2021; Jain, 2022). Additionally, sustainability offered firms a chance to differentiate their products from their competitors (Sharma & Rani, 2014; Fischer et al., 2021).

As part of the luxury market battle, there are not only economic and financial issues (customers, market share, sales, and profits) but also sustainable initiatives that meet the needs and expectations of new customers (Brandão & Cupertino de Miranda, 2022). According to Ko, Costello and Taylor (2019), luxury products may be attributed to developed markets, but their demand has significantly increased in emerging markets such as China, India, and the Middle East. It was reported in 2013 that the brand Hermès received negative publicity following Greenpeace's publication of the Fashion Duel results, a campaign aimed at raising awareness of fashion's detrimental effects on the environment, biodiversity, and humanity, and urging the luxury fashion industry to cease using hazardous chemicals (Mauer, 2014). However, the company was able to survive and still be successful with sales in Asia (especially China) with nearly 50% of the sales being made for colorful silk shawls and luxurious handbags. Known for its leather handbags and silk scarves that can be purchased for between £4,000 and £20,000 on the Hermès website, the Parisian firm stated that sales in its Asian business, including China and Korea, increased 47% in the last three months of 2020, compensating for the loss of sales during the Coronavirus outbreak earlier in the year (Wood, 2021).

Similarly, there are many instances of luxury marketing becoming successful in South Asia by balancing both profits and sustainability practices (Wood, 2021). Additionally, the brand Hermès renovated stores in Paris, Istanbul, and Brisbane, and opened new stores in Tokyo, Zurich, Detroit, and Miami (Wood, 2021). Further, it was reported that the brand Hermès fulfilled the two main sustainability practices of adopting high-quality materials and consumer-oriented marketing (Wei, 2022). This further illustrated, the ability of the brand Hermès in becoming consumer-oriented by viewing its marketing strategy from the perspective of the consumer (Wei, 2022).

Gucci, for example, reduces chromium and other hazardous chemicals in its leather tanning processes (this brand has a policy approved by Canopy Style) (Paul, 2022). As part of its "Gucci Off the Grid" circular line, Gucci uses some more eco-friendly materials (Paul, 2022). Also, China is popular for the green fashion brand "Icicle", which caters toward more sustainability by using natural fabrics made of natural yarns such as cashmere, linen, wool, and silk specifically using a brand slogan carrying "Made in Earth" (ICICLE, 2022). Similarly, the Indian luxury handloom clothing brand "No Nasties" followed this practice by using materials that are environmentally friendly by maintaining the brand as a vegan clothing brand with organic cotton (Sengupta & Sengupta, 2020).

Key Takeaways

- Historically, luxury consumers in South Asia used to travel to developed countries due to the lack of available luxury brands in the South Asian market. Due to the travel restrictions of the COVID-19 pandemic leads travelers to stay in their home countries and enjoy the existing brand outlets in their country (for example brand Hermès). This made a significant decrease in demand for luxury brands in developed countries and the new luxury brand outlets slowly started opening up in the South Asian context.
- Markets with a greater degree of local consumption and growth are experiencing a change in behavior such as the growth of the hub of Singapore. For example, L'Oréal, for instance, shifted its headquarters to Singapore from Hong Kong.
- The concern for more research is also raised in the South Asian context of luxury marketing. While Non-Asian context-based research has focused on sustainable supply chain practices, it has not fully explored how luxury firms manage and design sustainable supply chains within the South Asian context.
- Many instances of luxury marketing becoming successful in South Asia by balancing both profits and sustainability practices are the high-quality materials and consumer-oriented marketing of brands such as Hermès, Gucci, Icicle, and No Nasties.

1.2.3 Combining Sustainability Consumption with Luxury Marketing in the South Asian Context

Luxury products are traditionally consumed for purposes such as hedonism, higher quality standards, and unique features (Kumar et al., 2022). Sustainability in luxury sectors must also be approached cautiously (Kumar et al., 2022). A luxury context lacks clarity on what sustainability means in general (Wei, 2022). The perception of sustainable products is that they are not compatible with luxury products, which are seen as a result of aesthetics (Niinimäki, 2022). When considering luxury fashion items, the state of sustainability is found to be irrelevant in marketing the products (Niinimäki, 2022). A micro level of research indicates that consumers are pushing back against sustainable luxury products. There is a misconception among consumers that ethical/sustainable luxury products are of lower quality, as demonstrated by Achabou et al. (2022).

As consumption becomes more sustainable and buying behaviors become more eco-friendly, consumers are increasingly aware of their impact on the environment (Achabou et al., 2022). Most luxury brands have taken advantage of consumers' growing concerns about the impact of their consumption choices to sustain such consumption (e.g., Achabou et al., 2022). Conversely, Kapferer (2010) found that due to increasing consumer interest in sustainability issues, luxury and sustainability are convergent since both focus on rarity and high quality. Scholarly research has suggested that sustainable luxury branding and consumption may not have a negative meaning (e.g., in Achabou et al., 2022), although can provide the same product quality standards while preserving the environmental standards. LVMH and Kering are two of the few luxury sector organizations which frequently disclose sustainable practices with the company by considering it as a major element for brand reputation (Adamska, 2019).

Key Takeaways

- Several factors influence people's desire to consume luxury products, such as conspicuous consumption, hedonism, quality, uniqueness, and durability.
- Several gaps were identified within the luxury marketing literature such as the state of sustainability being irrelevant when marketing luxury fashion items.
- There has been a pushback on sustainable luxury products at a micro level, and consumers assume ethical/sustainable luxury products are of lower quality.

The following Figure 1.2 illustrates the overview of luxury marketing and sustainability-related practices in the South Asian Context.

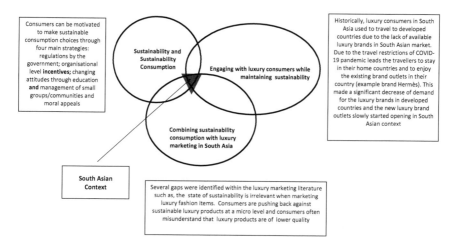

Figure 1.2 The overview of luxury marketing and sustainability-related practices in the South Asian Context.

1.3 Implications of Luxury Marketing and Sustainability Practices in the South Asian Context

The authors identified three broad practical implications for future researchers, policymakers, and administration bodies. First, the possibility of introducing innovation into luxury brands and products through sustainability needs to be focused on international perspectives such as cross-cultural differences among consumers in eastern and western counterparts. Brand experiences play a crucial role in connecting customers emotionally and hedonically with luxury organizations (Dion & Arnould, 2011). The global luxury market has significant differences between consumers in the Global North and the Global South (Ho & Wong, 2022). To examine how sustainable luxury consumption decisions differ across cultures (Ho & Wong, 2022) and how consumers perceive the negative effects of consumerist lifestyles, cross-cultural research is needed.

Second, sustainable activities of luxury producers focus on consumer behavior with less attention on consumer attitudes (Paul, 2022). In the South Asian context, luxury consumption is associated with ostentation, overconsumption (Berry, 2022), overproduction, indulgence, and personal pleasure, resulting in conflicts between luxury and sustainability. There are even researchers who state that sustainability does not apply to fashion items (Ho & Wong, 2022). Dean (2018) highlighted the incompatibility between luxury and sustainability; luxury values are often accompanied by pleasures, while sustainable consumption involves moderation and ethics by neglecting the fact that consumer attitude formation is based upon the likelihood of liking or disliking a luxury product.

Third, Mosca and Chiaudano (2022) proposed that luxury-brand managers do not have the proper knowledge in identifying the importance of sustainable practices in luxury marketing, as sustainability may increase consumers' positive perceptions of luxury goods in South Asia (such as lack of animal testing, limitations on forced labor) only if incorporated and precisely mentioned publicly. Hence, updated knowledge of brand managers becomes a major part of the sustainable luxury marketing process (Dion & Arnould, 2011; Berry, 2022).

Key Takeaways

- There are three broad implications for policymakers when catering to the South Asian market with both luxury marketing and sustainability practices.
- First, the need for higher consideration of international perspectives such as cross-cultural differences among consumers in eastern and western counterparts during the luxury marketing process.
- Cecond, focus on consumer attitudes during the sustainable activities of luxury producers by limiting the focus on consumer behavior
- Third, updated knowledge of the brand managers toward sustainable practices during the luxury marketing process is necessary to remain competitive as a brand in South Asia.

1.4 Summary

The purpose of this chapter is to provide an integrated review of the sustainability in the luxury marketing sector with consumer buying behavior toward luxury products in the South Asian context. The first part of this chapter provided a brief overview of the context of luxury products in South Asia. The second part revealed the concept of sustainability and sustainable consumption and the various ways in engaging with South Asian luxury consumers while maintaining sustainability. Furthermore, this section combined sustainability consumption with luxury marketing in the South Asian Context. The final section of this chapter is dedicated to the implications of luxury marketing and sustainability practices in the South Asian Context.

Key Takeaways

- Scholars in South Asia have focused more attention on CSR and sustainable activities mainly due to the reasons of climate change, declining natural diversity, and scarcity of the natural resources.
- Fast-moving economies such as China do have growing luxury brand marketing and this implies that the luxury industry is facing a shortage of resources, indicating the importance of conserving them.

- The need for research in communication theory and science, the use of virtual technologies, and experiential marketing tools, and the importance of high-end consumers to sustainably consume are among the factors contributing to environmental sustainability.
- It has been historically the case that luxury consumers in South Asia have traveled to developed countries due to the lack of luxury brands available in the South Asian market. Due to the travel restrictions associated with the COVID-19 pandemic, many travelers have opted to stay at home and take advantage of the existing brand outlets in their home countries (e.g., Hermès). As a result, the demand for luxury brands in developed countries decreased significantly, and new luxury brand outlets gradually began opening in South Asian countries.
- There are three broad implications for policymakers when catering to the South Asian market with both luxury marketing and sustainability practices namely consideration of international perspectives, focus on consumer attitudes during the sustainable activities of luxury producers by limiting the focus toward consumer behavior and updated knowledge of the brand managers toward sustainable practices during the luxury marketing process.

References

Achabou, M. A., Dekhili, S., & Hamdoun, M. (2022). How the country-of-origin cue affects consumer preference in the case of ecological products: An empirical study in two developing countries. *Journal of Strategic Marketing*, 1–17. doi.org/10.1080/0965254X.2021.2004207.

Achille, A., & Zipser, D. A. (2020). Perspective for the luxury-goods industry during—And after—Coronavirus. Retrieved from: https://www.mckinsey.com/industries/retail/our-insights/a-perspective-for-the-luxury-goods-industry-during-and-after-coronavirus. Accessed 15th October 2022.

Adamska, M. (2019). The positioning of the four most valuable luxury fashion brands – 2019 update. BrandStruck. Available at: https://brandstruck.co/blog-post/positioning-three-valuable-luxury-fashion-brands/. Accessed 8th May 2022.

Amatulli, C., De Angelis, M., Costabile, M., & Guido, G. (2017). *Sustainable luxury brands: Evidence from research and implications for managers*. Springer.

Athwal, N., Wells, V. K., Carrigan, M., & Henninger, C. E. (2019). Sustainable luxury marketing: A synthesis and research agenda. *International Journal of Management Reviews*, 21(4), 405–426.

Berry, C. J. (2022). The history of ideas on luxury in the early modern period. In *The Oxford handbook of luxury business* (p. 21). Oxford University Press.

Bossink, B. A. (2002). The development of co-innovation strategies: Stages and interaction patterns in interfirm innovation. *R&D Management*, 32(4), 311–320.

Brandão, A., & Cupertino de Miranda, C. (2022). Does sustainable consumption behaviour influence luxury services purchase intention? *Sustainability*, 14(13), 7906.

Choi, T. M. (2014). Luxury fashion branding: Literature review, research trends, and research agenda. In Choi, T. M. (ed.), (1st ed.), *Fashion branding and consumer science: Scientific models* (pp. 7–28). Springer. D'Arpizio, C., & Levato, F. (2017). The millennial state of mind. Bain & Company. Available at: https://www. bain. com/insights/the-millennial-state-of-mind/. Accessed 23rd April 2018.

Dean, A. (2018). Everything is wrong: A search for order in the ethnometaphysical chaos of sustainable luxury fashion. Retrieved from: http://www. fashionstudiesjournal.org/5-essays/2018/2/25/everything-is-wrong-a-search-for-order-in-the-ethnometaphysical-chaos-of-sustainable-luxury-fashion.Accessed 14th October 2022.

Dekhili, S. & Achabou, M.A. (2016). Is it beneficial for luxury brands to embrace CSR practices? In celebrating America's pastimes: Baseball, Hot Dogs, Apple Pie and Marketing? *Proceedings of the Academy of Marketing Science, Florida*, 18–21 May.

Dhaliwal, A., Singh, D. P., & Paul, J. (2020). The consumer behavior of luxury goods: A review and research agenda. *Journal of Strategic Marketing*, 28, 1–27.

Dion, D., & Arnould, E. (2011). Retail luxury strategy: Assembling charisma through art and magic. *Journal of Retailing*, 87(4), 502–520.

Donvito, R., Aiello, G., Grazzini, L., Godey, B., Pederzoli, D., Wiedmann, K. P.,… & Siu, N. Y. M. (2020). Does personality congruence explain luxury brand attachment? The results of an international research study. *Journal of Business Research*, 120, 462–472.

Fischer, D., Reinermann, J. L., Mandujano, G. G., DesRoches, C. T., Diddi, S., & Vergragt, P. J. (2021). Sustainable consumption communication: A review of an emerging field of research. *Journal of Cleaner Production*, 300, 126880.

Ghosh, A., & Varshney, S. (2013). Luxury goods consumption: A conceptual framework based on literature review. *South Asian Journal of Management*, 20(2), 146–159.

Gond, J. P., El Akremi, A., Swaen, V., & Babu, N. (2017). The psychological microfoundations of corporate social responsibility: A person-centric systematic review. *Journal of Organizational Behavior*, 38(2), 225–246.

Haider, M., Shannon, R., & Moschis, G. P. (2022). Sustainable consumption research and the role of marketing: A review of the literature (1976–2021). *Sustainability*, 14(7), 3999.

Haunschild, R., Leydesdorff, L., Bornmann, L., Hellsten, I., & Marx, W. (2019). Does the public discuss other topics on climate change than researchers? A comparison of explorative networks based on author keywords and hashtags. *Journal of Informetrics*, 13(2), 695–707.

Henninger, C. E., Alevizou, P. J., Tan, J., Huang, Q., & Ryding, D. (2017). Consumption strategies and motivations of Chinese consumers: The case of UK sustainable luxury fashion. *Journal of Fashion Marketing and Management: An International Journal*, 21(3), 419–434.

Ho, F. N., & Wong, J. (2022). Re-interpreting marketings role in the study of the Asian consumer. In Brodowsky, G. H., Schuster, C. P. & Perren, R. (eds.), *Handbook of research on ethnic and intra-cultural marketing* (pp. 170–180). Edward Elgar Publishing.

ICICLE (2022). Shanghai, where the journey begins. Retrieved from: https://www. icicle.com.cn/en/shanghai-where-the-journey-begins. Accessed 16th October 2022.

Isozaki, Y., & Donzé, P. Y. (2022). Dominance versus collaboration models: French and Italian luxury fashion brands in Japan. *Journal of Global Fashion Marketing*, 13(4), 394–408.

Jain, S. (2022). Factors influencing online luxury purchase intentions: The moderating role of bandwagon luxury consumption behavior. *South Asian Journal of Business Studies* (ahead-of-print).

Jain, V. K., Verma, H., Naithani, J., & Agarwal, S. (2022). Moving towards less-modeling enablers of responsible consumption for sustainable consumption in an emerging economy: An ISM approach. *International Journal of Social Ecology and Sustainable Development (IJSESD)*, 13(1), 1–21.

Kapferer, J. N. (2017). Managing luxury brands. In Kapferer, J. N., Kernstock, J., Brexendorf, T. & Powell, S. (eds.), *Advances in luxury brand management* (pp. 235–249). Palgrave Macmillan.

Kapferer, J. N. (2010). All that glitters is not green: The challenge of sustainable luxury. *European Business Review*, 2(4), 40–45.

Kapferer, J. N., & Michaut-Denizeau, A. (2017). Is luxury compatible with sustainability? Luxury consumers' viewpoint. https://doi.org/10.1007/978-3-319-51127-6_7

Kapferer, J. N., & Michaut-Denizeau, A. (2020). Are millennials really more sensitive to sustainable luxury? A cross-generational international comparison of sustainability consciousness when buying luxury. *Journal of Brand Management*, 27(1), 35–47.

Kale, G. Ö., & Öztürk, G. (2016). The importance of sustainability in luxury brand management. *Intermedia International E-Journal*, 3(4), 106–126.

Kilian, S., Pristl, A. C., & Mann, A. (2022). Understanding and raising consumers' normative motivation for sustainable consumption. In Bhattacharyya, J., Balaji M. S., Jiang, Y., Azer, J., & Hewege, C. R. (eds.), *Socially responsible consumption and marketing in practice* (pp. 35–49). Springer.

Ko, E., Costello, J. P., & Taylor, C. R. (2019). What is a luxury brand? A new definition and review of the literature. *Journal of Business Research*, 99, 405–413.

Kumar, B., Bagozzi, R. P., Manrai, A. K., & Manrai, L. A. (2022). Conspicuous consumption: A meta-analytic review of its antecedents, consequences, and moderators. *Journal of Retailing*, 98(3), 471–485.

Laukkanen, T., Xi, N., Hallikainen, H., Ruusunen, N., & Hamari, J. (2022). Virtual technologies in supporting sustainable consumption: From a single-sensory stimulus to a multi-sensory experience. *International Journal of Information Management*, 63, 102455.

Margolis, J. D., & Walsh, J. P. (2003). Misery loves companies: Rethinking social initiatives by business. *Administrative Science Quarterly*, 48(2), 268–305.

Mauer, E. (2014). Is green the new black? Sustainable luxury: Challenge or strategic opportunity for the luxury sector (Doctoral dissertation, Haute école de gestion de Genève).

Mosca, F., & Chiaudano, V. (2022). How could well-being-centered business strategies increase competitiveness and innovation among luxury firms? In Batat, W. (ed.), *The rise of positive luxury: Transformative research agenda for well-being, social impact, and sustainable growth* (1st ed.). Routledge. https://doi.org/10.4324/9781003163732

Niinimäki, K. (2022). Sustainable eco-luxury in the Scandinavian context. In: Henninger, C. E., & Athwal, N. K. (eds.) *Sustainable luxury: An international perspective* (pp. 35–57). Springer International Publishing.

Parris, T. M., & Kates, R. W. (2003). Characterizing and measuring sustainable development. *Annual Review of Environment and Resources*, 28(1), 559–586.

Paul, T. (2022). Gucci, Stella McCartney and 8 other sustainable luxury brands you should know about. Retrieved from: https://www.lifestyleasia.com/ind/style/fashion/best-sustainable-luxury-brands. Accessed 16th October 2022.

Prokopec, S. (2022). How to engage with the new Asian luxury consumer. Retrieved from: https://www.warc.com/newsandopinion/opinion/how-to-engage-with-the-new-asian-luxury-consumer/en-gb/5796. Accessed 15th October 2022.

Ranfagni, S., & Ozuem, W. (2022). Luxury and sustainability: Technological pathways and potential opportunities. *Sustainability*, 14(9), 5209.

Sengupta, M., & Sengupta, N. (2020). Sustainable fashion: The issues, challenges, and prospects. *Manthan: Journal of Commerce and Management*, 7(2), 74–94.

Sharma, M., & Rani, L. (2014). Environmentally sustainable consumption: A review and agenda for future research. *Global Journal of Finance and Management*, 6(4), 367–374.

Sun, J. J., Bellezza, S., & Paharia, N. (2021). Buy less, buy luxury: Understanding and overcoming product durability neglect for sustainable consumption. *Journal of Marketing*, 85(3), 28–43.

Testa, F., Pretner, G., Iovino, R., Bianchi, G., Tessitore, S., & Iraldo, F. (2021). Drivers to green consumption: A systematic review. *Environment, Development and Sustainability*, 23(4), 4826–4880.

Weber, H., Loschelder, D. D., Lang, D. J., & Wiek, A. (2021). Connecting consumers to producers to foster sustainable consumption in international coffee supply–a marketing intervention study. *Journal of Marketing Management*, 37(11–12), 1148–1168.

Wei, A. (2022). Has Hermès' strong momentum reached a tipping point in China? Retrieved from: https://www.luxurysociety.com/en/articles/2022/03/has-hermes-strong-momentum-reached-a-tipping-point-in-china. Accessed 16th October 2022.

Wells, V., Athwal, N., Nervino, E., & Carrigan, M. (2021). How legitimate are the environmental sustainability claims of luxury conglomerates? *Journal of Fashion Marketing and Management: An International Journal*, 25(4), 697–722.

Wood, Z. (2021), Luxury brand Hermès reports 'remarkable' rise in sales in Asia. Retrieved from: https://www.pressreader.com/usa/the-guardian-usa/20210220. Accessed 16th October 2022.

2 Digital Technologies in Luxury Industry

Identifying the Future Aspects of Luxury Brand Management

Md. Abdul Alim, Park Thaichon, Sara Quach, Scott Weaven, and Tusher Ghosh

2.1 Overview

The luxury management paradigm is experiencing huge shifting due to rapid technological advancement and its usages in businesses (Christodoulides & Wiedmann, 2022). The frequent usages of advanced technologies in businesses and the increasing trend of digital interactions between marketers and customers build more opportunities for luxury management (Kong, Witmaier, & Ko, 2021). Several studies focusing on digital technologies in the luxury industry have been conducted in the last few years. These studies address the issues of online sales (Liu, Perry, & Gadzinski, 2019; Beauloye, 2022; Rathi, Garg, Kataria, & Chhikara, 2022), Millennials and Gen Z consumers (Zollo, Filieri, Rialti, & Yoon, 2020; Beauloye, 2022; Monteros, 2022), global consumption (Gong, Wang, & Lee, 2020; Atwal, 2021; Parker, 2021; Christodoulides & Wiedmann, 2022; Rathi et al., 2022), second-hand luxury market (Turunen, Cervellon, & Carey, 2020; Christodoulides, Athwal, Boukis, & Semaan, 2021; Beauloye, 2022), culture in luxury brands (Correia, Kozak, & Kim, 2019; Correia, Kozak, & Del Chiappa, 2020; Shukla & Rosendo-Rios, 2021; Beauloye, 2022), seamless shopping (Aslanyan & Pesigan, 2021; Watanabe, Akhtar, Tou, & Neittaanmaki, 2021; Beauloye, 2022; Creevey, Coughlan, & O'Connor, 2022; Watanabe, Akhtar, Tou, & Neittaanmaki, 2022), and sustainability (Karaosman, Perry, Brun, & Morales-Alonso, 2020; Kong et al., 2021; Beauloye, 2022). However, the rapid change in luxury consumers' shopping preferences and the availability of information through different digital channels make them more aware than ever before. This calls for identifying the potential aspects of digital technologies for managing and promoting luxury brands. Therefore, this chapter attempts to identify the future aspects of digital technologies in luxury management.

2.2 Identification of Future Aspects of Luxury Brand Management

2.2.1 Digital Dominance in Online Luxury Sales

Online and digital commerce has emerged at a phenomenal rate in recent years. This rapid growth of digitalization and advanced technological

DOI: 10.4324/9781003321378-2

communication redefines the luxury sector in online retailing systems and social media marketing (Ko, Phau, & Aiello, 2016). More specifically, from the accessibility and democratization point of view, the sales and marketing activities through digital channels may extend the traditional strategy of luxury brands by enhancing exclusivity and creating higher control. As a result, many luxury brands are shifting from traditional ways of offering products to digitally selling concepts through using online and social media platforms (Liu et al., 2019).

Scholars also suggest some digital aspects of branding in the luxury industry to implement branding digitally for heritage luxury brands by offering different values. This initiative may open opportunities for firms to interact and engage with more customers using digital devices and technical strategies. Luxury brands can also create an omnichannel strategy in the marketing communication process to address seamless and integrated customer journeys (Rathi et al., 2022). In this regard, Rathi et al. (2022) suggested to use advanced technology, for example, Virtual Reality (VR), Augmented Reality (AR), and the Internet of Things (IoT), to obtain popularity in promoting luxury brands digitally and asked the researchers to investigate the effects of online celebrity endorsement on the brand-consumer relationships.

The recent pandemic situation of COVID-19 formed a new pace to boost online sales for luxury brands, the ratio of online sales was approximately doubled from 12% in 2019 to 22% in 2021, and it climbed up to $70.1 billion (Beauloye, 2022). Online sales of luxury brands continue to outplay the other sales channels in all industries in 2022 as the growth of online sales in all categories of luxury brands is evident. Digital technology influences almost 80% of the luxury market globally and it is expected that online sales in this sector will rise to 20% of all transactions by 2025 (McKinsey & Company, 2018). Therefore, greater marketing budgets and exclusive collections should be distributed to avail the support in terms of infrastructure for generating greater online sales. It is also reported that about 500 million consumers will be considered luxury fashion consumers by 2030 (D'Arpizio, Levato, Kamel, & de Montgolfier, 2017). Hence, online sales may have the opportunity to overpasses the other channels and generate the most revenue in the field of luxury brands. For example, by making a closer relationship with Alibaba, Richemont, a Swiss luxury brand, will be largely reliant on Alibaba for distributing its product to the largest marketplace of luxury brands and will consider views sales as transactions to enhance reach, revenues, traffic, and more (Selvanathan, 2021).

The Kering, a world-renowned French luxury company, can be an ideal example that the company has experienced continued growth of online sales at a rapid rate of 55% in 2021. And, in terms of geographical points of view, Asia-Pacific and North America achieved the highest growth rate of 101.9% in online sales (Kering, 2022). In addition, Farfetch received strength in using technology and has proficiency in brand coordination (Fernandez, 2020) where the company is expected to advance the luxury industry through digitalization by introducing new luxury retail stores (Roulet, 2020) to integrate both physical and digital entities.

Key Takeaways

- More investment is required to make a successful online management team where a talented media content specialist and Chief Data Officer can be recruited to develop a successful strategy on digital platforms (Liu et al., 2019).
- Luxury managers should relook to connect consumption with the changing behavior of consumers (Rathi et al., 2022).
- Luxury managers also should pay more attention to both offline and online channels (omnichannel) to understand the indulgent experience of consumers while shopping, particularly in multi-brand stores (Desmichel & Kocher, 2020).
- Managers need to modify their conventional marketing approaches in a more unique way on online platforms by making storytelling content and by interacting with consumers more actively to enhance the desirability of the brand in their minds (Liu et al., 2019).

2.2.2 Millennials and Gen Z-Driven Luxury Growth

Millennials characterize a specific group of people who were born from the years of 1980 to 1995 having common beliefs, values, and experiences (Howe & Strauss, 2009). And, Generation Z represents the group of people who were born between 1995 and the mid-2000s (Dingli & Seychell, 2015). This is also called the beginning of "digital natives" using computers or mobile devices to have access to social networking sites, and it is more than generation X or Y who are popularly known as "digital immigrants" (Gentina & Delecluse, 2018). Many studies have represented them as more modern buyers who are more attracted by the symbolic means of luxury brands (Shin, Eastman, & Motherbaugh, 2017), and they are more enthusiastic to use the brands for their social status in comparison with older buyers. As expected, brand experience is crucial; thus, cognitive, social integrative, personal integrative, and hedonic benefits are considered positive predictors of brand experience. Millennials are also very likely to seek sensory, affective, behavioral, and intellectual brand experiences from social media platforms (Zollo et al., 2020).

Providing up-to-date information and opportunities to satisfy the cognitive needs of Millennials is the most crucial marketing strategy for luxury brands (Zollo et al., 2020). Young consumers consider themselves "digital" by experiencing online shopping (Jain, 2018). However, despite the upward growth of the luxury market, less attention has been given to the consumption of luxury brands by these young consumers who have inimitable qualities such as brand consciousness, high public self-consciousness, and a propensity toward less self-esteem (Gentina & Chandon, 2013). Thereby, online communities especially on social media platforms should be designed carefully to ensure learning and cognitive experiences, social interactivity, and integrated opportunities that might increase consumers' social reputation, status, and self-presentation (Zollo et al., 2020). Therefore, more scholarly attention is highly desirable to understand young consumers' attitudinal development toward luxury brands (Kapferer & Laurent, 2016).

Consumers who are in Gen Z and Millennials (Gen Y) groups are likely to continue purchasing luxury brands (Beauloye, 2022). Statistics show that respectively 45% and 32% of the global personal luxury brands market are likely to be represented by these consumer groups (Millennials and Gen Z) (Shin et al., 2017). This substantial growth will result from thriving new markets such as in Asia, and evolving consumer segments with greater purchasing power for Millennials and Gen Z (Rathi et al., 2022). Together, these younger consumers are to occupy about 70% of the global luxury market by 2025 as well as help the luxury market grow by 130% whereas many luxury brands are not explored by these generations yet (Beauloye, 2022). Thus, it would be wise for luxury brands to provide opportunities to Millennials so that they can advance their sense of the rich and complex meaning of luxury products resulting in a greater quality of relationship and consumer-brand identification (de Kerviler & Rodriguez, 2019).

Practically, Gucci has recently purchased an unrevealed quantity of space on an online real estate site named "The Sandbox" which will make a virtual arena in the metaverse for Gen Z consumers (Monteros, 2022).

Key Takeaways

- The intrinsic value would be more meaningful than the extrinsic value for this generation (Bakir, Gentina, & de Araújo Gil, 2020).
- The emotional connection to luxury products for consumers can be fruitful (Kim, 2019).
- Managers should invest more in generating video content and more transparent and collaborative ways to engage the new Gen Z consumers and also remodify the conventional strategies on digital platforms (Bakir et al., 2020).

2.2.3 The Shift in Global Consumption

The notion of "luxury brands" is a comparatively modern innovation related to a particular version of branding and is a global influence behind the luxurious consumption lifestyle (Chevalier & Mazzalovo, 2008). The exponential rise in demand for luxury goods is also attributed to growing possibilities for wealth accumulation, global exposure, technological advancements, and economic integration (Okonkwo, 2009). The global luxury industry is radically changing and experiencing colossal growth. This transformation is not restricted to Europe and the West anymore and has entered Asian markets. This lucrative industry is expected to reach a whopping $1.5 trillion market across categories by 2025 (Rathi et al., 2022). Luxury brands consequently leave no stone unturned to meet growing consumer expectations (Rathi et al., 2022). In the course of global economic and social development, a shift in emphasis is taking place from traditional Western markets to new and emerging markets, primarily in Asia and the Middle East. For some years, for example, Chinese consumers mainly stimulate the demand for luxury goods (Christodoulides & Wiedmann, 2022).

With the concept of democratization and reasonable premium price products for middle-income people, a new strategy has been innovated which is called masstige (Truong, McColl, & Kitchen, 2009), although the strategy has not been empirically reviewed in the literature. Firms could initiate campaigns that facilitate consumers' absorption processes to enhance customer engagement and characterize their online communication either through social media or self-developed websites with features that allow customers to explore and fulfill their information exploration needs (Gong et al., 2020).

For instance, over the last two decades, the Chinese economy developed rapidly and China became the third biggest global luxury market after the United States and Japan (Euromonitor, 2016; Bain and Company, 2017). Beauloye (2022) reports that for the first domestic luxury sales in China surpassed international sales due to travel restrictions in the years 2020 and 2021. Domestic sales accounted for 21% of global sales in 2021 versus just 11% in 2019 (Beauloye, 2022). In parallel, it is also observed that US domestic sales surpass Chinese domestic sales, growing from 22% in 2019 to 31% in 2021 globally. But It is also predicted that Chinese consumers will fuel nearly half of global high-end sales by 2025 (Shukla & Rosendo-Rios, 2021). Chinese affluent consumers will come back to driving the majority of worldwide luxury sales between 2022 and 2023, but things might be about to change. Therefore, while attempting to engage with Chinese consumers, managers should employ tactics that demonstrate that their luxury goods are unique, are acceptable in the societal setting and that the possessor could get social mileage via the display of such objects. For instance, a personalized and authorized e-commerce experience and planning to exploit new retail points will create an enthusiastic digital ecosystem that is already practiced in different country settings (Williams, 2020). Meanwhile, India can be the x-factor as the economy of the country is expected to grow up in the future. Similarly, India continues to experience significant growth in the luxury goods market, which, following economic forecasts, will be worth more than US $30 billion by 2022 (Shukla & Rosendo-Rios, 2021). However, while targeting Indian consumers, managers should avoid the conspicuous display aspects of their products and focus more on the uniqueness and social approval associated with their products and brands.

A recent report shows that 45% of Chinese consumers in Tier-2 and Tier-3 cities were interested in purchasing luxury goods, versus 37% in Tier-1 cities (Parker, 2021). Ikea has helped bring affordable design into the homes of modern Chinese consumers through its 37 online stores, but there is still scope for significant growth as it is well behind its coverage of Germany and the United States (Atwal, 2021).

Key Takeaways

- Luxury management needs to recognize that masstige luxury brands have allowed luxury brands to be consumed by a wider group (Iyer, Babin, Eastman, & Griffin, 2022).
- Luxury management should adopt personalized and customized strategies to market their luxury products and services (Park, Hyun, & Thavisay, 2021).
- Management can emphasize the truly exclusive nature of their luxury offerings to their customers through "select viewing" or "by invitation only" in the world markets (Iyer et al., 2022).

2.2.4 Growing Trend of Luxury Sales

Although luxury brand was considered for rich people in the previous time, this preference no longer belonged to that particular segment only (Bilge, 2015). Nowadays the opportunities are expanding for luxury consumers. Today, relatively less financially affluent people are representing a growing and significant segment of the global luxury market (Brun & Castelli, 2013). Because of the increasing demand for luxury products by relatively less financially affluent consumers, online sales of luxury products are growing at a rapid pace. Some luxury products including cosmetics, fashion, jewelry, handbags, and other luxury goods such as luggage and watches have had tremendous growth worldwide in recent times (Satista, 2022a).

With the growth of the global economy and luxury market, luxury brands sometimes require to navigate the conventional marketing knowledge "upside down" to maintain their brand value and status (Kapferer & Bastien, 2012). Therefore, it is essential to introduce specific theories on the luxury market and develop frameworks that may help managers to withstand this growth. Experiencing the rapid and constant growth of the luxury market globally, many researchers pay attention to numerous studies on luxury brands. However, it is also observed that there is a deficiency in understanding the behavior of consumers while purchasing luxury brands online (Liu, Burns, & Hou, 2013). In addition, despite the significant growth of e-commerce sales of luxury brands by authorized online sites, few researchers have studied the e-performance and the perception of luxury brand consumers that have their online sites (Kim, 2019).

The growth of the luxury industry is noticeable in recent times. In 2019, the industry earned the best-ever profit of 309 billion USD till then and was expected to reach 350 billion USD in 2020 (D'Arpizio et al., 2021). The total sales volume of luxury brands was 1.44 trillion USD globally in 2019 (Beauloye, 2022). But the recent downfall of the global economy by imposing lockdowns and travel restrictions suffers the luxury markets at an extreme level like never before. A report also stated that the sales of luxury products were in degrowth of 25% in the first quarter of 2020 and the second quarter, the downfall was estimated from 20% to 35%. This degrowth of the global market was experienced in 2020 due to the restricted mobility of physical products enforced due to the global pandemic situation (Beauloye, 2022). But this situation may not last forever. The estimation by 2025 is expected to reach the 1.5 trillion USD market in the global range (Rathi et al., 2022). Therefore, luxury management should utilize the opportunity to grow luxury businesses in a more diversified way (Beauloye, 2022). It is also suggested that management for selling in the showroom and selling in the webroom would be more crucial for the luxury goods. Thus, the management of luxury brand providers should increase the in-store and online facilities as customer-friendly as possible by clicking and collecting goods, localizing inventory, clicking and returning or trying, seeking and sending, accessing Wi-Fi facilities in store, and introducing technology-based luxury custodian services (Deloitte, 2021).

In this regard, luxury stores can offer a fully innovative experience where a new way of emotional bonding between customers and shoppers, and the brand as well can be established and developed through new aesthetics, triggers, and touchpoints (CPP Luxury, 2020). Hence, customers will get more opportunities to be engaged with the brand through utilizing digital offerings (PwC, 2020). Moreover, as the mixed opinion about luxury consumers' engagement and behavior is evident in the literature, studies also focused on pro-environmental consumer behavior, and brands' corporate social responsibility as well (Raza, Farrukh, Iqbal, Farhan, & Wu, 2021). Thus, consumers' emotional attachment or bonding can be further explored whether this attachment leads positive attitude (Kay, Mulcahy, Sutherland, & Lawley, 2022), especially toward a pro-environmental attitude in luxury consumption.

Louis Vuitton, a renowned luxury fashion brand, recorded the highest brand value of 75.7 billion USD in 2021 (Satista, 2022a). In the future, the luxury fashion brand is also expected to grow at an incomparable rate.

Key Takeaways

- Luxury management should be rapidly adopted to grow their businesses in a more diversified way (Beauloye, 2022).
- Firms should establish strong omnichannel facilities for luxury consumers (Gomes, 2021).

- The luxury management should increase the in-store and online customer-friendly facilities (Deloitte, 2021).
- The effect of luxury consumers' emotional attachment on pro-environmental attitudes can be further explored (Raza et al., 2021).

2.2.5 Second-Hand Market: Resold Luxury Is the First Priority for Many

Second-hand luxury product refers to products that were previously used or owned and the sales of these items are seen on secondary alternative channels. Generally, these items are sold at much lesser prices than the intake products in the luxury market except for antique and iconic products or limited-edition products (Turunen et al., 2020). People are getting accustomed to second-hand luxury products, for instance; personal luxury products are capturing the attention of younger consumers across the globe. A recent report by Boston Consulting Group (BCG, 2019) showed that the market of personal second-hand luxury products was valued at over 20 billion Euros with 12% annual growth in the European market.

Studies also acknowledged how luxury consumers evaluate luxury brands to show their social status by purchasing and consuming luxury products (Berger & Ward, 2010). A specific customer segment also desires to use the latest model while deciding to resell the used products. As a result, a 21 billion market of second-hand luxury products has been exploited as a new dimension of consuming luxury products comprising a growth rate of 8% which is greater than the overall growth rate of the luxury market (BCG, 2019). Selling second-hand luxury goods creates an unfamiliar way of addressing consumers' social status. The first-hand users perceived that selling second-hand luxury products is a modern way to demonstrate and display a greater status than representing as a user of luxury products (Turunen et al., 2020). However, the scarcity of insight is found in the literature on how consumers examine these second-hand products in terms of transportation and accommodation as well (Camilleri & Neuhofer, 2017).

The second-hand luxury industry is growing by increasing demand from affluent marketing from first-hand consumers which makes more circulation of economic activities and enriches consumerism with more consciousness. It is also predicted that the resale market of luxury products will be reached up to USD 77 billion in the global market in 2025 (Beauloye, 2022), with a remarkable growth rate. Some incredible features of luxury products like enduring desirability, timelessness, durability, and sometimes scarcity will make the resale market more promising and well-suited. Therefore, new partnership business models, more acquisitions, and new technology solutions may be introduced into the attractive and rapidly growing luxury market for reselling. At the same time, the authenticity and tracking of luxury products may play an important role in this rapidly growing to resell market (Beauloye, 2022). On the other hand, the supply of reselling products is expanding by creating online sending-hand platforms where a competitive approach is seen. Thus, the researchers can examine how different kinds of consumption of luxury goods affect different aspects such as the economic, social, and sustainability of the environment (Christodoulides et al., 2021). Studies also acknowledged that a particular segment of consumers is more aware of the environmental impact of second-hand luxury consumption (Rolling, Seifert, Chattaraman, & Sadachar, 2021), the absence of luxury consumers' pro-environmental behavior is also evident in the literature (Vanhamme, Lindgreen, & Sarial-Abi, 2021). These situations call to explore deeper insights into this innovative creation of product value process in second-hand renting luxury market in different country settings and evaluate the sustainability of different luxury products.

For instance, 69% of eBay luxury consumers purchase online second-hand luxury brands in the United States followed by Facebook Marketplace where 53% of the users purchase resale luxury products in 2021 (Satista, 2022b).

Key Takeaways

- The resale market of luxury products will be reached up to 77 billion USD in the global market in 2025 (Beauloye, 2022).
- Second-hand luxury products are sold at much lesser prices than the intake products in the luxury market except for antique and iconic products or limited-edition products (Turunen et al., 2020).
- As a rapidly growing reselling market, the authenticity and tracking of luxury products will play an important role (Beauloye, 2022).

2.2.6 Adoption of Advanced Technologies

The advancement of technology and digital information system open new horizons for virtual communication for luxury brands. Luxury brand promoters can be able to demonstrate product features such as the rarity of the product, product quality, and personality by using digital devices (Park et al., 2021). For example, some promotional activities like celebrity endorsement, public relations, influencers, and stories are introduced to advertise the quality features to the consumers (Chu, Kamal, & Kim, 2019). AR also becomes a new agenda for digital marketing. AR technology makes the advertised products visible by integrating the virtual components into real-time environment interactivity (Javornik, 2016). It would be interesting to see how consumers adapt to new technology while purchasing.

Advanced technologies can be important weapons for luxury goods to increase exclusivity. For example, facial recognition or the IoT can be integrated, with the customers' permission, into customers' loyalty cards and select luxury items (e.g., a handbag) and connected to the brand's loyalty program (Holmqvist, Wirtz, & Fritze, 2020). The technology could immediately alert employees when an elite customer enters a boutique.

This would heighten customers' exclusive treatment as they would be recognized in any of the brand's boutiques worldwide, rather than just the boutique they usually visit. Thus, luxury-brand managers must pay special attention to creating visualizations that convey the luxuriousness of their products to continue to differentiate from mainstream brands. Rather than using emerging semi-automated processes for creating AR content, managers should explore how to capture the exceptional craftsmanship and superior material textures of luxury products (Javornik et al., 2021). Advances in photogrammetry may be a particularly important area to consider. On the one hand, robotic service can improve the intellectual experience by engaging the curiosity of customers, but in contrast, there is potential that robotic service could be too complicated for guests to operate (Chan & Tung, 2019).

Consequently, managers need to be cognizant of the level of difficulty from robots that could affect the overall brand experience. For example, the target market of a luxury brand using such technology can be an important factor in determining such a level of difficulty. The younger individuals could be more receptive to potential intellectual experiences from robotic service than the older ones. To that end, brand managers should collaborate with experts who possess relevant technical expertise, either in-house or through external partners. Furthermore, the investments in blockchain technology, in particular, is an interesting approach to improve the authentication process from the moment a new product is sold to ensure greater traceability and transparency, track a product's sustainable credentials and tackle counterfeiting, ultimately boosting consumer trust (Beauloye, 2022). However, common standards remain to be developed collaboratively for this new technology to be truly effective at scale. But the question remains how deep the relationship between luxury's primary and secondary markets is set to grow deeper in the future.

Despite the traditional lag behind in using technologies for luxury brand manufacturers, nowadays they are acquiring integrated advanced technologies like material science, AI, AR, additional production concepts, and analytics in their production processes (Satista, 2022c). Recently, LVMH, a giant luxury company, has planned to promote the migration of brands by shared technology like AI and leverage data management system (Williams, 2020).

Key Takeaways

- AR technology makes the advertised products visible by integrating the virtual components into real-time environment interactivity (Javornik et al., 2021).
- Facial recognition or the IoT can be integrated, with the customers' permission, into customers' loyalty cards and select luxury items, and connected to a brand's loyalty program (Holmqvist et al., 2020).

- Robotic service can improve the intellectual experience by engaging the curiosity of customers; but in contrast, there is potential that robotic service could be too complicated for guests to operate (Chan & Tung, 2019).

2.2.7 Cultural Change Explore New Opportunities for the Luxury Market

Nowadays, cultural modernization is observed in most countries, and consumers are becoming more conscious of brand values (Beauloye, 2022). Consumers are also becoming crazy to prefer more luxury products to adapt themselves to this changing environment. This trend contributes to social attributes and develops the intention to purchase luxury brands. Moreover, the open and frequent access to information via the internet makes the consumers' lifestyle more elite which will increase the overall market volume of luxury brands in the future (Beauloye, 2022). Thereby, marketers need to emphasis more to the cultural aspects of the luxury market (Shukla & Rosendo-Rios, 2021).

The combination of numerous aspects, such as value magnitudes that determine the consumption of luxury brands (Correia et al., 2019), cultural behavior, and motivations (Correia et al., 2020), is still unexplored in luxury brand studies. It is also observed that the customers are more attracted to Western culture, thereby, they are fonder of Western luxury brands by connecting with retailers and marketers (Zupan et al., 2015).

For example, Indian consumers prefer Western brands like Louis Vuitton dress over the domestic brand, and there is no issue of patriotism (Devanathan, 2020). Hence, luxury marketers should focus on the fundamental components of culture and make the products the shape of a more modern outlook to attract luxury consumers (Beauloye, 2022).

Key Takeaways

- The open and frequent access to information via the internet makes the lifestyle of the consumers more elite which will increase the overall market volume of luxury brands in the future (Beauloye, 2022).
- Customers are more attracted to Western culture, thereby, they are fonder of Western luxury brands by connecting with retailers and marketers (Zupan et al., 2015).
- Indian consumers prefer Western brands like Louis Vuitton dress over domestic brands, and there is no issue of patriotism (Devanathan, 2020).

2.2.8 Seamless and Live-Streaming Shopping

The customers' desire for immediate gratification can be raised by a seamless experience (Watanabe et al., 2022). An integrated retail experience allows the customer to make seamless switching comparing different channels. Therefore, an innovative integration of online and offline channels called omnichannel is developed intending to provide customers an opportunity to experience seamless shopping in any channel (Piotrowicz & Cuthbertson, 2014). Omnichannel shopping refers to a new business model where a customer can experience the brands seamlessly through the integration of numerous channels throughout his/her lifetime (Brynjolfsson, Hu, & Rahman, 2013). On the other hand, social media platforms are continuing to develop as a more shoppable digital space where live-streaming sales with developed features motivate customers to experience seamless shopping with more engagement and entertainment (Beauloye, 2022).

Luxury management is expected to establish their exclusive selling point along with offering their products on integrated e-commerce platforms like Amazon with non-contact orientation which will help the customers to experience seamless shopping with more availability of products within their network (Watanabe et al., 2021). Seamless shopping requires the availability of products in all possible channels where customers can look for the products. So, the availability of the product in all channels consistently is necessary for seamless switching with the help of the internet dilemma in the case of luxury brands (Watanabe et al., 2021). Moreover, the effect of social media with a complete review in the context of luxury brands is yet to be addressed (Creevey et al., 2022).

As a result, the development of seamless shopping in border fields is expected to introduce a new dimension by developing a process with growing characteristics (Watanabe et al., 2021). The integration of technology with non-technological aspects could be a solution for developing seamless shopping (Aslanyan & Pesigan, 2021). At the same time, luxury management should bring flexible strategies into business with sustainable growth by integrating the developing seamless shopping function (Watanabe et al., 2021). Luxury company structure needs to be more elastic and agile in their structure with the collaboration of multi-departmental teams with new ways of working and mindsets and the management need to be assertive, quick and bold as innovation is all about taking a risk at the right time (Aslanyan & Pesigan, 2021). Although almost every brand is pushing itself to be more digitalized, the brick and mortar concept is still important for customers to take decisions regarding purchasing luxury goods and it will be crucial in the future (Selvanathan, 2021). In that case, the supra-omnichannel concept can be extensively used for every product and service (Watanabe et al., 2021). This concept may provide opportunities for customers to experience seamless shopping of luxury products through redesigning, implementing, and prioritizing (Selvanathan, 2021). Therefore, the combination of all channels in retailing in both offline and online selling will be necessary for gaining a seamless experience (Aslanyan & Pesigan, 2021).

Amazon is the best example of seamless shopping with the facilities of a complete integrated online service, fast and free delivery 24/7, digital marketing tools with full visualization technology, global availability, and an online store-to-door (Watanabe et al., 2021).

Key Takeaways

- The omnichannel is developing with the objective to allow customers to experience seamless shopping in any channel (Piotrowicz & Cuthbertson, 2014).
- Social media platforms are continuing to develop as a more shoppable digital space where live-streaming sales with developed features help customers to experience seamless shopping with more engagement and entertainment (Beauloye, 2022).
- The integration of technology with non-technological aspects could be a solution for developing seamless shopping (Aslanyan & Pesigan, 2021).
- The supra-omnichannel concept can be extensively used for every product and service (Watanabe et al., 2021).

2.2.9 Luxury Goods Marketing Strategies

A combination of innovation, creativity, technology, and personalization will be the important elements to create a successful marketing strategy for luxury goods (Adam, 2020). The functions, experience, and symbols of a luxury brand create value for the product. The meaning of brand (Oswald, 2010) as well as the strategies (Keller, 2017) meaningfully capture product line extensions (Boisvert & Ashill, 2018), co-branding (Wang, Soesilo, & Zhang, 2015) and brand extension (Reddy, Terblanche, Pitt, & Parent, 2009) more dominantly. With the expansion of the digital world remarkably, strategies relating to virtual images have become a major issue (Jin & Ryu, 2020). While offering brand values, management needs to adapt and respond as quickly as possible to the changing trends more significantly. Thus, luxury management should focus on the individuality and inclusivity of the generation that they are approaching (Adam, 2020). Adam (2020) also added that some luxury brands recognize the present situation at the survival stage, but those who are adapting to the quickly changing environment, focusing on innovation, and making complete use of the latest technologies in their marketing activities will be the ultimate survivors.

The growth strategies of luxury brands have been focused on in a few recent studies (Keller, 2017). These studies especially focused on acquisitions and mergers (Strach & Everett, 2006), brand equity and performance (Guzman & Paswan, 2009), and marketing communication (Massara, Scarpi, & Porcheddu, 2020) in different country contexts. In terms of luxury brand product categories, watches (Donze, 2020), luxury automobiles (Tournois & Chanaron, 2018), wines and spirits (Taplin, 2016), and fashion (Skorobogatykh, Saginova, & Musatova, 2014) were mainly focused in previous studies. Choi (2019) also suggested blockchain technology to increase the authentication in the supply chain of luxury brands. But these studies lack the clarity of social media strategies for luxury brands (Creevey et al., 2022). Therefore, in-depth studies are required to see the complete picture of luxury brands especially in developing market settings (Yu, Rahman, & Yan, 2019).

The interaction through digital channels with the consumers will require more intellectual strategies to engage with the customer more often. So, an online communication strategy for luxury brands creates an opportunity for scholars in the future (Rathi et al., 2022). But a question remains about what technologies exactly need to be utilized to maintain the vibe of luxury brands and to make the customer experience more reflective (Baker, Ashill, Amer, & Diab, 2018). The demographical change of consumers indicates the introduction of innovative models for business including combined consumption like renting or sharing or using reused luxury products (Adam, 2020). But customers often misuse the promotion of second-hand luxury products as many enterprises sells unsold products named second-hand product in the form of drop shipping which threatens the image of the brand. Thereby, luxury management should modify their strategies by involving in rotating consumption focusing on changing consumer behavior although they may experience criticism (Rathi et al., 2022). Therefore, an integration of all available online channels in the organization's business strategy of a luxury firm needs the engagement of top-level management (Heine & Berghaus, 2014). As a result, marketing strategies should focus on giving customers more opportunities to obtain knowledge and skills by creating a positive attitude in their minds (de Kerviler & Rodriguez, 2019). De Kerviler and Rodriguez (2019) also suggest that marketers should target consumers who have more interest in innovation and exploration like lead users, key opinion leaders, and trendsetters by whom customers may get attracted to giving themselves opportunities for self-expansion and more positive interest can be created among their followers.

A holistic approach to the new ways of luxury consumption is used in different circumstances in the product-service economy (i.e., Rent the Runway), in second-hand use (i.e., Luxury closet), in the on-demand economy (i.e., Airbnb Luxe) and co-ownership (SeaNet) (Christodoulides et al., 2021).

Key Takeaways

- Luxury management should focus on the individuality and inclusivity of the generation that they are approaching (Adam, 2020).
- Luxury management should modify their strategies by involving in rotating consumption focusing on changing consumer behavior (Rathi et al., 2022).

- Integration of all available online channels in the organization's business strategy of a luxury company needs the engagement of top-level management (Heine & Berghaus, 2014).

2.2.10 Sustainable Sustainability: Towards a More Holistic Approach to Values

Nowadays, consumers are more aware of sustainability and desire to buy products that sustain for a long time and this mindset of consumers brings a change to management objectives and prioritizes sustainability as a major concern (Kim & Hall, 2015). Sustainability is associated with ethics, moderation, and altruism (Kong et al., 2021). As consumers are paying attention to environmental and social issues, luxury brands promote their exertion to make sustainable products (Han, Seo, & Ko, 2017). Sustainable products especially fashion and luxury products need to address local tradition, diversity, and heritage (Soini & Dessein, 2016). In fact, consumers are willing to see more transparency on the social and environmental effects of the purchased products (Beauloye, 2022). Thus, future studies should focus on the sustainability and environmental issues of luxury products.

It is also expected to introduce more luxury products with new technology innovations like digital passports of the products to ensure products have sustainable credentials such as production process, materials, and origins to offer more personal value to the consumers (Beauloye, 2022). Besides, external factors like uncertain situations and the complexity of the market can affect the planned strategies of sustainability. Thus, further needs to be focused on rapidly changing circumstances by which luxury brands can reconfigure, build, and integrate both internal and external competencies to make the supply chain more sustainable (Karaosman et al., 2020). Luxury brands may acquire innovative ways for the sustainability of materials that are ethical and environmentally friendly, as luxury consumers demand. Therefore, a more holistic approach ensuring sustainability from water waste to human rights needs to be acquired by luxury brands (Beauloye, 2022). The mission of luxury brands will continue to expand beyond excellence and innovation while adapting to cultural and social change. On the other side, the increasing impact of social media on consumers will make luxury brands (i.e., fashion brands) understand the acceptability and response of consumers to sustainable and environmental advertisements on digital platforms (Kong et al., 2021). Hence, more inclusive and sustainable interaction may help luxury brands to maintain relevance and attract young consumers (Beauloye, 2022). The State of Fashion (2022) also reports that 43% of Gen Z consumers who purchase fashion products are more loyal to companies having a strong reputation for sustainability.

For example, Gucci, Chanel, Cartier, and Armani, world-renowned luxury fashion brands, are showing their commitment to making sustainable communication strategies in their marketing activities (Han et al., 2017).

Key Takeaways

- Consumers want more transparency on the social and environmental effects of the purchased products (Beauloye, 2022).
- Luxury brands can reconfigure, build, and integrate both internal and external competencies to make the supply chain more sustainable (Kara-osman et al., 2020).
- Sustainability can be used as an influencer while making communication strategies (Kong et al., 2021).

2.3 Summary

This chapter focuses on the applications of digital technologies in luxury brand management drawn from the existing literature and industry practices. The chapter mainly focused to identify the future aspects of luxury brand management. Specifically, how digital devices are being used in the luxury industry, and their potential applications for promoting and managing luxury brands. How marketers handle digital channels for smooth marketing communication, and how luxury consumers perceive these channels for digital interactions. In this chapter, every section was articulated by stressing its key concept, drawing at least one example from the industry, and developing key takeaways, from which readers can skim the key aspects of digital technologies in luxury brand management. In summary, the following key aspects were focused on in this chapter:

- The rapid growth of digitalization and advanced technological communication in online retailing systems in the luxury industry (Ko et al., 2016).
- Technology-based customized services in luxury brands (Deloitte, 2021).
- The luxury management strategies in changing consumer behavior (Rathi et al., 2022).
- Sustainability-driven communication strategies in luxury brands (Kong et al., 2021).
- Luxury consumers' perceptions, ethical marketing practices, and pro-environmental behavior (Raza et al., 2021; Kay et al., 2022).

2.4 Acknowledgment

This study was funded by the Griffith University Postgraduate Research Scholarship.

References

Adam, C. (2020). 'Luxury marketing': What's ahead in the future? October 22, 2020, available at https://recommend.pro/luxury-marketing-future/.

Aslanyan, E., & Pesigan, L. (2021). *When COVID-19 changes the rules: Interplay of innovation and crisis in the luxury fashion industry: A case study of an Italian fashion brand.* Digitala Vetenskapliga Arkivet: Sweden.

Atwal, G. (2021). 3 unexpected luxury growth categories coming to China. December 7, 2021, available at https://jingdaily.com/luxury-growth-categories-china-fragrances-winter-sports/.

Bain & Company (2017). Luxury goods worldwide market study, Fall–Winter 2017, available at www.bain.com/insights/luxury-goods-worldwide-market-study-fall-winter-2017/ (accessed September 4, 2022).

Baker, J., Ashill, N., Amer, N., & Diab, E. (2018). The internet dilemma: An exploratory study of luxury firms' usage of internet-based technologies. *Journal of Retailing and Consumer Services, 41*, 37–47.

Bakir, A., Gentina, E., & de Araújo Gil, L. (2020). What shapes adolescents' attitudes toward luxury brands? The role of self-worth, self-construal, gender and national culture. *Journal of Retailing and Consumer Services, 57*, 102208.

BCG, A. (2019). The true-luxury global consumer insight. April 17, 2019, available at https://media-publications.bcg.com/france/True-Luxury%20Global%20Consumer%20Insight%202019%20-%20Plenary%20-%20vMedia.pdf.

Beauloye, F. E. (2022). 'The future of luxury': 7 trends to stay ahead in 2022. New frontiers. Our predictions for 2022. Retrieve from https://luxe.digital/business/digital-luxury-trends/luxury-future-trends.

Berger, J., & Ward, M. (2010). Subtle signals of inconspicuous consumption. *Journal of Consumer Research, 37*(4), 555–569.

Bilge, H. A. (2015). Luxury consumption: Literature review. *Khazar University Press, 18*(1), 35–45, available at http://hdl.handle.net/20.500.12323/3250.

Boisvert, J., & Ashill, N. J. (2018). The impact of branding strategies on horizontal and downward line extension of luxury brands: A cross-national study. *International Marketing Review, 35*(6), 1033–1052.

Brun, A., & Castelli, C. (2013). The nature of luxury: A consumer perspective. *International Journal of Retail & Distribution Management, 41*(11/12), 823–847.

Brynjolfsson, E., Hu, Y. J., & Rahman, M. S. (2013). *Competing in the age of omnichannel retailing.* Cambriidge: MIT.

Camilleri, J., & Neuhofer, B. (2017). Value co-creation and co-destruction in the Airbnb sharing economy. *International Journal of Contemporary Hospitality Management, 29*(9), 2322–2340.

Chan, A. P. H., & Tung, V. W. S. (2019). Examining the effects of robotic service on brand experience: The moderating role of hotel segment. *Journal of Travel & Tourism Marketing, 36*(4), 458–468.

Chevalier, M., & Mazzalovo, G. (2008). *Luxury brand management.* Milano: Franco Angeli.

Choi, T. M. (2019). Blockchain-technology-supported platforms for diamond authentication and certification in luxury supply chains. *Transportation Research Part E: Logistics and Transportation Review, 128*, 17–29.

Christodoulides, G., Athwal, N., Boukis, A., & Semaan, R. W. (2021). New forms of luxury consumption in the sharing economy. *Journal of Business Research, 137*, 89–99.

Christodoulides, G., & Wiedmann, K. P. (2022). Guest editorial: a roadmap and future research agenda for luxury marketing and branding research. *Journal of Product & Brand Management, 31*(3), 341–350.

Chu, S. C., Kamal, S., & Kim, Y. (2019). Re-examining of consumers' responses toward social media advertising and purchase intention toward luxury products from 2013 to 2018: A retrospective commentary. *Journal of Global Fashion Marketing, 10*(1), 81–92.

Correia, A., Kozak, M., & Del Chiappa, G. (2020). Examining the meaning of luxury in tourism: A mixed-method approach. *Current Issues in Tourism, 23*(8), 952–970.

Correia, A., Kozak, M., & Kim, S. (2019). Investigation of luxury values in shopping tourism using a fuzzy-set approach. *Journal of Travel Research, 58*(1), 77–91.

CPP Luxury (2020). What's ahead for the luxury industry – Newly released "Future Luxe" book (Erwan Rambourg). September 30, 2020. Retrieved from https://cpp-luxury.com/whats-ahead-for-the-luxury-industry-newly-released-future-luxe-book-erwan-rambourg/.

Creevey, D., Coughlan, J., & O'Connor, C. (2022). Social media and luxury: A systematic literature review. *International Journal of Management Reviews, 24*(1), 99–129.

D'Arpizio, C., Levato, F., Kamel, M. A., & de Montgolfier, J. (2017). Insights: The new luxury consumer: why responding to the millennial mindset will be key. Bain and Co, available at http://www. bain.com/publications/articles/luxury-goods-worldwide-marketstudy-fall-winter-2017.aspx (accessed March 19, 2018).

D'Arpizio, C., Levato, F., Prete, F., Del Fabbro, E., & de Montgolfier, J. (2021). The future of luxury: A look into tomorrow to understand today, available at https://www.bain.com/insights/luxury-goods-worldwide-market-study-fall-winter-2018/.

de Kerviler, G., & Rodriguez, C. M. (2019). Luxury brand experiences and relationship quality for Millennials: The role of self-expansion. *Journal of Business Research, 102*, 250–262.

Deloitte (2021). Global powers of luxury goods 2021: Breakthrough luxury, available at https://www2.deloitte.com/content/dam/Deloitte/ch/Documents/consumer-business/deloitte-ch-en-global-powers-of-luxury-goods-2021.pdf.

Desmichel, P., & Kocher, B. (2020). Luxury single-versus multi-brand stores: The effect of consumers' hedonic goals on brand comparisons. *Journal of Retailing, 96*(2), 203–219.

Devanathan, S. (2020). Indian consumers' assessment of 'luxuriousness': A comparison of Indian and Western luxury brands. *IIM Kozhikode Society & Management Review, 9*(1), 84–95.

Dingli, A., & Seychell, D. (2015). *The new digital natives. Cutting the chord.* Berlin/Heidelberg: Springer.

Donze, P. Y. (2020). The transformation of global luxury brands: The case of the Swiss watch company Longines, 1880–2010. *Business History, 62*(1), 26–41.

Euromonitor (2016). 'Luxury goods in Russia.' Euromonitor International, Chicago, available at https://www.euromonitor.com/luxury-goods-in-russia/report.

Fernandez, C. (2020). What the Farfetch-Alibaba-Richemont mega-deal means for luxury e-commerce. November 06, 2020. Retrieved from https://www.businessoffashion.com/articles/luxury/farfetch-alibaba-investment-richemont-artemis-kering-ynap.

Gentina, É., & Chandon, J. L. (2013). Adolescent shopping behaviour: Different assimilation and individuation needs in France and the United States. *Journal of Retailing and Consumer Services, 20*(6), 609–616.

Gentina, E., & Delecluse, M. E. (2018). *Génération Z: Des Z consommateurs aux Z collaborateurs.* Paris: Dunod.

Gomes, M. H. A. F. (2021). *Online resale of luxury goods-The new luxury* (Doctoral dissertation, ISCTE-Instituto Universitario de Lisboa (Portugal)).

Gong, T., Wang, C. Y., & Lee, K. (2020). The consequences of customer-oriented constructive deviance in luxury-hotel restaurants. *Journal of Retailing and Consumer Services, 57*, 102254.

Guzman, F., & Paswan, A. K. (2009). Cultural brands from emerging markets: Brand image across host and home countries. *Journal of International Marketing, 17*(3), 71–86.

Han, J., Seo, Y., & Ko, E. (2017). Staging luxury experiences for understanding sustainable fashion consumption: A balance theory application. *Journal of Business Research, 74*, 162–167.

Heine, K., & Berghaus, B. (2014). Luxury goes digital: How to tackle the digital luxury brand–consumer touchpoints. *Journal of Global Fashion Marketing, 5*(3), 223–234.

Holmqvist, J., Wirtz, J., & Fritze, M. P. (2020). Luxury in the digital age: A multi-actor service encounter perspective. *Journal of Business Research, 121*, 747–756.

Howe, N., & Strauss, W. (2009). *Millennials rising: The next great generation.* Vintage.

Iyer, R., Babin, B. J., Eastman, J. K., & Griffin, M. (2022). Drivers of attitudes toward luxury and counterfeit products: The moderating role of interpersonal influence. *International Marketing Review, 39*(2), 242–268.

Jain, V. (2018). Luxury: Not for consumption but developing extended digital self. *Journal of Human Values, 24*(1), 25–38.

Javornik, A. (2016). Augmented reality: Research agenda for studying the impact of its media characteristics on consumer behaviour. *Journal of Retailing and Consumer Services, 30*, 252–261.

Javornik, A., Duffy, K., Rokka, J., Scholz, J., Nobbs, K., Motala, A., & Goldenberg, A. (2021). Strategic approaches to augmented reality deployment by luxury brands. *Journal of Business Research, 136*, 284–292.

Jin, S. V., & Ryu, E. (2020). Instagram fashionistas, luxury visual image strategies and vanity. *Journal of Product & Brand Management, 29*(3), 355–368.

Kapferer, J. N., & Bastien, V. (2012). *The luxury strategy: Break the rules of marketing to build luxury brands.* London, Philadelphia, New Delhi: Kogan Page.

Kapferer, J. N., & Laurent, G. (2016). Where do consumers think luxury begins? A study of perceived minimum price for 21 luxury goods in 7 countries. *Journal of Business Research, 69*(1), 332–340.

Karaosman, H., Perry, P., Brun, A., & Morales-Alonso, G. (2020). Behind the runway: Extending sustainability in luxury fashion supply chains. *Journal of Business Research, 117*, 652–663.

Kay, S., Mulcahy, R., Sutherland, K., & Lawley, M. (2022). Disclosure, content cues, emotions and behavioural engagement in social media influencer marketing: an exploratory multi-stakeholder perspective. *Journal of Marketing Management*, 1–35.

Keller, K. L. (2017). Managing the growth tradeoff: Challenges and opportunities in luxury branding. *Advances in Luxury Brand Management*, 179–198.

Kering (2022). Excellent 2021 performances well ahead of 2019 levels. February 17, 2022. https://keringcorporate.dam.kering.com/m/491ca96e5fc7cfbf/original/KERING.pdf.

Kim, H. S., & Hall, M. L. (2015). Green brand strategies in the fashion industry: Leveraging connections of the consumer, brand, and environmental sustainability. In Choi, T-M. & Cheng, T.C. (eds.), *Sustainable fashion supply chain management* (pp. 31–45). Cham: Springer.

Kim, J. H. (2019). Imperative challenge for luxury brands: Generation Y consumers' perceptions of luxury fashion brands'e-commerce sites. *International Journal of Retail & Distribution Management, 47*(2), 220–244.

Ko, E., Phau, I., & Aiello, G. (2016). Luxury brand strategies and customer experiences: Contributions to theory and practice. *Journal of Business Research, 69*(12), 5749–5752.

Kong, H. M., Witmaier, A., & Ko, E. (2021). Sustainability and social media communication: How consumers respond to marketing efforts of luxury and non-luxury fashion brands. *Journal of Business Research, 131*, 640–651.

Liu, S., Perry, P., & Gadzinski, G. (2019). The implications of digital marketing on WeChat for luxury fashion brands in China. *Journal of Brand Management, 26*(4), 395–409.

Liu, X., Burns, A. C., & Hou, Y. (2013). Comparing online and in-store shopping behavior towards luxury goods. *International Journal of Retail & Distribution Management, 41*(11/12), 885–900.

Massara, F., Scarpi, D., & Porcheddu, D. (2020). Can your advertisement go abstract without affecting willingness to pay? Product-centered versus lifestyle content in luxury brand print advertisements. *Journal of Advertising Research, 60*(1), 28–37.

McKinsey & Company (2018). Is apparel manufacturing coming home? McKinsey & Company, New York. Retrieved March 16, 2021 from https://www.mckinsey.com/~/media/McKinsey/Industries/Retail/Our%20Insights/Is%20apparel%20manufacturing%20coming%20home/Is-apparel-manufacturing-coming-home_vf.pdf.

Monteros, M. (2022). 'The consumer of the future': Luxury brands place their bets on Gen Z. Published on April 15, 2022. https://www.modernretail.co/retailers/the-consumer-of-the-future-luxury-brands-place-their-bets-on-gen-z/.

Okonkwo, U. (2009). The luxury brand strategy challenge. *Journal of brand management, 16*(5), 287–289.

Oswald, L. (2010). Developing brand literacy among affluent Chinese consumers: A semiotic perspective. *ACR North American Advances, 37*, 413–419.

Park, J., Hyun, H., & Thavisay, T. (2021). A study of antecedents and outcomes of social media WOM towards luxury brand purchase intention. *Journal of Retailing and Consumer Services, 58*, 102272.

Parker, J. (2021). Luxury brands review their strategy for China's tier 2 and 3 cities, available at https://luxe.digital/digital-luxuryreports/luxury-brands-review-strategy-china-tier-2-3-cities/ (accessed September 30, 2022).

Piotrowicz, W., & Cuthbertson, R. (2014). Introduction to the special issue information technology in retail: Toward omnichannel retailing. *International Journal of Electronic Commerce, 18*(4), 5–16.

PwC (2020). Mainland China/Hong Kong luxury goods market – "Get ready for the next wave". *PricewaterhouseCoopers*, June 2020. Retrieved from https://dokumen.tips/documents/mainland-china-hong-kong-luxury-goods-market-get-ready-mainland-chinahong.html.

Rathi, R., Garg, R., Kataria, A., & Chhikara, R. (2022). Evolution of luxury marketing landscape: A bibliometric analysis and future directions. *Journal of Brand Management, 29*(3), 241–257.

Raza, A., Farrukh, M., Iqbal, M. K., Farhan, M., & Wu, Y. (2021). Corporate social responsibility and employees' voluntary pro-environmental behavior: The role of organizational pride and employee engagement. *Corporate Social Responsibility and Environmental Management, 28*(3), 1104–1116.

Reddy, M., Terblanche, N., Pitt, L., & Parent, M. (2009). How far can luxury brands travel? Avoiding the pitfalls of luxury brand extension. *Business Horizons, 52*(2), 187–197.

Rolling, V., Seifert, C., Chattaraman, V., & Sadachar, A. (2021). Pro-environmental millennial consumers' responses to the fur conundrum of luxury brands. *International Journal of Consumer Studies, 45*(3), 350–363.

Roulet, C. (2020). Top spot for online luxury up for grabs. December 06, 2020. Retrieved from https://journal.hautehorlogerie.org/en/top-spot-for-online-luxury-up-for-grabs/.

Satista (2022a). Brand value of the leading 10 most valuable luxury brands worldwide in 2021. July 27, 2022, available at https://www.statista.com/statistics/267948/brand-value-of-the-leading-10-most-valuable-luxury-brands-worldwide/.

Satista (2022b). Most popular online marketplaces for buying secondhand luxury items in the United States in 2021. June 24, 2022, available at https://www.statista.com/statistics/1259090/most-popular-online-marketplaces-for-second-hand-luxury-us/.

Satista (2022c). 'Luxury goods': In-depth market insights & data analysis. August 2022, available at https://www.statista.com/study/61582/in-depth-report-luxury-goods/.

Selvanathan, S. (2021). *What is the future of Richemont, Kering and Lvmh's online-offline strategies in China?* (Doctoral dissertation).

Shin, H., Eastman, J. K., & Mothersbaugh, D. (2017). The effect of a limited-edition offer following brand dilution on consumer attitudes toward a luxury brand. *Journal of Retailing and Consumer Services, 38*, 59–70.

Shukla, P., & Rosendo-Rios, V. (2021). Intra and inter-country comparative effects of symbolic motivations on luxury purchase intentions in emerging markets. *International Business Review, 30*(1), 101768.

Skorobogatykh, I. I., Saginova, O., & Musatova, Z. (2014). Comparison of luxury brand perception: Old (UK) vs. modern (Russia) consumers' perception toward Burberry brand. *Journal of Eastern European and Central Asian Research (JEECAR), 1*(1), 1–7.

Soini, K., & Dessein, J. (2016). Culture-sustainability relation: Towards a conceptual framework. *Sustainability, 8*(2), 167.

Strach, P., & Everett, A. M. (2006). Brand corrosion: Mass-marketing's threat to luxury automobile brands after merger and acquisition. *Journal of Product & Brand Management, 15*(2), 106–120.

Taplin, I. M. (2016). Crafting an iconic wine: The rise of "cult" Napa. *International Journal of Wine Business Research, 28*(2), 105–119.

The State of Fashion (2022). The Business of Fashion and McKinsey & Company. November 2021, available at https://cdn.luxe.digital/media/2022/The-State-of-Fashion-2022-The-Business-of-Fashion-and-McKinsey-Company-luxe-digital.pdf.

Tournois, L., & Chanaron, J. J. (2018). Car crisis and renewal: How Mercedes succeeded with the A-Class. *Journal of Business Strategy, 39*(1), 3–14.

Truong, Y., McColl, R., & Kitchen, P. J. (2009). New luxury brand positioning and the emergence of masstige brands. *Journal of Brand Management, 16*(5), 375–382.

Turunen, L. L. M., Cervellon, M. C., & Carey, L. D. (2020). Selling second-hand luxury: Empowerment and enactment of social roles. *Journal of Business Research, 116*, 474–481.

Vanhamme, J., Lindgreen, A., & Sarial-Abi, G. (2021). Luxury ethical consumers: Who are they? *Journal of Business Ethics*, 1–34.

Wang, S. C., Soesilo, P. K., & Zhang, D. (2015). Impact of luxury brand retailer co-branding strategy on potential customers: A cross-cultural study. *Journal of International Consumer Marketing, 27*(3), 237–252.

Watanabe, C., Akhtar, W., Tou, Y., & Neittaanmäki, P. (2021). Amazon's new supra-omnichannel: Realizing growing seamless switching for apparel during COVID-19. *Technology in Society, 66*, 101645.

Watanabe, C., Akhtar, W., Tou, Y., & Neittaanmäki, P. (2022). A new perspective of innovation toward a non-contact society-Amazon's initiative in pioneering growing seamless switching. *Technology in Society, 69*, 101953.

Williams, G. A. (2020). Is chanel's offline strategy paying off in China? November 11, 2020. Retrieved from https://jingdaily.com/china-chanel-e-commerce-karl-lagerfeld-virginie-viard-hermes/#.X9CpLVs_rYA.linkedin.

Yu, H., Rahman, O., & Yan, Y. (2019). Branding strategies in transitional economy: The case of Aimer. *Journal of Global Fashion Marketing, 10*(1), 93–109.

Zollo, L., Filieri, R., Rialti, R., & Yoon, S. (2020). Unpacking the relationship between social media marketing and brand equity: The mediating role of consumers' benefits and experience. *Journal of Business research, 117*, 256–267.

Zupan, N., Kase, R., Rašković, M., Yao, K., & Wang, C. (2015). Getting ready for the young generation to join the workforce: A comparative analysis of the work values of Chinese and Slovenian business students. *Journal of East European Management Studies, 20*(2), 174–201.

3 Ethical and Sustainability Issues of Artificial Intelligence (AI) in the Luxury Industry

Lars-Erik Casper Ferm, Sara Shawky, Park Thaichon, and Sara Quach

3.1 Introduction

The term Artificial Intelligence (AI) is utilized to describe information systems that allow machines or software to endow the intellectual processes of human behaviors (Nilsson, 1980). Since its inception, AI has demonstrated the power of programming data-driven digital technologies to perform activities that used to be solely associated with intelligent human beings (Quach et al., 2022), such as problem-solving, decision-making, drawing generalizations, communication, perception of meaning, and reasoning (Ayoko, 2021; Balajee, 2020). Organizations have continued to embrace the adoption of AI technologies for their accelerated progress in algorithms, the internet, interconnectedness, and big data storage (Ayoko, 2021; Hanelt et al., 2021). This is why the luxury sector, and firms such as Prada (Lang, 2022), have jumped on the limitless capabilities of AI.

However, debates on the ethicality of AI have proliferated and lack a consensus on what "ethics" means for AI (Jobin et al., 2019). As AI is supposed to augment or replicate human intelligence, often AI is left to its own devices in its decision-making and has been found to cause harm, with little clarity on how an AI reached a particular unethical decision (Lawton & Wigmore, 2023). Indeed, AI bias is said to emerge on the basis of the data that feeds it and may exclude people shown particular recommendations, such as women not seeing ads for an executive coaching service (Tucker, 2019), or mistaking black models' legs as dark jeans (Steiner-Dicks, 2020). Moreso, the use of AI is often not disclosed to end users and thus their data is disseminated and used for purposes beyond their knowledge such as Sephora's Visual Artist app feature which sold customers' data to third parties without end users' knowledge (Thompson, 2022).

On a sustainability front, by 2030 AI has been proposed to reduce annual CO_2 emissions to the equivalent of Australia, Canada, and Japan combined (Herweijer et al., 2020). In particular, there is an urgent need for greater sustainability in the luxury and fashion industries which currently contribute 10% of annual global carbon emissions, but this number is rising astronomically (Milton, 2022). Between fast-moving trends and brands churning out

DOI: 10.4324/9781003321378-3

collections people don't buy, AI offers a sustainable solution through means such as upcycling, 3D modeling, predictive modeling, and sustainable supply chains (Milton, 2022). AI has propagated throughout the fashion and luxury industry with its spending predicted to reach $7.3 billion in 2022 (Gosselin, 2019) and globally add $16 trillion to the global economy overall (Intelistyle, 2022).

It is at the intersection of AI ethics and sustainability within the luxury industry that this book chapter situates itself. This chapter strives to provide readers with an overview of ethical issues facing the luxury industry in their adoption and usage of AI via the lens of transparency whilst looking at sustainability issues through AI's potential to reduce waste. Utilizing these two areas, this chapter will delve into what transparency and sustainability mean and provide case studies demonstrating issues regarding these areas. Of importance is our proposed strategic framework to address the prevalence of AI ethics and sustainability and how firms can concretely address any issues based on datasets and AI behaviors (Manyika et al., 2019) or a lack of transparency (Jobin et al., 2019). The framework is specifically split into parts to emphasize how luxury firms can take the appropriate steps to first address where AI ethical and sustainability issues may lie and how to address them.

As such, this chapter is structured as follows. First, this chapter will analyze the most pertinent AI ethical issues, firstly via the lens of transparency and the case of Sephora's Virtual Artist app feature and secondly through AI sustainability as evidenced by the case of Stitch Fix. Second, a strategic framework is proposed to guide future researchers and practitioners in how to be proactive in preventing AI ethically and sustainability issues, namely through (1) discovering, (2) discussing, and (3) disclosing as it relates to AI ethics. Lastly, this chapter will offer a conclusion and summary.

3.2 Types of Ethical and Sustainability Issues Emerging from AI Adoption

In this section, some of the most pressing AI ethical issues are discussed. Drawing on case studies to demonstrate the extent to which these ethical issues can play a role in jeopardizing values in business operations, we further identify relevant strategic solutions associated with every case. Of particular note, transparency and AI bias will be thoroughly discussed along with accompanying case studies from Sephora and Stitch Fix, respectively.

3.2.1 AI Ethics – Transparency

A key issue present in most ethical debates of AI applications is how transparent firms are in their communication of AI's role in their (1) use of data, (2) interactions with customers, (3) decision-making, and (4) purpose of use (Jobin et al., 2019). First, corporations need to be clear on how they *use* the data of customers, and in the cases of B2B corporations, how their algorithms work. For example, some companies, such as IBM, are transparent in how AI is being applied and the sources of its data and methods of learning (IBM, 2017). However, considering the case of an AI designed to read X-rays to determine cancerous tumors and save doctors time (Blackman & Ammanath, 2022). The data scientists who built the program determined the AI's detection model sensitivity should be *low* to avoid flagging X-rays that do have evidence of cancer, as not. Unfortunately, this led to the AI model being *too* sensitive and displaying many false positives, an algorithmic quality not communicated to the doctors. This ultimately led to a waste of doctors' time as they overanalyzed X-rays which the AI said were cancerous but were, in fact, non-cancerous. If the company had been more transparent, the doctors would have been able to quickly determine the presence of cancerous tumors (Blackman & Ammanath, 2022). As a result, being transparent and informing other firms and customers about the *use* of their data can, in the above case, avoid potentially life-threatening situations.

Second, ethical AI frameworks, such as that by MI Garage (2022, para. 12), state that firms, within any interaction between humans and AI, should *"be able to communicate clearly the benefits and potential risks of their products and the actions they have taken to deliver benefits and avoid, minimize, or mitigate the risks"*. However, it remains unclear what should be communicated – the *use* of AI, the code of the AI, or the laws surrounding AI (e.g., Europe's General Data Protection Regulation (GDPR)) (Jobin et al., 2019). Along these lines, Luo et al. (2019) found that, whilst AI chatbots are as effective as trained salespeople (and four times more than untrained salespeople), once it is disclosed that the customer is interacting with an AI, purchase rates drop by 75%. It is clear that users feel uncomfortable with AI interactions and clear transparency of their use is a necessity.

Third, AI can boost analytical and decision-making abilities through ML algorithms (Wilson & Daugherty, 2019). For instance, AI systems can aid decision-making in credit approval for personal or business loans using predictive analytics, but this has been found to be rife with ethical issues such as discrimination (Hale, 2021). For example, risk-equivalent minority group borrowers paid higher interest rates (up to 7.8%) and were rejected for loans 14% more than privileged borrowers (Bartlett et al., 2022; Zewe, 2022). This inequality stems from the source of ML algorithms data – that of inherently biased historical lending data (Zewe, 2022). A similar factor occurred in Amazon where an AI hiring tool, initially created to find the best candidate, drew ten years of Amazon-hired candidates' resumes to determine terms and functions that best predicted company and skill-fit candidates (Lauret, 2019). It can be assumed that prior candidates were predominantly male, and the AI thus favored those with similar qualities. Overall, the ethics of AI decision-making in such cases are indiscriminate, but the data that it draws upon is not.

Lastly, being transparent about the reasons and purpose for utilizing AI systems is paramount (Jobin et al., 2019). If the use and reason for AI's usage are explicitly stated, individuals will tend to react more favorably to its usage (Aguirre et al., 2015). For instance, the Commonwealth Bank Australia (CBA) participated in a government AI ethics framework program and provided insights into its AI solution program *Bill Sense* (Department of Industry, Science and Resources, 2022a). CBA uses *Bill Sense* to help customers determine their saving patterns and bill frequency to predict and plan their future bills (Department of Industry, Science and Resources, 2022b). Of note, CBA makes clear *what* they are providing and assures customers that it aligns with the bank's and government's ethical and legal guidelines. *Bill Sense* is transparent as it allows for feedback and uses minimal data that only the customer provides (Department of Industry, Science and Resources, 2022b). As a result, being clear on not only the fact that AI is being used but also *why* it is used is an emerging ethical consideration.

Overall, and combining all four of the above elements of transparency, we will turn to Sephora's Visual Artist app feature to represent transparency (or lack thereof) in the AI luxury space.

3.2.1.1 Sephora Virtual Artist

Sephora is an international retailer of beauty and luxury products with a 2021 profit of $11 billion making them one of the largest luxury and makeup brands in the world (LVMH, 2022). No stranger to innovation, in 2016 Sephora introduced its Virtual Artist feature in its native app which uses facial recognition to allow users to test lipstick and eye shadow products, along with their variety of colors, to then purchase them using the app (Jaekel, 2017). Specifically, Sephora's Virtual Artist uses augmented reality (AR) to create a highly personalized and engaging experience for the customer (Nikumb, 2020). For instance, Sephora claims customers *"…get virtual step-by-step tutorials customized to your own face, color match your makeup to your outfit, and compare hundreds of color swatches instantly"* (Sephora, 2022, p. 3). Thus, Sephora's Virtual Artist can be thought of as placing the locus of the luxury experience with customers.

However, Sephora has faced ethical backlash, particularly due to a clear lack of transparency – a fact expanded as per the transparency guidelines discussed prior (Table 3.1). In 2018, a customer alleged that Sephora was collecting users' biometric data without complying with Illinois state laws (Gonzales, 2018). These laws require informing customers that their biometric data would be captured, collected, stored, and used as per Illinois' Biometric Information Privacy Act (BIPA) (Gonzales, 2018). Sephora further sold customers' personal information and failed to allow customers to opt out of the sale (Thompson, 2022). As of 2021, Sephora has agreed to pay a $1.25 million settlement to all those affected – a paltry sum when compared to Sephora's $11 billion annual profit (LVMH, 2022). In Sephora's settlement statement, Sephora states it will now inform customers that it sells their data and allow them to not be part of this sale – a fact where third-party companies are

Table 3.1 Virtual Artist app and issues of transparency

Use of data	Sephora did not inform customers how their data would be used
Interaction with customers	• It was unclear what specific data was being used to personalize experiences for customers or how their data will be stored/disseminated
Decision-making	• The Virtual Artist app may impede the decision-making of customers with incorrect shades
Purpose of use	• Whilst the Virtual Artist features do mention the use of facial recognition, greater transparency in its features and why they use specific types of data are needed

purported to build consumer profiles using the collected biometric data and personal information (Thompson, 2022).

Sephora demonstrated a lack of transparency in their utilization of customers' data – in particular by impeding on the autonomy of individuals and transparency on how their sensitive data is used (Department of Industry, Science and Resources, 2022c). As the capabilities of technology are fast outpacing that of laws and regulations (Weisinger, 2022), and draw upon vast amount of data points from a large number of databases (Hollebeek et al., 2021), it is important for firms to be transparent in terms of (1) *disclosing* the presence of AI (2) communicating *how* the AI is using data provided by customers (3) disclosing *why* the AI collects particular data and how it is stored. Without being transparent and ethical in the use of customers' data, Sephora faced legal backlash.

Key Takeaways

• AI Transparency involves (1) being clear on how their data will be used, (2) how data will be stored or disseminated, (3) how data will inform AI in their decision-making, and (4) being clear on the purpose of using specific customer data
• Sephora's Visual Artist app feature was unclear how they used customer data and thus faced legal backlash
• Companies must be transparent in (1) disclosing the presence of AI, (2) communicating how customers' data will be used, and (3) telling customers what data they use to personalize their experience

3.2.2 AI & Sustainability

AI has great potential to reduce greenhouse gas emissions as well as create 38.2 million jobs worldwide (Herweijer et al., 2020). However, there are critics of AI stating that the electricity requirements of AI and its algorithms (such as Deep Learning (DL) or Natural Language Processing (NLP)) may use up to 626,155 CO_2e lbs of emissions for AI with neural architecture, which is astronomical in comparison with the average human who emits 11,023 CO_2e lbs of emissions annually (Strubell et al., 2019). The training of AI has thus been approached cautiously where a pause is needed to consider the appropriate need for training advanced AI systems in comparison to the vast environmental impact of these processes (van Wynsberghe, 2021). For example, AI data processing uses a large amount of energy that is supported by diesel-powered generators and the use of AI across all sectors is said to emit as much CO_2 as the aviation industry (Jones & Easterday, 2022). Moreover, Google's AlphaGo Zero, an advanced AI that played an ancient Chinese game of Go, whilst showing a highly advanced capability of AI and learning capacity – generated 96 tons of CO_2 in its 42 days of training, which is the equivalent of 1,000 hours of air travel (van Wynsberghe, 2021). Whilst the advancement of AI is necessary, the use of AI has given way to sustainability concerns overall.

Turning towards the luxury industry, the UN Environment Programme estimated 20% of global wastewater comes from textile dyeing, 10% of global carbon emissions are emitted by the apparel industry and cotton farming is responsible for 24% and 11% of insecticides and pesticides respectively (Chen, 2022). Further, general clothing consumption is an already devastating environmental threat, yet its sales doubled from 100 to 200 billion units a year from 2000 to 2015 (Chen, 2022), as such the sustainability of the clothing industry has considerably worsened over time. A root cause of such waste can be drawn from the fact that fashion brands simply make things people don't buy, with luxury and high street brands burning unsold stock which is in perfect condition (Gosselin, 2019). It is the fashion and luxury houses that are simply missing the mark in what customers want and are exorbitantly wasteful in the production and disposal of their goods. However, there have been vast movements in these industries – particularly with the use of AI to combat such sustainability concerns. Epitomizing this is Stitch Fix as discussed in the next section.

3.2.2.1 Stitch Fix

Founded in 2011, Stitch Fix is an online styling service that uses AI algorithms and human stylists working together to make recommendations to clients and their clothing (Davenport, 2021). Stitch Fix has built its service around recommendation engines which help users filter out items they do not want and reduces their burden of choice (MultiThread, 2022). The goal of the company is to provide clients with a "Fix" which entails the mailing of personalized clothes that match customers' requirements – which they can keep or return (Davenport, 2021). The individual then keeps (i.e., buys) the clothes they want and returns those they do not (Stitch Fix, 2022a). In other words, the customer provides their size requirements, preferences, and price range and then Stitch Fix sends a multitude of options to the individual who returns the clothes they do not want. In such scenarios, Stitch Fix's AI works by curating and understanding customers' inputs (e.g., "I want a summer dress") using NLP and their preferences, upon which stylists interpret and select the required clothes in tandem with the AI (Davenport, 2021).

Stitch Fix is a pioneer in not only personalized fashion but also sustainability. Stitch Fix claims they only partner with sustainable partners and aim to source 100% of their materials from sustainable alternatives by 2025, which as of FY22 Stitch Fix has achieved 59% of their goal (Stitch Fix, 2022b). Furthering Stitch Fix's sustainability efforts, their AI reduces the number of clothes needlessly created by marrying AI and human stylists to help customers make better buying decisions and reduce the overall carbon footprint of customers and fashion supply chains (Gosselin, 2019). Through AI personalizing fashion based on customer requirements, Stitch Fix is able to sell its stock at higher rates than the industry average and thus reduce waste overall (Stitch Fix, 2022b).

However, AI cannot always be accurate, which is where human stylists are involved and can override algorithmic decisions – as stated by Stitch Fix's engineering team *"while machines are great for tasks involving rote calculations, there are other tasks that require improvising, knowledge of social norms and the ability to relate to clients. These tasks are in the purview of humans. This is where our stylists perform the type of computation that only humans can do."* (MultiThread, 2022, para. 27) But recently Stitch Fix stylists are claiming that the AI has been pushing out-of-season clothing, is recommending clothes to stylists that need to be cleared from inventory, and not taking into account customers' preferences (Lamare, 2021). Therefore, contrasting the initial declaration of collaboration of AI and stylists (Davenport, 2021), Stitch Fix has been found to prioritize the acquisition of greater data scientists and engineers whilst their stylists are quitting en masse (Lamare, 2021). Therefore, the sustainability initiatives Stitch Fix is most known for are in stark contrast to their practices.

Removing internal human judgment from Stitch Fix's downstream outputs can result in (1) inaccurate recommendations, and (2) wastage due to recommending stock the customer does not want. In fact, Stitch Fix's reliance on AI over stylists leads to scenarios where Stitch Fix tells their stylists to *"take ownership of the [customers] disappointment, no matter the role the data played"* (Howland, 2022a, para. 6). From a sustainability perspective, this leads to stock being sent back as the algorithms are not as effective as human stylists at picking up customers nuanced requests or fashion trends overall (Howland, 2022b). This ultimately results in a negative feedback loop for the company as they send customers stock they don't want, which the customers send back, which then will be disposed of due to not being purchased. Figure 3.1 illustrates this ineffectual process in more depth.

Figure 3.1 depicts the key issues with Stitch Fix and fundamental issues that may arise. In red we can see the fundamental issues facing Stitch Fix

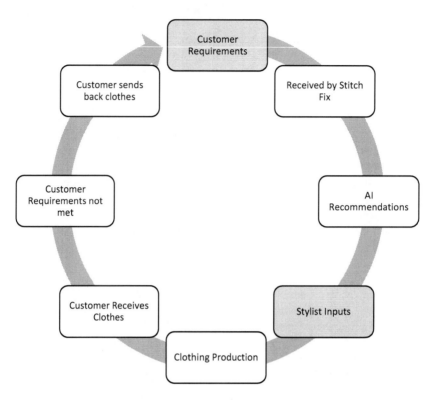

Figure 3.1 Stich Fix sustainability issues.

which would impact their overall sustainability. For instance, customers first give their requirements for what style they desire, but if ultimately ignored or misinterpreted by the AI, will lead to an incorrect styling being sent. This leads to the next point of the issue – "Stylist Inputs". It is here a human can intervene for any misinterpretations by the AI and to provide a second glance at the customers' requirements. However, if these crucial steps are missed or ignored, the wrong clothes will be sent to customers – ultimately leading to potential sustainability issues. Therefore, if humans cannot override the decisions of the AI recommendations (e.g., at the "Stylist Inputs" point in Figure 3.1), then there is a systematic breakdown all throughout.

Key Takeaways

- AI can help aid in making the fashion and luxury industries more environmentally sustainable by helping reduce wastage and emissions
- Stitch Fix uses AI to personalize fashion choices for customers which reduces

- Not including humans in the AI decision-making process may lead to greater environmental wastage as AI is not as effective in determining individuals' subtler requirements

3.3 Reconciling AI Ethics and Sustainability

The prolific use of AI in the luxury space has given way to a variety of ethical issues. When deploying AI systems it is important to determine areas where bias may occur – be that through areas such as a lack of transparency in the AI's purpose (i.e., Sephora's Visual Artist) or sustainability issues that may emerge (i.e., Stich Fix). We thus propose the below framework (Figure 3.2) could potentially minimize these issues going forward. The figure below encapsulates the ideas presented in this chapter's discussion and represents important questions that luxury and fashion brands should ask themselves before implementing AI, or when scrutinizing their current usage of AI.

3.3.1 A Framework for AI Bias and Sustainability

3.3.1.1 AI & Ethics

3.3.1.1.1 DISCOVER

We propose brands must *discover* areas where AI ethical issues may occur. It is here that firms can implement systems, build specific in-house teams or hire third parties that actively seek to identify where, when, and how ethical AI issues might arise. To aid this, management teams can stay up to date with

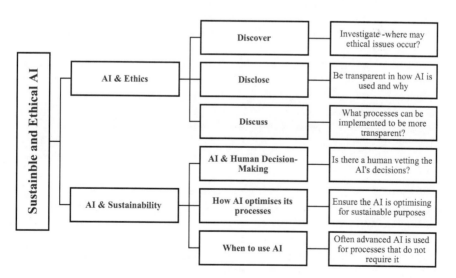

Figure 3.2 Proposed framework.

the fast-moving arena of AI research to identify potential emerging areas of ethical concerns or conduct research identifying where issues have been found to occur (Manyika et al., 2019). This can be further done through the internal education of data scientists and the implementation of ethical values within the AI's algorithms (Marr, 2022). Further, establishing frameworks and strategies to optimize the collection of customer data and ongoing sampling would be useful (Silberg & Manyika, 2020). For instance, Cosco aims to reduce bias in AI algorithms and found brands such as Nike perform well in diversity, but Chanel does not (Mallon, 2022). Therefore, luxury brands should attempt to discover any biases their algorithms may have – be this via the content they post, the promotions of new campaigns, or the algorithms they utilize.

3.3.1.1.2 DISCUSS

Next, we have to *discuss*. After the identification of areas of ethical issues, firms can discuss what processes led to this point and how to remedy this. It is important here to establish dialogues amongst a variety of stakeholders such as management, data scientists, and end users. For example, Stitch Fix has begun to focus predominantly on the data scientists and analytics portion of its business model, with a lesser focus on its stylists – it is here that incorporating employees' insights is key to ensuring ethical decisions as well as accurate outputs. For example, without feedback processes that have direct and tangible inputs from humans, inaccurate and potentially unethical AI decisions emerge – with one Stitch Fix customer stating *"…the reason why they struggle so much is that the stylists don't actually pick out your clothes. It's all the computer algorithm"* (Jake, 2022, Comments section). To avoid this particular scenario, it is important to always have a human-in-the-loop (Silberg & Manyika, 2020) who can always vet the decisions the AI makes. In terms of end users, whilst Stitch Fix claims they take customer feedback seriously (MultiThread, 2022), emerging are complaints that Stitch Fix's recommendations are inaccurate to a customer's requirements (Jake, 2022; Lamare, 2021). Enforcing this ideal at multiple stakeholder levels will create a stronger and more accurate AI learning process as it is learning within the parameters set by humans who are (1) impacted by its decisions (i.e., end users), or (2) can shift the way it makes decisions (i.e., employees), thus reducing potential bias.

3.3.1.1.3 DISCLOSE

Lastly, the *disclosure* relates to being transparent with customers about how and why their data will be used by AI systems. Transparency about the processes of the AI can help individuals take steps to ensure they are treated ethically, or at the very least, understand why they receive specific recommendations from the AI (Silberg & Manyika, 2020). Turning to Sephora, who were found selling users' data to third parties without their consent, was not transparent in (1) how the AI uses their data, (2) how AI is used during interactions,

(3) how the AI goes about its decision-making, and (4) the purpose of using an AI at all (Jobin et al., 2019). There has been a push for ML models to release the documentation of their intended use to discern what the model's purpose is as those that venture beyond their intended characteristics may incorporate biases (Mitchell et al., 2019). Disclosing a model's intended purpose may help prevent the 'mixing and matching' of ML models that foundationally have different purposes which may lead to discriminatory outcomes. Lastly, ensuring end users are made aware that an AI is using and disseminating/storing their data is important – this may be done via a pop-up warning them (a) an AI is using their data, (b) for what purpose the AI will use their data, and (c) how their data will be stored and disseminated.

3.3.1.2 AI & Sustainability

3.3.1.2.1 AI & HUMAN DECISION-MAKING

AI was initially designed to assist humans to make decisions, but it has slowly become an element left unchecked and over-relied on in businesses – a prominent issue in areas an AI operates in such as dealing with morality or general life at large (McKendrick & Thurai, 2022). It is important to keep humans in the loop and be able to override any decisions AI has made. For instance, Stitch Fix has been favoring the decisions of AI over that of their stylists, but for a highly subjective domain such as fashion, the input of a human would (1) prevent AI mistakes and (2) help the AI learn and become more consistent and ethical. It is therefore important for AI to be an augmenting tool, rather than the sole one (Meissner & Keding, 2021). For luxury brands, it is therefore important to allow humans and AI to work in tandem – thus potentially reducing the wastage of clothes and poor recommendations overall.

3.3.1.2.2 HOW AI OPTIMIZES ITS PROCESSES

AI optimization can be thought of as AI improving its capabilities via learning. For example, chatbots communicate from a variety of interactions with multiple individuals and improve their interactional capabilities based on feedback (Hollebeek et al., 2021). However, AI's method of optimizing its processes can lead to ethical concerns (such as Amazon's AI hiring practices) or sustainability concerns (such as Stitch Fix) (McKendrick & Thurai, 2022). An example of AI optimizing its processes can be seen through Google search, which ranks pages and displays results based on (1) what others click/ what is popular and (2) the user's prior search behaviors. Whilst the benefit/ risk of this optimization is beyond the scope of this chapter, turning towards Stitch Fix – it is imperative that the AI optimizes itself from a sustainability standpoint rather than that of trying to clear stock (Lamare, 2021). Therefore integrating human values into its decision-making as pure data and optimization processes should only be part of, not the sole reason, for decisions.

3.3.1.2.3 WHEN TO USE AI

AI comes in differing levels of learning. First, NLP is used to understand, learn and create language content (e.g., Amazon's Alexa); second, ML learns and adapts through trial and error (e.g., personalization algorithms); and third, DL uses neural networks and billions of data points to make a decision (e.g., autonomous cars) (Casper Ferm et al., 2023). Each type of AI uses a lot more electricity than the other with experimental NLP emitting 60% of the annual CO_2 of the average car and DL architecture emitting 500% more CO_2 annually (Strubell et al., 2019). It is therefore imperative that managers do not simply use AI for the sake of it, but to be purposeful and deliberate in determining if AI is necessary. For instance, developing and training a neural architecture would be wasteful in the development of a chatbot to interact with customers. As a result, knowing when to use AI and what type is an imperative discussion.

3.4 Conclusion

This chapter has discussed what AI ethical issues are occurring in the luxury space via the lens of (1) transparency and (2) AI sustainability. Complementary case studies of Sephora's Visual Artist app feature and Stitch Fix were provided to illustrate the importance of these issues. A framework was further provided to provide insights to firms and practitioners on how to address AI ethics and sustainability in their companies. Overall, this chapter has provided insights into AI bias in the luxury industry and provided a framework for future research.

Key Takeaways

- AI, whilst highly beneficial, comes with a slew of ethical and sustainable issues.
- Transparency is key in the use of AI wherein people who are not aware of its usage may feel violated and can also breach laws and regulations.
- AI being utilized for sustainability is a double-edged sword, whilst it can reduce environmental impacts, more complicated systems emit a large amount of CO_2.
- Luxury firms should think and discuss where in their processes unethical or unsustainable practices emerge in their use of AI – or if it is required at all.

References

Aguirre, E., Mahr, D., Grewal, D., De Ruyter, K., & Wetzels, M. (2015). Unraveling the Personalization Paradox: The Effect of Information Collection and Trust-Building Strategies on Online Advertisement Effectiveness. *Journal of Retailing, 91*(1), 34–49.

Ayoko, O. B. (2021). Digital Transformation, Robotics, Artificial Intelligence, and Innovation. *Journal of Management and Organization, 27*, 831–835.

Balajee, N. (2020). What Is Artificial Intelligence? Retrieved January 21, 2022, from https://nanduribalajee.medium.com/what-is-artificial-intelligencec68579db123.

Bartlett, R., Morse, A., Stanton, R., & Wallace, N. (2022). Consumer-Lending Discrimination in the FinTech Era. *Journal of Financial Economics, 143*(1), 30–56.

Blackman, R., & Ammanath, B. (2022). When – and Why – You Should Explain How Your AI Works. *Harvard Business Review.* Retrieved November 7, 2022, from https://hbr.org/2022/08/when-and-why-you-should-explain-how-your-ai-works

Casper Ferm, L. -E., Quach, S., & Thaichon, P. (2023). Data privacy and artificial intelligence (AI): How AI collects data and its impact on data privacy. In *Artificial Intelligence for Marketing Management* (pp. 163-174). Routledge.

Chen, A. (2022). 5 Ways Artificial Intelligence Is Transforming the Fashion Industry for Sustainability. *Matters Academy.* Retrieved November 14, 2022, from https://www.matters.academy/blog/5-ways-ai-is-transforming-the-fashion-industry-for-sustainability.

Davenport, T. (2021, March 12). The Future of Work Now: Ai-Assisted Clothing Stylists at stitch fix. *Forbes.* Retrieved October 24, 2022, from https://www.forbes.com/sites/tomdavenport/2021/03/12/the-future-of-work-now-ai-assisted-clothing-stylists-at-stitch-fix/?sh=64d1be383590.

Department of Industry, Science and Resources. (2022a). Ai Ethics Case Study: Commonwealth Bank of Australia. *Department of Industry, Science and Resources.* Retrieved October 26, 2022, from https://www.industry.gov.au/publications/australias-artificial-intelligence-ethics-framework/testing-ai-ethics-principles/ai-ethics-case-study-commonwealth-bank-australia.

Department of Industry, Science and Resources. (2022b). Australia's AI Ethics principles. *Department of Industry, Science and Resources.* Retrieved October 18, 2022, from https://www.industry.gov.au/publications/australias-artificial-intelligence-ethics-framework/australias-ai-ethics-principles.

Department of Industry, Science and Resources. (2022c). Artificial Intelligence. *Department of Industry, Science and Resources.* Retrieved October 26, 2022, from https://www.industry.gov.au/science-technology-and-innovation/technology/artificial-intelligence.

Gonzales, B. (2018). Sephora Customer Alleges Virtual Artist Kiosks Don't Inform Customers in Writing of Biometrics Collection. *Cook County Record.* Retrieved October 13, 2022, from https://cookcountyrecord.com/stories/511659209-sephora-customer-alleges-virtual-artist-kiosks-don-t-inform-customers-in-writing-of-biometrics-collection.

Gosselin, V. (2019). How Artificial Intelligence Can Help Fashion Brands Be More Sustainable. *Heuritech.* Retrieved November 14, 2022, from https://www.heuritech.com/articles/fashion-solutions/how-artificial-intelligence-can-help-fashion-brands-be-more-sustainable/.

Hale, K. (2021). A.I. Bias Caused 80% of Black Mortgage Applicants to Be Denied. *Forbes.* Retrieved October 21, 2022, from https://www.forbes.com/sites/korihale/2021/09/02/ai-bias-caused-80-of-black-mortgage-applicants-to-be-denied/?sh=1fd73f6436fe.

Hanelt, A., Bohnsack, R., Marz, D., & Antunes Marante, C. (2021). A Systematic Review of the Literature on Digital Transformation: Insights and Implications for Strategy and Organizational Change. *Journal of Management Studies, 58*(5), 1159–1197.

Hollebeek, L. D., Clark, M. K., & Macky, K. (2021). Demystifying Consumer Digital Cocreated Value: Social Presence Theory-Informed Framework and Propositions. *Recherche et Applications En Marketing (English Edition), 36*(4), 24–42.

Howland, D. (2022a). Stitch Fix to Stylists: 'Take Ownership of the Disappointment, No Matter the Role the Data Played'. *Retail Dive*. Retrieved November 15, 2022, from https://www.retaildive.com/news/stitch-fix-to-stylists-take-ownership-of-the-disappointment-no-matter-th/623132/.

Howland, D. (2022b). Stitch Fix to Close Factory, Cease Production of Sustainable, Size-Inclusive Private Label. *Retail Dive*. Retrieved November 14, 2022, from https://www.retaildive.com/news/stitch-fix-close-factory-cease-production-sustainable-size-inclusive/633503/.

IBM. (2017). Transparency and Trust in the Cognitive Era. *IBM*. Retrieved October 11, 2022, from https://www.ibm.com/blogs/think/2017/01/ibm-cognitive-principles/.

Intelistyle. (2022). Fashion AI in 2022: An Exenstive Guide. *Intelistyle*. Retrieved November 15, 2022, from https://www.intelistyle.com/fashion-ai-in-2022-what-should-we-expect-to-see-this-year/.

Herweijer, C., Combes, B., & Gillham, J. (2020). How AI Can Enable a Sustainable Future. *PwC*. Retrieved October 14, 2022, from https://www.pwc.co.uk/services/sustainability-climate-change/insights/how-ai-future-can-enable-sustainable-future.html.

Jaekel, B. (2017). Sephora's Virtual Artist Brings Augmented Reality to Large Beauty Audience. *Retail Dive*. Retrieved November 13, 2022, from https://www.retaildive.com/ex/mobilecommercedaily/sephoras-virtual-artist-brings-augmented-reality-to-larger-beauty-audience.

Jake. (2022). Stitch Fix Review (2022): Why I Returned Everything in the Box. Twice. *Modern Fellows*. Retrieved October 21, 2022, from https://www.modernfellows.com/stitch-fix-review/.

Jobin, A., Ienca, M., & Vayena, E. (2019). The Global Landscape of AI Ethics Guidelines. *Nature Machine Intelligence, 1*(9), 389–399.

Jones, E., & Easterday, B. (2022). Artificial Intelligence's Environmental Costs and Promise. *Council on Foreign Relations*. Retrieved November 14, 2022, from https://www.cfr.org/blog/artificial-intelligences-environmental-costs-and-promise.

Lang, K. (2022). The Prada Story: Ensuring the Brand's Future by Creating Unified Customer Experiences. *Forbes*. Retrieved February 9, 2023, from https://www.forbes.com/sites/sprinklr/2022/01/21/the-prada-story-ensuring-the-brands-future-by-creating-unified-customer-experiences/?sh=6292fc862001.

Lamare, A. (2021). Why Stitch Fix's Human Stylists are in Revolt (It's Not Just Over Ending Flexible Hours). *Business of Business*. Retrieved October 29, 2022, from https://www.businessofbusiness.com/articles/why-stitch-fixs-human-stylists-are-in-revolt-its-not-just-over-ending-flexible-hours/.

Lauret, J. (2019). Amazon's Sexist AI Recruiting Tool: How Did It Go So Wrong? *Medium*. Retrieved October 11, 2022, from https://becominghuman.ai/amazons-sexist-ai-recruiting-tool-how-did-it-go-so-wrong-e3d14816d98e.

Lawton, G., & Wigmore, I. (2023). AI Ethics (AI Code of Ethics). *TechTarget*. Retrieved October 27, 2022, from https://www.techtarget.com/whatis/definition/AI-code-of-ethics.

Luo, X., Tong, S., Fang, Z., & Qu, Z. (2019). Frontiers: Machines vs. Humans: The Impact of Artificial Intelligence Chatbot Disclosure on Customer Purchases. *Marketing Science, 38*(6), 937–947.

LVMH. (2022). *LVMH Annual Report 2021.* Retrieved October 14, 2022, from https://r.lvmh-static.com/uploads/2022/03/lvmh_rapport-annuel-2021-va.pdf.

Mallon, J. (2022). Female-Led Start-Up Removes the Bias from Artificial Technology in Fashion. *Fashion United.* Retrieved October 28, 2022, from https://fashionunited.com/news/fashion/female-led-start-up-removes-the-bias-from-artificial-technology-in-fashion/2022041347079.

Manyika, J., Silberg, J., & Brittany, P. (2019, October 25). What Do We Do About the Biases in Ai? *Harvard Business Review.* Retrieved October 21, 2022, from https://hbr.org/2019/10/what-do-we-do-about-the-biases-in-ai.

Marr, B. (2022). The Problem with Biased AIS (and How to Make Ai Better). *Forbes.* Retrieved October 26, 2022, from https://www.forbes.com/sites/bernardmarr/2022/09/30/the-problem-with-biased-ais-and-how-to-make-ai-better/?sh=45866e924770.

McKendrick, J., & Thurai, A. (2022). AI Isn't Ready to Make Unsupervised Decisions. *Harvard Business Review.* Retrieved November 15, 2022, from https://hbr.org/2022/09/ai-isnt-ready-to-make-unsupervised-decisions.

Meissner, P., & Keding, C. (2021). The Human Factor in AI-Based Decision-Making. *MIT Sloan Management Review.* Retrieved November 15, 2022, from https://sloanreview.mit.edu/article/the-human-factor-in-ai-based-decision-making/.

MI Garage. (2022, April 26). Learn More About AI Ethics Framework: Digital Catapult. *MI Garage.* Retrieved October 11, 2022, from https://migarage.digicatapult.org.uk/ethics/ethics-framework/#section-7.

Milton, L. (2022). How AI Is Making the Fashion Industry More Sustainable. *Sustainability-Chic.* Retrieved November 14, 2022, from https://www.sustainably-chic.com/blog/how-ai-is-making-the-fashion-industry-more-sustainable.

Mitchell, M., Wu, S., Zaldivar, A., Barnes, P., Vasserman, L., Hutchinson, B.,... & Gebru, T. (2019, January). Model Cards for Model Reporting. In *Proceedings of the Conference on Fairness, Accountability, and Transparency* (pp. 220–229). Association for Computing Machinery.

MultiThread. (2022). Stitch Fix Algorithms Tour. *MultiThread.* Retrieved October 26, 2022, from https://algorithms-tour.stitchfix.com/#human-computation.

Nikumb, S. (2020). Understanding the End-To-End UX of the Sephora Virtual Artist App-A UX Case Study. *Medium.* Retrieved October 13, 2022, from https://uxdesign.cc/understanding-the-end-to-end-user-experience-of-the-sephora-virtual-artist-app-product-try-on-d8ae3f8d1fcf.

Nilsson, N. J. (1980). *Principles of Artificial Intelligence.* Palo Alto, CA: Tioga Pub. Co.

Quach, S., Thaichon, P., Martin, K. D., Weaven, S., & Palmatier, R. W. (2022). Digital technologies: Tensions in privacy and data. *Journal of the Academy of Marketing Science, 50*(6), 1299–1323.

Sephora. (2022). Sephora Virtual Artist: Try On Makeup Instantly | Sephora Australia. *Sephora.* Retrieved October 14, 2022, from https://www.sephora.com.au/pages/virtual-artist.

Silberg, J., & Manyika, J. (2020, July 22). Tackling Bias in Artificial Intelligence (and in Humans). *McKinsey & Company.* Retrieved October 21, 2022, from https://www.mckinsey.com/featured-insights/artificial-intelligence/tackling-bias-in-artificial-intelligence-and-in-humans.

Steiner-Dicks, K. (2020, September 16). Algorithms Are Biased, and It Looks Like Designers Could Be to Blame. *Freelance Informer.* Retrieved October 26, 2022, from https://www.freelanceinformer.com/bs-tech/algorithms-are-biased-looks-like-designers-are-to-blame/.

Stitch Fix. (2022a). Sustainability. *Stitch Fix.* Retrieved November 15, 2022, from https://impact.stitchfix.com/sustainability/.

Stitch Fix. (2022b). Fashion Styling: How Does Stitch Fix Work? *Stitch Fix.* Retrieved October 25, 2022, from https://www.stitchfix.com/how-it-works.

Strubell, E., Ganesh, A., & McCallum, A. (2019). Energy and Policy Considerations for Deep Learning in NLP. In *Proceedings of the 57th Annual Meeting of the Association for Computational Linguistics*, Florence, Italy (pp. 3654–3650). Association for Computational Linguistics.

Thompson, D. (2022). Cosmetics Giant Sephora Settles Customer Data Privacy Lawsuit. *PBS.* Retrieved October 11, 2022, from https://www.pbs.org/newshour/economy/cosmetics-giant-sephora-settles-customer-data-privacy-lawsuit.

Tucker, C. (2019). Privacy, Algorithms, and Artificial Intelligence. In A. Ajay, G. Joshua, & G. Avi (Eds.), *The Economics of Artificial Intelligence: An Agenda* (pp. 423–438). University of Chicago Press.

Van Wynsberghe, A. (2021). Sustainable AI: AI for Sustainability and the Sustainability of AI. *AI and Ethics, 1*(3), 213–218.

Weisinger, D. (2022). Responsible AI: Doing it the Right Way. *Formtek.* Retrieved September 22, from, https://formtek.com/blog/responsible-ai-doing-it-the-right-way/.

Wilson, J., & Daugherty, P. (2019, November 19). How Humans and Ai Are Working Together in 1,500 Companies. *Harvard Business Review.* Retrieved October 11, 2022, from https://hbr.org/2018/07/collaborative-intelligence-humans-and-ai-are-joining-forces.

Zewe, A. (2022). Can Machine-Learning Models Overcome Biased Datasets? *MIT News.* Retrieved November 4, 2022, from https://news.mit.edu/2022/machine-learning-biased-data-0221.

4 Luxury Brands and Pro-environmental Behaviour through Commitment

The (Un)Awareness Perspective

Nadezhda Lisichkova and Cecilia Lindh

4.1 Introduction

Luxury brands continue to be in demand and seem to have a universe of their own; regardless of crises and wars in the world we see prices rising and some premium brands have waiting lists for their buyers. Despite representing a somewhat small economic sector they embody quite visible and attractive industries (Kapferer & Michaut, 2015; Cabigiosu, 2020). The market for luxury goods is on the rise: various reports show a high current market value (more than $250 billion) with high accelerated growth expected to reach more than $400 billion by 2026 (Research and Markets, 2022). Globalisation and digitalisation made it possible for more people to have access to what was quite a limited market: the one for luxury goods, thus impacting the demand worldwide. But does that really mean that luxury goods are accessible? How are they positioned, and how do they impact on the consumers' behaviour?

In this chapter we seek to discuss a framework for understanding luxury brand marketing, as opposed to that of premium or upmarket brands, in a context where sustainability is growing in importance. We start out by presenting our brand-prestige pyramid, which in turn entails a discussion on the theoretical view of its three levels. We propose that the old marketing mix may be obsolete or irrelevant for luxury brands, even for premium brands, but potentially not for upmarket brands, and instead companies should focus on commitment. As an alternative theory and practice for the premium and particularly luxury brands we suggest a relationship view with commitment as the main marketing concept. We also introduce the idea that the luxury brands, since they are in demand, can contribute to pro-environmental behaviour, by circularity through second-hand shopping.

4.2 Luxury Brands: Affective and Valuable

Luxury goods and brands signal that the feeling is of something expensive, that is desirable but yet unattainable. Luxury is quite a complex concept, evolving through the centuries and it is considered rather hard to define (Berry, 1994; Vickers & Renand, 2003; Christodoulides et al., 2009; Becker et al., 2018). In general, the luxury market consists of luxury goods and

DOI: 10.4324/9781003321378-4

experiences. Luxury goods are apparel, accessories, hard luxury, cosmetics, and others – luxury cars for example. The luxury experiences refer to luxury gourmet dining, fine art, luxury hospitality, private yachts and jets (D'Arpizio et al., 2021). Basically, it is agreed that the concept of luxury goods is not so much about the value, but rather about exclusivity and experience for those able to consume them (Chan et al., 2015). They touch upon self-esteem and the desire to be different than the masses: the show-off of wealth, success, and hedonistic drive, to be perceived as exclusive (Kapferer, 2012; Kapferer & Valette-Florence, 2019). Luxury brands are the opposite to low-price seeking consumers; they are for those who need not care about the price, who are not money/price sensitive (Kauppinen-Räisänen et al., 2018). Luxury brands allude to the "luxury" as a status, as an experience. Consumers feel that if the price is high this transcribes to luxury, consequently making the expensive appealing to the consumers and separating them from non-luxury products or fake ones (Vigneron & Johnson, 2004). Luxury fashion goods maintain high profit margins despite the costs of the craftsmanship involved and the materials. Commonly, when a price of a commodity goes up the demand for it decreases, and vice versa, but that is not the case with luxury goods. Rather, they are the perfect example of a Veblen commodity, with the increase in demand directly reflecting the increase in price, contradicting the basic law of demand (Bagwell & Bernheim, 1996; Finkle, 2020). The more expensive an item is, the more demand there is, even when the starting selling point is expensive. With luxury goods the supply is kept low, the prices increase, and demand follows the increase as the craving for exclusivity appeal by the consumers persists (Corporate Finance Institute, 2021).

The entire ecosystem of the luxury brand emulates the feeling of luxury, personal and personalised experience, having a class, appealing strong aesthetically, relying on how much the people feel sophisticated, traditions and long history. Additionally, luxury brands are used by people in certain circles to signal their status quo. The increase and diversification of global wealth, including amongst youth, made it possible for a larger number of shoppers globally to be able to afford luxury, thus leading to a wider variety of consumers buying exclusive products as a result of the descending democratisation of luxury (Plażyk, 2015).

4.3 The Brand-Prestige Pyramid

The market diversification as per Vigneron and Johnson (1999) operationalised luxury brands using prestige as a measure of their degree of luxury. If a certain brand is perceived as having high quality value, high social and hedonistic value, strongly unique and conspicuous – all these benchmarks being at the top of the prestige brand category, then such a brand is considered a luxury brand. We suggest developing it by putting the three categories as levels in a pyramid, to depict the increasing number of consumers when moving down as well. The axis of prestige puts the upmarket brands at the

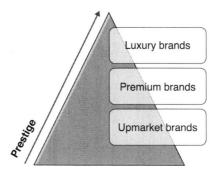

Figure 4.1 The brand-prestige pyramid.

lowest point, followed by premium brands in the middle, and on the top the luxury brands (Figure 4.1).

This figure is an interpretation of Vigneron and Johnson (1999), constructed with the purpose of providing a framework for comparing marketing practices and theory. Starting from the bottom with the upmarket brands, they are those positioned primarily by low price, which can be maintained thanks to the ability to mimic more luxurious brands, thus creating a feeling of being "known" by potential consumers. This entails lower marketing costs, since they can be desired simply because a more luxurious brand is desired but cannot be afforded. Consumers buying these perceive some of the value of a better brand, although they purchase the cheaper one. These products can be "copies" of those from more expensive brands but can also have their own identity and marketing, still being positioned as cheaper and of lower quality. H & M is such an example; they build identity with their customers to create a strong brand, still being one of low price, mediocre quality and available to most people all over the world.

The premium brands, in the middle of the brand-prestige pyramid, are brands that are of high quality and higher price and desirable, but not very hard to attain by their target group. The customers buy because the items are beautiful and there is a relationship with the brand, which is positioned as an exclusive and expensive brand – because it is that to many people – but still the quality, price and limited supply is not an issue. Fewer people can be consumers of these than the upmarket brands, although there is a broad market in this sector. Examples here are Tommy Hilfiger and Michael Kors, whose products are perceived as high quality and elegant, often luxurious by their target group (Bivens, 2019; Segura, 2019). Most people cannot buy these brands, but still there are so many that they can be seen worn in many contexts.

On top of the brand-prestige pyramid there are the luxury brands. These do not advertise widely, like premium or high-street brands; the customers are often on a waiting list and the supply is very limited. In contrast to the premium and upmarket brands, the luxury brands are pulled rather than pushed. This is a necessity if the feeling of exclusivity is to be maintained. In this category there can be handmade items, some even produced specifically for one customer, thus being unique, although similar articles are made. Luxury brands are not widely distributed, having a small market in terms of individuals and limited production, with limited quantity. Despite fewer items being produced, and the expensive materials and hours of manual labour put into making one haute-couture piece of clothing are staggering, very often the luxury garment is worn a couple of times only (Willett-Wei, 2015). A dress worn on the Oscars' award night is not seen again (or very rarely re-worn), although admired at length during the evening it is worn (Harwood, 2017; Roos, 2022).

Luxury brands rely on top-of-the-top raw materials and, for example, HERMES bags are mainly handmade and hand-stitched. Recently HERMES announced the creation of the waiting list, no matter if one has money and can afford to buy a bag it would be that simple: you have to be on the list (Cary, 2021; Kim, 2021; Marinelli, 2021). From a marketing point of view that is somehow a smart move, again touching on the hedonistic and emotional side of the consumer to increase the demand and profit. CHANEL also announced a somewhat similar policy: one consumer cannot buy an unlimited amount of goods; there is a limit to the number bought, as well as waiting and invitation-only lists for some rare and limited-edition items (TFL, 2021; Aloisi & Spencer, 2022). Scarcity is the key and not always the price, again working quite well as positioning and advertising strategy. (Example: Supreme, or Travis Scott x Jordan (Nike shoes), or Yeezy – not expensive shirts, shoes, garments, but a very limited supply (McKinnon, 2020; The Irregular Report by Irregular Labs, 2021)). The second-hand market – becoming quite popular – might be reviewed as the answer from a sustainability point of view with younger consumers: they are more sustainability-focused, and for some of them, that is the way in (more accessible) to the world of luxury goods.

To compare, luxury brands and premium brands do not only possess different brand positioning, but they also have different prices, target markets, and advertising. Examples of luxury brands include, but are not limited to, HERMES (Paris), CHANEL, SAINT LAURENT, Dior, ROLEX, PRADA, Louis Vuitton, etc. (Bivens, 2019). The brand-prestige pyramid calls for new considerations of strategy, with subsequent development of theory.

4.4 From 4Ps towards Relationship Strength

Luxury brands do not solve a problem and do not meet a need. In contrast to the premium and upmarket brands, their marketing cannot purposefully be analysed with the traditional four Ps (cf. Kotler, 2001); at least it is not meaningful to do when considering sales strategies. Although many people buy what they already like and desire, and we can argue that there is a relationship behaviour, or at least a relationship-like behaviour for most brands and products in consumer as well as industrial settings (cf. Quach et al., 2020; Khodabandeh & Lindh, 2021), the strengths and formations of the relationships may vary. A company selling the exclusive luxury brands often know who their customers are and there is an awareness from both parties that there is a relationship, and the feeling of importance is mutual. This is not the case with premium or upmarket brands, where the clientele is a broad audience consisting of a great number of people. For these there is a necessity to have large-scale production, and of course those buying are unknown to managers of the brand producing companies. Nevertheless, all companies need customers who re-purchase to survive economically, and thus the strategy to create unity and identity among customers prevails; loyalty programmes and clubs are the landmarks of premium brands' strategies (Becker et al., 2018). This enables us to study them from a relationship perspective as well as from a marketing mix perspective. For an understanding and strategising of luxury, as well as premium brands, we suggest a more relationship-oriented view, and there are also signs of this entering the scene in marketing theory since the issue of sustainability has become key (Lunde, 2018).

4.5 Sustainability Integration in Strategy and Theory

Belz and Peattie introduced a more sustainable marketing mix as early as 2009, one which suggests a focus shift from e.g. product to solution for the customer and rather convenience for customers than place, and communication rather than promotion. Although we may argue that the content is the same, it is another way to view the exchanges with customers that focus on relationship aspects, promoting them to be more sustainable than single transactions. This is from an economic point of view: keeping customers is more financially healthy than recruiting new ones. Since then, the issue of also being sustainable concerning the environment has become a concern for many consumers, and thus also companies (Papadas & Avlonitis, 2014).

In addition to the question of what strategy is applicable for the marketing of products in consideration of the brand-prestige pyramid, the new condition of sustainable development, as presented by e.g. Papadas and Avlonitis (2014), is as important as ever. This is one of many sources expressing the urge for marketers to think more sustainably and to maintain markets and desired consumption, while saving the planet's resources at the same time.

Another stream of development suggests a switch from the traditional 4Ps of marketing to the four Es – emotions, experiences, engagement and exclusivity – in order to successfully compete on the market (a replacement suggested by Olivier Robert-Murphy from Universal Music Group (Dawson, 2016)). From a scientific point of view, they may still seem to have the same content, but they do focus more on emotion and experience than the traditional mix of the four Ps. This is interesting because it suggests that the need for merchandise is not the only thing relevant for our markets; today other values – those that give feelings and experiences – are more important. In a worldwide increase in purchasing power, marketing is concerned with new thinking, and is in line with our proposed idea to revisit relationship marketing (cf. Bejou, 1997; Yoganathan et al., 2015) for at least the luxury and premium brands. This relationship view is applicable to brands of very strong commitment – they are desired and waited for, and the companies selling them cannot afford any mistakes in design or production. We define commitment in the established way, that is that something of value is pledged to obtain another value (Allen & Meyer, 1990; Anderson & Weitz, 1992; Gustafsson et al., 2005). In this case resources from the selling companies are devoted to creating unique items, reciprocated from customers by doing everything in their power to obtain the right item. This commitment is also connected to the potential show-off among friends and others, implying that there is a strong social effect through this commitment.

4.5.1 How Can Luxury Brands Induce Pro-environmental Behaviour?

As the prices for some luxury brand goods are already twice what they were before the pandemic (and with the tendency to rise even more) they are considered a top-investment product to fight the upcoming recession and inflation, as confirmed by a report recently published by the Credit Suisse Research Institute in collaboration with Deloitte Luxembourg (Credit Suisse, 2022). Such goods, such as Rolex watches, or CHANEL bags, are credited as stores of value with low volatility, and their annual returns are outpacing fluctuation rates. One may speculate that being sustainable is also a way to avoid inflation, and protect from it, as investment items will presumably increase their value, and being sustainable will pay off in the long run. Luxury brands are hiking up prices constantly, and continue to flourish even when the world is in crisis, according to (Cristoferi, 2022; Reuters, 2022). This may seem a contradiction to what politicians aim to achieve with the 2030 Agenda: to end poverty and save the planet, compelling brands globally to become more sustainable. (see Ozdamar-Ertekin, 2019, Kunz et al., 2020). Is there a way for luxury brands to work towards sustainability, and be pro-environmental, or at least induce such behaviour? This concept has been used to analyse effects of behaviours that favour the environment for some time (cf. Videras et al., 2012) and has also reached the realm of luxury brands (Quach et al., 2022).

Luxury brands not only represent an actual market for those buying them but also provide a desire for those shopping as part of the premium brand market. Arguably, most consumers of premium brands never become consumers of the luxury brands, but as they strive and supply eagerly tries to follow, there is an aspect of sustainability relevant to discuss. High quality products last longer and have a high second-hand value (Heine, 2012). Buyers of premium brands can afford them, but they still need to be economical and recognise the value of passing on items they no longer use. In this way, the premium brands contribute to more sustainable consumption thereby becoming a pro-environmental act, both by buying high quality and passing it on. Although this principle may be at work in the luxury brand market too, to some extent (as e.g. celebrities selling clothing at auctions) it is rather small as compared with the premium brand market. Nevertheless, the existence of the luxury brands must be there to create incitement to strive for exclusivity and high quality.

Using recyclable and recycling materials and/or adopting fair labour practices is rarely of marketing concern for luxury brands. Nevertheless, sustainability and luxury brands in combination raise concerns of ethical production and positioning. Looking at attitudes in general, we observe a heightened sense of living ethically and sustainably. People are concerned about saving the planet, recycling, and reducing food and material waste, meaning the customers, in general, are more responsible and thus pro-environmental in their consumption. Despite that trend in consumer behaviour, research has found that luxury and sustainability do not mix well together, meaning that the consumers of luxury brands might perceive brands that are engaged in CSR activities and practices negatively (Achabou & Dekhili, 2013). To an extent, such findings are not surprising as the concept of luxury branding (relying on the hedonistic drive about being exclusive and showing off wealth and status) is on the opposite side of the spectrum of sustainability and CSR (caring about others and the good of all, being altruistic and ethical) (Vigneron & Johnson, 1999; Tynan et al., 2010; Bianchi & Birtwistle, 2011).

According to Lipovetsky (2006), our society's hyper-consumption has changed the way consumers view luxury brand purchases. As hyper-consumption is characterised by widespread consumption at all levels and spheres, it entails the hedonistic dimension of the buying process. People are buying for the sake of it, as it pleases them, rather than enhancing their own status. Buying for pleasure shows a socio-cultural change but, in some societies, it is just a slight shift, or almost non-existent. For example, in Brazil, Russia, and China, consumers are still driven and motivated by the appearance and status the luxury goods are connected to. Furthermore, social media play an increasingly important role, especially for the new consumers entering the market, such as Millennials and Generations Y and Z, who behave differently (Goldring & Azab, 2020). They research more (Arora et al., 2020), are prolific internet users (Anshari et al., 2021), and are very aware of marketing and branding tactics, so they connect with the experience and sharing rather than the product itself (Guerrier & Maria, 2012; Woo, 2018; Kamath, 2022). Consumers are focusing on value and experience; luxury is an outlet to express oneself – it is about emotionality rather than garishness.

The fashion industry is relatively a complex one, especially luxury fashion; there are hand-crafted items, unique designs, exquisite craftsmanship, and exquisite quality that all lead to prolonged usage and emphasised durability (Heine, 2012; Hennigs et al., 2012). Such characteristics are associated with sustainability, which in recent years has led more and more researchers to address the connection between luxury fashion and sustainability (Achabou & Dekhili, 2013; Hennigs et al., 2013; Arrigo, 2015; Kapferer, 2015; Godart & Seong, 2017; Quach et al., 2022). Therefore, this conceptual chapter aims to discuss whether luxury brands and sustainability are still a paradox or whether this relationship has moved towards a solution to more aware consumption and increasing sustainability for the environment.

4.5.2 Second Hand, Sustainability and Luxury Brands

People buying second-hand luxury items are unconsciously acting sustainably. When buying second hand they abstain from other, brand-new items, and hence there is no new production cost to the environment. Various resources are being used in the production of a new item, such as basic materials (for example new leather, new stitching, new metal hardware; none of these that are used are usually from sustainable sources). There is also the cost of manufacturing, including but not limited to electricity, man labour, logistics, etc.), as well as costs for distribution and sales. But all these costs relate to electricity spending, CO_2 emissions, and earth pollution, since basically most of the goods that the luxury brands are producing and selling are far from sustainable. This further supports that when a consumer buys second-hand luxury goods they are acting sustainably. Some do that on purpose, as their purchasing behaviour is sustainable-focused (Kessous & Valette-Florence, 2019). Others buy second-hand for different reasons: due to limited purchasing resources (Ducasse et al., 2019), or due to the desire to buy a vintage item that is no longer available or produced brand new. Some buy luxury goods due to their status as a top-investment product to fight inflation, as a majority of even second-hand bags for instance; bags hold their value on the secondary market (Turunen & Leipämaa-Leskinen, 2015; Turunen & Pöyry, 2019). Thirds are doing this due to the recent policy some brands implicated on buying their items. For example, CHANEL implicated a policy of "no more than two per year", limiting clients to being able to obtain only 2/two/ CHANEL bags during a calendar year (Bondarenko, 2022; Stewart, 2022). Behind such a decision, the brand's officials explained the desire to keep the brand exclusive and hard to get. Such a decision will limit the amount personal assistants/shoppers were buying and stashing for their clients, thus leading to limited supply for the rest of the consumers, and higher resale values. Additionally, CHANEL bags can only be bought in physical stores, and not online, unlike Gucci or Prada (TFL, 2017; Fifth Avenue Girl, 2020). Having in mind that CHANEL does not have a store in every country worldwide, it makes it harder for potential customers to purchase even if they have the means to, thereby forcing them to look elsewhere in a way to secure the item (Handbagholic, 2022). Recently, Amazon announced a partnership with the reseller What Goes Around Comes Around to launch Amazon Luxury Store, where there will be pre-owned items from CHANEL, Louis Vuitton, Rolex available for sale (Zerbo, 2022)

Unknowingly, the luxury brands induce behaviour that is pro-environmental, through the vast activities of second-hand usage. There is not just selling used or worn products, there is also the phenomenon of rentals. If you cannot buy a luxury bag, you can rent one. This is exemplified in the popular "Sex and the City" movie from 2009 (https://www.youtube.com/watch?v=rUVgcCB_SwA) where a person who has little money (Carrie Bradshaw's assistant, Louise) has a very exclusive Louise Vuitton bag. The television series and movie encouraged millions of viewers to rent what they cannot buy; hence, the renting services are growing (Scott, 2021; Murphy, 2022; Post, 2022).

In analysing the relationships between the luxury brand and the customer, it is fruitful to use relationship marketing theory with commitment as a key concept. The above highlights that there is a path to environmental sustainability, supported by the existence of luxury brands. The strong commitment of these brands, which also spreads to premium brands as they are all about desiring luxury, entails not only that they are used longer and cared for, but there is also a second-hand market of buyers who are even more prone to care about their items. The commitment is contingent on the high quality and good looks of products, both traits of longevity, the first by allowing the item to last, the latter by allowing the desire to possess to last. And this is nurtured by the desire to enjoy products and show everyone else that they are in possession (Balabanis & Stathopoulou, 2021). This latter function of the commitment, that is, the social status signals and word-of-mouth, may become increasingly apparent as our markets go through digital transformation. Looking outside the relationships, which create the strength that makes the second-hand and rental market bloom, a greater effect on sustainability is achieved, and the luxury brands' commitment can also be interpreted as pro-environmental. In marketing it is becoming a concept of increasing importance. Pro-environmental is important in this context as the surrounding and context of luxury brands cause pro-environmental behaviour (Quach et al., 2022). The activity that is sustainable behaviour, that is the circularity that second-hand and rental entails, is a consequence of the strong commitment to the luxury brands purchased by those who can.

4.5.3 Luxury Brand Commitment and Spread through the Internet

The Metaverse is expanding rapidly, especially within the Generation Z population. According to a recent report, the young financially struggling customers in China are obsessed with buying affordable luxury goods, for example, hats for $300, or sneakers for $700 (Ivanova, 2022). Their splurge is hampering the luxury brands as they are not prepared for such a high demand, especially having in mind how big the Chinese market is, and that the average age of the consumers in the high luxury class is lower than the world average of 38 years of age. According to Zhan and He (2012) the market with the largest consumption power for luxury goods is China. Likewise,

China is predicted to convey 65% of the growth in the global market by 2025 (McKinsey & Company, 2019). Luxury brands are also worried that such purchases are aggravating even more the already worse financial status of these young customers, particularly the recent reports and predictions of a worldwide recession. Despite these reports though, the brands are continuing their price increases, and CHANEL even announced that they will open special boutiques for VIP clients. The young consumers, to be able to continue buying luxury goods, are turning towards the Metaverse, a hypothetical iteration of the internet as a universal world, or a place where numerous virtual worlds are connected. In the Metaverse the prices are cheaper: a pair of Gucci sneakers sells for under $20 USD. Even at these prices, the brands are still making profits; analysts at Morgan Stanley predict that the virtual luxury goods market could be worth $50 billion by 2030 (Marr, 2022).

In practice, we also see the use of influencers for many premium brands, but with luxury brands, it is limited or done differently. Luxury brands usually have brand ambassadors: superstars, actors, sports stars, and people famous for being famous, such as CHANEL-using influencers to promote CHANEL beauty, but not the brand's clothes or bags. Research on marketing influencers has shown that authenticity and being honest are key features to be heard and to grow in today's digitalised world (Lisichkova & Othman, 2017). Even the Italian designer Giorgio Armani suggested that in the crisis following the Covid-19 pandemic it is time to return to the value of authenticity (Nicoletti, 2020).

Luxury brands are usually brands that established a name for themselves a long time ago and they rely on the reputation built during the years as an elite brand. The exclusivity in making the luxury goods hard to attain is a counter-intuitive marketing strategy that works brilliantly. The harder to get the more desired it becomes! While premium and upmarket brands can use influencers or have celebrity endorsements, the luxury brands would work in the opposite way with this strategy. A celebrity can be seen wearing the brand or its accessories but would most likely not be paid to do so, that is there would be no intended marketing behind it.

4.6 Concluding Remarks

With increasing digitalisation and information exchanges, there is a new realm to flourish and show off, as well as new products difficult to attain. There are also new possibilities for second-hand purchasing.

Luxury brands and sustainable products have a lot in common. Both are expensive, as ethically produced goods usually are. Furthermore, they are of higher quality, the producers are proud of their brands and their objective of leaving a heritage. But relying only on those common grounds will not be helpful in shaping the future, rather sustainable one, for the luxury brand industry. In order to move to a greener future, transparency is the key. Adopting fair trade principles and/or using recycled materials might be a little push

Figure 4.2 The commitment to pro-environmental behaviour chain.

in the right direction and it must be done carefully, so as to not put out consumers who might consider that as greenwashing (Achabou & Dekhili, 2013).

Finally, given the idea that commitment plays a major role in the value of brands, we propose a simple chain of value creation based on the discussions in this chapter. In this value chain, commitment is first, and the final, dependent variable is not value or money, it is pro-environmental behaviour (Figure 4.2).

Although all companies need at least a small profit to survive, there is a great interest to do good, to nurture personal relationships and personal interest, which when taken into consideration open for new models of value, which include pro-environmental behaviour, without excluding profit or value. The line of argument in this chapter is that the strong commitment created by the desire to possess items that are wonderful, and which also adds to a personal position in a personal network, creates customer value that demands high-quality products. This also creates incitement for others with less money to possess, or at least be able to use, the products. The inherent value of the products makes them last, and also makes them attractive in the second-hand market. In this way the *desire* to have luxury – although not necessarily aimed at achieving a better environment – engenders high quality, which in turn increases environmental sustainability, and is thereby pro-environmental. The merchandise is popular in second-hand markets, and often sold more than just once. Higher quality would yield higher prices and hence the selling companies need not get less profit, despite selling fewer items. The world market, however, is growing, as we have seen in our examples, and thus there is plenty of room for increasing sales although prices increase with quality. This may seem paradoxical, that is, that there is more sold when we just suggested that selling fewer newer things would increase sustainability. This is, however, not the case; the population and purchasing power increases constantly and thus the more consumption that is moved to second hand, the better it would be for the environment. The suggestion here is that the share of purchased goods that are circulated needs to increase, to maintain consumption as pro-environmental.

- Strong commitment in the relationships between the buyer of the luxury brand and the consumer is a key concept.
- The commitment is spread, much thanks to the societal integration of different media, and thereby affects others who want the products.

- The desire to use the luxury brands nurtures second-hand markets and sustains circularity, which ultimately is pro-environmental.
- Being transparent is a key to staying relevant in business, and to be pro-environmental.

There is still much to learn and further studies are needed. We propose to apply the perspective we suggested and study circular economy using the prestige pyramid. Such research should include a deeper study of commitment and go into its types (cf. Arriaga & Agnew, 2001); Gustafsson et al., 2005); clearly affective commitment is key when it comes to the desire of luxury goods, but when a second-hand value is weighed in, or when the amount of money pledged (for consumers of premium brands and presumably also of upmarket brands), this also makes calculative commitment central to buying behaviour. Research should approach the luxury brand theme as a global and interesting problem for our economy as well as our ecology, through study on the topic from the view that the strong commitment is connected to other relationships and thus induces pro-environmental behaviours.

References

Achabou, M. A., & Dekhili, S. (2013). Luxury and Sustainable Development: Is There a Match? *Journal of Business Research*, *66*(10), 1896–1903. https://doi.org/10.1016/j.jbusres.2013.02.011.

Allen, N. J., & Meyer, J. P. (1990). The Measurement and Antecedents of Affective, Continuance and Normative Commitment to the Organization. *Journal of Occupational Psychology*, *63*(1), 1–18. https://doi.org/10.1111/j.2044-8325.1990.tb00506.x.

Aloisi, S., & Spencer, M. (2022). *Chanel May Limit Purchases More in Exclusivity Drive.* Reuters. Retrieved October 23, 2022, from https://www.reuters.com/markets/financials/chanel-upbeat-2022-growth-despite-china-recession-risk-2022-05-24/.

Anderson, E., & Weitz, B. (1992). The Use of Pledges to Build and Sustain Commitment in Distribution Channels. *Journal of Marketing Research*, *29*(1), 18. https://doi.org/10.2307/3172490.

Anshari, M., Alas, Y., Razzaq, A., Shahrill, M., & Lim, S. A. (2021). Millennials Consumers' Behaviors between Trends and Experiments. *Research Anthology on E-Commerce Adoption, Models, and Applications for Modern Business*, 1492–1508. https://doi.org/10.4018/978-1-7998-8957-1.ch076.

Arora, T., Kumar, A., & Agarwal, B. (2020). Impact of Social Media Advertising on Millennials Buying Behaviour. *International Journal of Intelligent Enterprise*, 7(4), 481. https://doi.org/10.1504/ijie.2020.110795.

Arrigo, E. (2015). Corporate Sustainability in Fashion and Luxury Companies. *Symphonya. Emerging Issues in Management*, *4*, 9–23. https://doi.org/10.4468/2015.4.02arrigo.

Arriaga, X. B., & Agnew, C. R. (2001). Being Committed: Affective, Cognitive, and Conative Components of Relationship Commitment. *Personality and Social Psychology Bulletin*, *27*(9), 1190–1203. https://doi.org/10.1177/0146167201279011.

Bagwell, L. S., & Bernheim, B. D. (1996). Veblen Effects in a Theory of Conspicuous Consumption. *The American Economic Review*, *86*(3), 349–373. http://www.jstor.org/stable/2118201.

Balabanis, G., & Stathopoulou, A. (2021). The Price of Social Status Desire and Public Self-Consciousness in Luxury Consumption. *Journal of Business Research, 123,* 463–475. https://doi.org/10.1016/j.jbusres.2020.10.034.

Becker, K., Lee, J. W., & Nobre, H. M. (2018). The Concept of Luxury Brands and the Relationship between Consumer and Luxury Brands. *The Journal of Asian Finance, Economics and Business, 5*(3), 51–63. https://doi.org/10.13106/jafeb.2018. vol5.no3.51.

Bejou, D. (1997). Relationship Marketing: Evolution, Present State, and Future. *Psychology & Marketing, 14*(8), 727–735.

Belz, F.M., & Peattie, K. (2009). *Sustainability Marketing.* Chichester: Wiley & Sons.

Berry, C. J. (1994). *The Idea of Luxury: A Conceptual and Historical Investigation (Ideas in Context, Series Number 30).* Cambridge: Cambridge University Press.

Bianchi, C., & Birtwistle, G. (2011). Consumer Clothing Disposal Behaviour: A Comparative Study. *International Journal of Consumer Studies, 36*(3), 335–341. https://doi.org/10.1111/j.1470-6431.2011.01011.x.

Bivens, M. (2019). *The Pyramid of Luxury Consumption.* Rude Baguette. Retrieved October 23, 2022, from https://www.rudebaguette.com/en/2014/10/rudevc-pyramid-of-luxury-consumption/.

Bondarenko, V. (2022). *Chanel Mulls Not Letting People Buy More Than Two Bags a Year.* TheStreet. Retrieved July 20, 2022, from https://www.thestreet.com/lifestyle/chanel-mulls-not-letting-people-buy-more-than-two-bags-a-year.

Cabigiosu, A. (2020). An Overview of the Luxury Fashion Industry. *Palgrave Advances in Luxury,* 9–31. https://doi.org/10.1007/978-3-030-48810-9_2.

Cary, A. (2021). *How to Buy an Hermès Bag: Vogue's Ultimate Guide.* British Vogue. Retrieved October 23, 2022, from https://www.vogue.co.uk/article/buying-an-hermes-bag.

Chan, W. Y., To, K. M., & Chu, W. C. (2015). Materialistic Consumers Who Seek Unique Products: How Does Their Need for Status and Their Affective Response Facilitate the Repurchase Intention of Luxury Goods? *Journal of Retailing and Consumer Services, 27,* 1–10. https://doi.org/10.1016/j.jretconser. 2015.07.00127.

Christodoulides, G., Michaelidou, N., & Li, C. H. (2009). Measuring Perceived Brand Luxury: An Evaluation of the BLI Scale. *Journal of Brand Management, 16*(5–6), 395–405.

Corporate Finance Institute. (2021). *Veblen Goods.* Retrieved October 23, 2022, from https://corporatefinanceinstitute.com/resources/knowledge/economics/veblen-goods/.

Credit Suisse Research Institute. (2022). Collectibles Amid Heightened Uncertainty and Inflation. Retrieved July 20, 2022, from https://www2.deloitte.com/lu/en/pages/art-finance/articles/collectibles-amid-heightened-uncertainty-inflation. html.

Cristoferi, C. (2022). *Prada Points to Pent-Up Luxury Demand with 2021 Sales Surge.* Reuters. Retrieved September 27, 2022, from https://www.reuters.com/business/retail-consumer/pradas-2021-sales-bounce-back-above-pre-pandemic-levels-2022-01-18/.

D'Arpizio, C., Levato, F., Gault, C., de Montgolfier, J., & Jaroudi, L. (2021). *From Surging Recovery to Elegant Advance: The Evolving Future of Luxury.* Bain. Retrieved August 1, 2022, from https://www.bain.com/insights/from-surging-recovery-to-elegant-advance-the-evolving-future-of-luxury/.

Dawson, A. (2016). *"The Days of the 4 Ps Are Over", Head of Universal Music Group Tells Marketers*. Mumbrella. https://mumbrella.com.au/the-four-ps-are-over-head-of-universal-music-group-tells-marketers-407370.

Ducasse, P., Finet, L., Gardet, C., Gasc, M., & Salaire, S. (2019). *Why Luxury Brands Should Celebrate the Preowned Boom*. BCG Global. https://www.bcg.com/publications/2019/luxury-brands-should-celebrate-preowned-boom.

Fifth Avenue Girl. (2020). *How to Buy Chanel Bags Online: A Complete Guide | FifthAvenueGirl.com*. Retrieved October 23, 2022, from https://fifthavenuegirl.com/2020/05/18/can-you-buy-a-chanel-bag-online/.

Finkle, C. (2020). *Veblen Goods: The Economics of Diamonds and Ferrari's - BMB*. BMB: Brand Marketing Blog. Retrieved October 23, 2022, from https://brandmarketingblog.com/articles/branding-definitions/veblen-good/.

Godart, F., & Seong, S. (2017). Is Sustainable Luxury Fashion Possible? In *Sustainable Luxury: Managing Social and Environmental Performance in Iconic Brands*, M. A. Gardetti, & A. L. Torres, eds. London: Routledge.

Goldring, D., & Azab, C. (2020). New Rules of Social Media Shopping: Personality Differences of U.S. Gen Z versus Gen X Market Mavens. *Journal of Consumer Behaviour, 20*(4), 884–897. https://doi.org/10.1002/cb.1893.

Guerrier, L., & Maria, N. (2012). *Generation Y and Luxury Brands: A High Stake Rendez-vous*. New York: Luxe Avenue Publication.

Gustafsson, A., Johnson, M. D., & Roos, I. (2005). The Effects of Customer Satisfaction, Relationship Commitment Dimensions, and Triggers on Customer Retention. *Journal of Marketing, 69*(4), 210–218. https://doi.org/10.1509/jmkg.2005.69.4.210.

Handbagholic. (2022). *Where to Buy a Chanel Bag*. Retrieved October 23, 2022, from https://www.handbagholic.co.uk/blog/where-to-buy-a-chanel-bag/.

Harwood, E. (2017). *Here's What Happens to Oscar Gowns after the Big Night*. Vanity Fair. Retrieved October 23, 2022, from https://www.vanityfair.com/style/2017/02/tanya-gill-oscar-dresses-after-the-show.

Heine, K. (2012). The Identity of Luxury Brands. https://doi.org/10.14279/DEPOSITONCE-3122.

Hennigs, N., Wiedmann, K. P., Klarmann, C., & Behrens, S. (2013). Sustainability as Part of the Luxury Essence: Delivering Value through Social and Environmental Excellence. *Journal of Corporate Citizenship, 2013*(52), 25–35.

Hennigs, N., Wiedmann, K. P., Klarmann, C., Strehlau, S., Godey, B., Pederzoli, D., Neulinger, A., Dave, K., Aiello, G., Donvito, R., Taro, K., Táborecká-Petrovičová, J., Santos, C. R., Jung, J., & Oh, H. (2012). What Is the Value of Luxury? A Cross-Cultural Consumer Perspective. *Psychology & Marketing, 29*(12), 1018–1034. https://doi.org/10.1002/mar.20583.

Ivanova, A. (2022). Шапки за *300$* и маратонки за *900$* - поколението *Z* и апетитът му към лукса. Dnes.bg. Retrieved August 20, 2022, from https://www.dnes.bg/index/2022/08/20hapkai-za-300-i-maratonki-za-900-pokolenieto-z-i-apetityt-mu-kym-luksa.540896.

Kamath, S. (2022). *Experience over Ownership – The Millennials' Way!* BHIVE Workspace. https://bhiveworkspace.com/blog/experience-over-ownership-the-millennials-way/.

Kauppinen-Räisänen, H., Björk, P., Lönnström, A., & Jauffret, M. N. (2018). How Consumers' Need for Uniqueness, Self-monitoring, and Social Identity Affect Their Choices When Luxury Brands Visually Shout versus Whisper. *Journal of Business Research, 84*, 72–81. https://doi.org/10.1016/j.jbusres.2017.11.012.

Kapferer, J. N. (2012). Abundant Rarity: The Key to Luxury Growth. *Business Horizons*, *55*(5), 453–462. https://doi.org/10.1016/j.bushor.2012.04.002.

Kapferer, J. N. (2015). *Kapferer on Luxury: How Luxury Brands Can Grow Yet Remain Rare*. London: 344 Kogan Page Publishers.

Kapferer, J. N., & Michaut, A. (2015). Luxury and Sustainability: A Common Future? The Match Depends on How Consumers Define Luxury. *Luxury Research Journal*, *1*(1), 3. https://doi.org/10.1504/lrj.2015.069828.

Kapferer, J. N., & Valette-Florence, P. (2019). How Self-Success Drives Luxury Demand: An Integrated Model of Luxury Growth and Country Comparisons. *Journal of Business Research*, *102*, 273–287. https://doi.org/10.1016/j.jbusres.2019.02.002.

Kessous, A., & Valette-Florence, P. (2019). "From Prada to Nada": Consumers and Their Luxury Products: A Contrast between Second-Hand and First-Hand Luxury Products. *Journal of Business Research*, *102*, 313–327. https://doi.org/10.1016/j.jbusres.2019.02.033.

Khodabandeh, A., & Lindh, C. (2021). The Importance of Brands, Commitment, and Influencers on Purchase Intent in the Context of Online Relationships. *Australasian Marketing Journal*, *29*(2), 177–186.

Kim, A. (2021). *How to Buy an Hermès Bag: Everything You Need to Know*. Madison Avenue Couture. Retrieved October 23, 2022, from https://madisonavenuecouture.com/blogs/news/how-to-buy-an-hermes-bag-the-hard-way-and-the-easy-way.

Kotler, P. (2001). *Marketing Management, Millenium Edition*. Upper Saddle River, NJ: Prentice-Hall, Inc.

Kunz, J., May, S., & Schmidt, H. J. (2020). Sustainable Luxury: Current Status and Perspectives for Future Research. *Business Research*, *13*(2), 541–601. https://doi.org/10.1007/s40685-020-00111-3.

Lisichkova, N., & Othman, Z. (2017). The Impact of Influencers on Online Purchase Intent (Dissertation). Retrieved from http://urn.kb.se/resolve?urn=urn:nbn:se:mdh:diva-35754.

Marr, B. (2022). *How Luxury Brands Are Making Money in the Metaverse*. Forbes. Retrieved August 20, 2022, from https://www.forbes.com/sites/bernardmarr/2022/01/19/how-luxury-brands-are-making-money-in-the-metaverse/.

McKinnon, T. (2020). *How Supreme & Yeezy Use Scarcity to Drive Sales*. Indigo9 Digital Inc. Retrieved October 23, 2022, from https://www.indigo9digital.com/blog//how-the-use-of-scarcity-is-driving-the-growth-of-popular-retail-brands.

Lipovetsky, G. (2006). *Le bonheur paradoxal: Essai sur la société d'hyperconsommation (NRF Essais Paradoxical happiness: Essay on hyperconsumption society)* (GALLIMARD). Paris: GALLIMARD.

Lunde, M. B. (2018). Sustainability in Marketing: A Systematic Review Unifying 20 Years of Theoretical and Substantive Contributions (1997–2016). *AMS Review*, *8*(3), 85–110.

Marinelli, G. (2021). *Hermes Birkin Bags Are Famously Expensive and Difficult to Buy — So We Asked an Expert How to Find Them and What Makes Them So Elusive*. Insider. Retrieved October 23, 2022, from https://www.insider.com/guides/style/how-to-buy-a-birkin-bag.

McKinsey & Company. (2019). *China Luxury Report 2019: How Young Chinese Consumers Are Reshaping Global Luxury*. Retrieved August 20, 2022, from https://www.mckinsey.com/~/media/mckinsey/featured%20insights/china/how%20young%20chinese%20consumers%20are%20reshaping%20global%20luxury/

mckinsey-china-luxury-report-2019-how-young-chinese-consumers-are-reshaping-global-luxury.pdf.

Murphy, W. (2022). *Is Renting a Designer Bag a Good Idea?* Clever Girl Finance. Retrieved October 23, 2022, from https://www.clevergirlfinance.com/blog/is-renting-a-designer-bag-a-good-idea/.

Nicoletti, S. (2020). *Opinion: Giorgio Armani Is Leading Luxury towards New Paths.* Retrieved September 25, 2022, from https://luxurysociety.com/en/articles/2020/04/opinion-giorgio-armani-leading-luxury-towards-new-paths.

Ozdamar-Ertekin, Z. (2019). Can Luxury Fashion Provide a Roadmap for Sustainability? *Markets, Globalization & Development Review, 4*(1). https://doi.org/10.23860/mgdr-2019-04-01-03.

Papadas, K. K., & Avlonitis, G. J. (2014). The 4 Cs of Environmental Business: Introducing a New Conceptual Framework. *Social Business, 4*(4), 345–360. https://doi.org/10.1362/204440814x14185703122928.

Plażyk, K. (2015). *The Democratization of Luxury – A New Form of Luxury.* Retrieved July 1, 2022, from https://www.academia.edu/9557814/The_democratization_of_luxury_a_new_form_of_luxury.

Post, T. J. (2022). *No Fakes, Just Rentals: How Young Indonesians Sport Luxury Bags without Breaking the Bank.* The Jakarta Post. Retrieved October 23, 2022, from https://www.thejakartapost.com/culture/2022/01/14/no-fakes-just-rentals-how-young-indonesians-sport-luxury-bags-without-breaking-the-bank.html.

Quach, S., Septianto, F., Thaichon, P., & Nasution, R. A. (2022). The Role of Art Infusion in Enhancing Pro-environmental Luxury Brand Advertising. *Journal of Retailing and Consumer Services, 64,* 102780-90.

Quach, S., Thaichon, P., Lee, J. Y., Weaven, S., & Palmatier, R. W. (2020). Toward a Theory of Outside-in Marketing: Past, Present, and Future. *Industrial Marketing Management, 89,* 107–128.

Research and Markets. (2022). *Global Luxury Goods Market, by Type (Jewelry & Watches, Clothing & Footwear, Bags & Accessories, Cosmetics & Fragrances), by Distribution Channel, by Region, Competition, Forecast & Opportunities, 2026.* Retrieved August 19, 2022, from https://www.researchandmarkets.com/reports/5450281/global-luxury-goods-market-by-type-jewelry-and.

Reuters. (2022). *Chanel Increases Prices Again in Europe and Asia.* Retrieved October 23, 2022, from https://www.reuters.com/business/retail-consumer/chanel-increases-prices-again-europe-asia-2022-03-04/.

Roos, D. (2022). *What Happens to Red Carpet Dresses after Celebrities Wear Them?* HowStuffWorks. Retrieved October 23, 2022, from https://lifestyle.howstuffworks.com/style/fashion/celebrity/red-carpet-dresses-celebrities-wear-them.htm.

Scott, N. (2021). *The Surprising Luxury of Designer Handbag Rentals.* Byrdie. Retrieved October 23, 2022, from https://www.byrdie.com/designer-handbag-rental-5206677.

Segura, A. (2019). *The Fashion Retailer the Fashion Pyramid of Brands.* The Fashion Retailer. Retrieved October 23, 2022, from https://fashionretail.blog/2019/03/11/the-fashion-pyramid-of-brands/.

Stewart, K. (2022). *This Is Why Chanel Has Implemented a One-Bag-per-Year Policy.* Editorialist. https://editorialist.com/news/chanel-handbags-one-per-year/.

TFL. (2017). *Chanel Will Not Sell Ready-to-Wear, Bags Online Any Time Soon.* The Fashion Law. Retrieved October 23, 2022, from https://www.thefashionlaw.com/chanel-will-not-sell-ready-to-wear-bags-online-any-time-soon/.

TFL. (2021). *Chanel Is Reportedly Putting a Quota System in Place for Some of Its Bags.* The Fashion Law. Retrieved October 23, 2022, from https://www.thefashionlaw.com/following-in-the-footsteps-of-hermes-chanel-is-putting-a-quota-system-in-place-for-some-of-its-bags/.

The Irregular Report by Irregular Labs. (2021). *The Illusion of Scarcity: Supreme, Fluid Values, and Drops.* Medium. Retrieved October 24, 2022, from https://medium.com/irregular-labs/the-illusion-of-scarcity-supreme-fluid-values-and-drops-f113d84f7bd8.

Turunen, L. L. M., & Leipämaa-Leskinen, H. (2015). Pre-loved Luxury: Identifying the Meanings of Second-Hand Luxury Possessions. *Journal of Product & Brand Management, 24*(1), 57–65. https://doi.org/10.1108/jpbm-05-2014-0603.

Turunen, L. L. M., & Pöyry, E. (2019). Shopping with the Resale Value in Mind: A Study on Second-Hand Luxury Consumers. *International Journal of Consumer Studies, 43*(6), 549–556. https://doi.org/10.1111/ijcs.12539.

Tynan, C., McKechnie, S., & Chhuon, C. (2010). Co-creating Value for Luxury Brands. *Journal of Business Research, 63*(11), 1156–1163. https://doi.org/10.1016/j.jbusres.2009.10.012.

Vickers, J. S., & Renand, F. (2003). The Marketing of Luxury Goods: An Exploratory Study -Three Conceptual Dimensions. *The Marketing Review, 3*(4), 459–478.

Videras, J., Owen, A. L., Conover, E., & Wu, S. (2012). The Influence of Social Relationships on Pro-environment Behaviors. *Journal of Environmental Economics and Management, 63*(1), 35–50.

Vigneron, F., & Johnson, L. W. (1999). A Review and Conceptual Framework of Prestige Seeking Consumer Behavior. *Academy of Marketing Science Review, 1*(1), 1–15.

Vigneron, F., & Johnson, L. W. (2004). Measuring Perceptions of Brand Luxury. *Journal of Brand Management, 11*(6), 484–506. https://doi.org/10.1057/palgrave.bm.2540194.

Willett-Wei, M. (2015). *Here's the Hierarchy of Luxury Brands around the World.* Business Insider. Retrieved October 23, 2022, from https://www.businessinsider.com/pyramid-of-luxury-brands-2015-3?international=true&r=US&IR=T.

Woo, A. (2018). *Understanding the Research on Millennial Shopping Behaviors.* Forbes. https://www.forbes.com/sites/forbesagencycouncil/2018/06/04/understanding-the-research-on-millennial-shopping-behaviors/.

Yoganathan, D., Jebarajakirthy, C., & Thaichon, P. (2015). The Influence of Relationship Marketing Orientation on Brand Equity in Banks. *Journal of Retailing and Consumer Services, 26*, 14–22.

Zerbo, J. (2022). *Chanel, Hermès Bags Are Shoppable on Amazon Thanks to Tie-Up with Reseller.* The Fashion Law. Retrieved October 24, 2022, from https://www.thefashionlaw.com/chanel-hermes-bags-are-shoppable-on-amazon-thanks-to-a-tie-up-with-wgaca/.

Zhan, L., & He, Y. (2012). Understanding Luxury Consumption in China: Consumer Perceptions of Best-Known Brands. *Journal of Business Research, 65*(10), 1452–1460.

5 Attention toward Sustainability in Premium Food Packaging

An Eye-Tracking Study on Red Meat

Reyhane Hooshmand, Billy Sung, Joo Hee Kim and Felix Septianto

5.1 Introduction

Premium food consumption is no longer the preserve of the wealthy and famous (Shukla et al., 2022). Many consumers these days are willing to purchase premium food products (Istenič & Bajec, 2021; Lee et al., 2019; Shukla et al., 2022). This growing trend has led to the emerging demand for premium food, where consumers value prestige in their food consumption (Hartman et al., 2016; Lee et al., 2019). Premium food sellers integrate the food purchasing experience with superior services such as wide aisles, smaller footprints, or food delivery (Consumer Report, 2017; Epicurious, 2017). They mainly offer rare and unique types of food, such as plant-based, sustainable, or healthy low-fat food (Food Business News, 2017). The superior services and high-quality products have led to significant growth in purchasing premium food products (Lee et al., 2019; Statista, 2022). For example, in the United States, on average, 40% of individuals stated that they buy premium brands when they want to purchase meat or sausages (Statista, 2020). However, despite the increased attention to purchasing premium food, understanding which product attributes inspire consumers to purchase premium food, especially premium meat, has remained limited.

Sustainability is one of the food product attributes that has gained significant attention from the demand and supply side over recent years (Hartmann et al., 2017). Consumers expect premium food brands to reduce their negative impacts on the environment and future generations by operating their businesses sustainably (De Angelis et al., 2017; Hartmann et al., 2017; Janssen et al., 2017). In accordance with consumers' demand for more sustainable products, many premium brands have started practising sustainability at different stages of their supply chain (Kapferer & Michaut-Denizeau, 2017). For example, Gucci has decreased its environmental impacts by 21% in 2019 and aims to diminish Carbon emissions by 50% by 2025 (CPP-Luxury, 2020). In the food industry, Alara Wholefoods, as a cereal brand, has practised

DOI: 10.4324/9781003321378-5

sustainability and reached zero waste in its food practices and manufacturing in 2008. Island Bakery is another example of a sustainable food brand producing biscuits free of pesticides or artificial flavours. In addition, they use milk from cows grown based on the highest standard of animal welfare (Earth.org., 2022). However, apart from developing sustainability practices in premium brands, they also face several barriers in their sustainability communications (Cervellon & Shammas, 2013; Kapferer & Michaut-Denizeau, 2017; Janssen et al., 2013; Winston, 2016). A major barrier is the misalignment between the concept of premium or luxury and sustainability. Hence, most premium brands are forced to keep their sustainability practices silent as consumers perceive premium and sustainability as incompatible concepts (Beckham & Voyer, 2014; Kang & Sung, 2022). Researchers also believe that consumers develop negative attitudes toward purchasing premium products that have been produced sustainably as such products made with sustainable materials are no longer unique or perceived by consumers to be unique (Achabou & Dekhili, 2013; De Barnier et al., 2012; Kapferer & Michaut-Denizeau, 2017). Furthermore, consumers value premium brands' image more than sustainability initiatives, as the conspicuousness of the brand is the main reason that justifies its premium price (Kang & Sung, 2022; Truong & McColl, 2011).

Due to this misalignment between sustainability and luxury or premium, the number of premium brands practising sustainability, especially in the food context, is limited (Lee et al., 2019). It is surprising given that the food industry has the biggest impact on the environment and community (Franceschelli et al., 2018; Garzón-Jiménez & Zorio-Grima, 2021; Matzembacher & Meira, 2018). Food production results in significant and detrimental environmental impacts, such as water waste (Golini & Gualandris, 2018) and air pollution (Al-Odeh et al., 2021). A European industrial report has shown that food companies are responsible for approximately 30% of the environmental damages caused by food consumption (European Commission, 2006). Thus, it is critical for food brands to consider, adopt, and create a market for sustainability practices (Bloomberg, 2017; Hartmann et al., 2017; Pearson & Henryks, 2008). However, the understanding of consumers' attitudes toward sustainability practices, especially in premium food brands, is still limited (Lee et al., 2019).

One way to examine whether consumers demand sustainability in premium food products is to measure their visual attention to sustainability claims on the product packaging of premium food (Van Loo et al., 2021). Previous studies have emphasized the importance of visual attention in consumers' purchasing decisions (e.g., Behe et al., 2015; Maughan et al., 2007; Wang et al., 2018). For instance, Orquin et al. (2020) suggested that the visual claims on product packaging are strong drivers of visual attention, affecting consumers' choices. Likewise, Danner et al. (2016) reported that attention measures, such as the number of fixations and dwell duration, positively correlate with consumer choices. It is also reported that price and sustainability claims are two product attributes that significantly impact consumers' visual attention (Van Loo et al., 2015, 2018). However, despite the previous attempts, it is still unclear whether consumers pay attention to sustainability in premium food products or whether consumers tend to pay more attention to sustainability information when the food products are premium. In fact, from a consumer perspective, does sustainability matter in premium food products?

Against this backdrop, the current study examines consumers' attention toward sustainability information in premium vs. non-premium food brands. To our knowledge, no study examines consumers' visual attention to the sustainability logo in premium food products, especially red meat. Thus, the current study is the first to explore whether consumers pay more attention to the sustainability initiatives of food brands when it is positioned to be a premium vs. non-premium food brand. The findings of this research fill the current gap in understanding whether consumers expect and therefore pay more attention to sustainability information on premium vs. non-premium food.

5.2 Literature Review

5.2.1 Sustainability Conceptualization

The notion of sustainability was first conceptualized by World Commission's view on Environment and Development (WCED) in 1987. According to WCED conceptualization, "sustainability meets the present needs without compromising the future generation's abilities to meet their own needs" (Brundtland Report, 1987, p. 8). Sustainability has been mainly studied based on three pillars: environmental, social, and economic sustainability (WSSD, 2002). Goodland (1995) believes that environmental sustainability refers to protecting nature by conserving materials and diminishing human impacts on the environment. Social sustainability encompasses social concerns, such as social justice and human well-being (Missimer et al., 2016; Suopajärvi et al., 2016; Vallance et al., 2011). Economic sustainability also focuses on preserving a business from financial instability and disruption (Costanza & Patten, 1995). All three pillars have been identified as essential, and sustainability has been studied as both a multidimensional and individual concept previously (e.g., Becker, 2009; McDonough & Braugart, 2010). This study mainly focuses on the environmental aspect of sustainability with less focus on social and economical sustainability.

5.2.2 Sustainability in Premium Brands

Sustainability has been practised across many companies to reduce their negative impacts on the environment and society (see Olofsson & Mark-Herbert, 2020; SanMiguel et al., 2021; Schrobback & Meath, 2020; Singh & Misra, 2021; Torkayesh et al., 2021; Tseng et al., 2018; Yang et al., 2017). Consumers have also shown interest in purchasing products or services from brands committed to the environment and society (Moscovici et al., 2022; Pomarici & Vecchio, 2014; Valenzuela et al., 2022). Along with increasing supply and demand interest in sustainability practices, several studies have examined consumers' attitudes toward sustainability in premium brands and the importance of communicating companies' sustainability initiatives to consumers (e.g., Al-Qudah et al., 2022; Amatulli et al., 2021; Olofsson & Mark-Herbert, 2020; Siano et al., 2016). For example, Amatulli et al. (2021) found that sustainability communication cultivates a higher willingness to book a room in a luxury hotel. Furthermore, they suggested that sustainability practices improve consumers' perceptions of the hotel's integrity. However, most recent studies argue that consumers are reluctant to adopt sustainability in luxury brands (see Han et al., 2017; Keller et al., 2014). For example, Han et al. (2017) interviewed luxury consumers regarding their attitudes toward sustainability in luxury and premium brands. Based on their findings, consumers' limited knowledge of sustainability in luxury and premium brands has led to negative sentiments toward sustainability in premium brands. Despite the previous attempts, little attention has been paid to how consumers perceive sustainability claims on premium food brands (Valenzuela et al., 2022).

In the food industry, companies have also started to operate their supply chain sustainably (Franceschelli et al., 2018; Kücükgül et al., 2022; Matzembacher & Meira, 2018; Orazalin, 2019; Schrobback & Meath, 2020; Tseng et al., 2018). Regardless of the significant efforts of food brands in practising sustainability, understanding of sustainability orientation in premium food companies has remained limited. This has happened potentially because of the incongruency between consumers' perceptions of sustainability and premium products. Hence, examining the consumers' attention to sustainability claims, especially in premium food brands, has gained prominence among academics and practitioners to predict consumers' attitudes toward sustainability initiatives. For example, Balconi et al. (2019) have emphasized consumers' attention to the sustainability claims of luxury brands using the neuromarketing technique. They found that consumers psychologically process the sustainability orientation of a brand in their mind before purchasing a premium product. However, they did not examine consumers' attention to sustainability labels on premium products' packaging. Therefore, more research is needed to understand how neuromarketing tools can effectively measure consumers' attitudes toward sustainability information in premium food brands (Tait et al., 2019).

5.2.3 Binomial Identity of Premium vs. Sustainability

The existing literature has identified significant contradictions between the concept of premiumness and sustainability. Premium or luxury emphasizes conspicuousness, pleasantness, and superficiality (Achabou & Dekhili, 2013; Ko et al., 2019). In contrast, sustainability is associated with scarifying, modernism, and ethics (Bray et al., 2011; Talukdar & Yu, 2020). Hence, consuming premium products encourages materialistic behaviours making consumers self-centred or indifferent to social concerns, while sustainability concerns make a person behave humbler and more ethically (Talukdar & Yu, 2020). In fact, the primary aim of consuming premium brands is to display the sumptuousness of items (Lee et al., 2021; Li et al., 2013). On the contrary, by consuming sustainable products, consumers aim to show that they have ethical consumption and care about the environment and society (Talukdar & Yu, 2020). Therefore, sustainable consumption fundamentally contradicts premium consumption regarding the meaning and consumers' perspectives. Under this circumstance, integrating high sustainability and premium rating might lead to conflict (Liu et al., 2019a, b).

Prior studies also postulated that consumers perceive sustainability and premium as incompatible product attributes, mainly when a premium product manifests selfishness and indulgence (Kong et al., 2021; Osburg et al., 2021). In fact, consumers tend to negatively evaluate sustainability efforts by premium brands (Achabou & Dekhili, 2013). For example, they perceive sustainability promotion in a premium brand as an indication of providing low-quality products (Achabou & Dekhili, 2013). However, consumers also intend to signal their identity and personal values by consuming premium products. Hence, it is unsurprising if they expect premium brands to reflect their concerns and aspirations for a better world (Bendell & Kleanthous, 2007). Following this belief, consumers might reward (punish) companies that emphasize (ignore) their commitment to the environment and society (Axsen et al., 2013; Grail Research, 2010; Osburg et al., 2019). For example, some consumers take the sustainability claim of a premium brand as an opportunity to introduce their identity and commitment to the environment (Bendell & Kleanthous, 2007; Chan & Wong, 2012). Therefore, the existing literature is contradictory on whether sustainability practices enhance consumers' attitudes, purchase intention, and willingness to pay (WTP) toward premium brands.

Furthermore, few studies have focused on evaluating consumers' responses to sustainability practices in premium food brands. A potential explanation for the contradiction is the use of self-reported measures. Self-reported measures are limited to measuring consumers' unconscious responses to marketing stimuli. This limitation is even wider when examining ethical or sustainable beliefs and attitudes (Yogesh & Ravindran, 2018). The potential reason is instability in consumers' ethical beliefs and sustainable consumption (Wang et al., 2017). For example, although some consumers believe in sustainability and preserving the environment, they still refuse to recycle their waste (Wang et al., 2017). Furthermore, it is reported that self-measured methods are insufficient to measure consumers' attitudes toward sustainability due to the instability of consumers' attitudes and beliefs (Wang et al., 2017). Although there are some efforts to examine consumers' self-reported attitudes toward sustainability in premium brands (e.g., Achabou & Dekhili, 2013; Davies et al., 2012; Ki & Kim, 2016; Kong et al., 2021; Kumagai & Nagasawa, 2017), no research has applied psychophysiological and neuromarketing methods to examine consumers' implicit responses and attitudes toward sustainability practices in premium food brands.

Thus, the current study aims to explicitly compare consumers' perceptions of sustainability in premium food brands vs. non-premium food brands through eye-tracking. Specifically, we examine the following research question using eye-tracking technology:

RQ: Do consumers expect and therefore pay more attention to sustainability information in premium (vs. non-premium) food products?

5.2.4 Attention toward Sustainability in Premium Food Brands

Consumers' visual attention has been recognized as an important factor in evaluating the effectiveness of marketing initiatives (Kahn, 2017; Oliveira et al., 2016; Strong, 1925). Many brands attempt to capture consumers' visual attention and direct them to specific attributes of their products which eventually leads to higher purchasing decisions (Huddleston et al., 2018). Therefore, marketing stimuli's ability to attract consumers' attention is crucial in improving sales and marketing effectiveness (Huddleston et al., 2018; King et al., 2019). This necessity is remarkably high in premium food products as consumers are more likely to choose low-cost and familiar brands once they shop for groceries (Canavari & Coderoni, 2019; White et al., 2019). Visual labels and claims on product packaging play a significant role in drawing consumers' attention to the product's attributes and provide sufficient information that may affect their choices (Drexler et al., 2018; Peschel et al., 2019). Previous studies on the impact of attention on consumers' purchasing choices suggested that longer fixation and a higher number of fixations (i.e., higher attention) are associated with a greater likelihood of purchase (Bialkova & van Trijp, 2011; Graham & Jeffery, 2012; Van Loo et al., 2015). Prior attempts to use eye-tracking to capture consumers' attention have also suggested that greater visual attention positively affects marketing outcomes such as positive attitudes and higher purchasing intentions (Allen et al., 2013; Sciulli et al., 2017; Sung et al., 2021). For instance, Clement et al. (2015) reported a significant relationship between the level of consumers' attention toward the information on the product's packaging and the likelihood of purchasing decisions. Van Loo et al. (2021) have also used eye-tracking to measure consumers' attention toward the information on the product packaging regarding using nutritious ingredients and sustainability commitment. Based on their findings, consumers' visual attention to nutrition and sustainability claims positively affects their choices. In fact, more visual attention to these claims resulted in a higher choice likelihood (Van Loo et al., 2021). Hence, sustainability information on product packaging might be one of the product's attributes that captures consumers' attention before purchasing (Liu et al., 2019a). Adding to the previous findings, Liu et al. (2019a) have found that the type of sustainability a producer practises also affects consumer choices.

Based on their findings, consumers pay greater attention to the certification related to environmental friendliness rather than the fair-trade logo on product packaging (Liu et al., 2019a). Prior evidence supporting the relationship between consumers' visual attention toward sustainability claim on the chicken meat packaging and purchasing intentions indicates that the higher visual attention toward sustainability and the possibility of purchasing the product is positively interrelated (Samant & Seo, 2016). Although previous research has demonstrated the effectiveness of sustainability information in capturing attention (see Grebitus et al., 2015; Orquin et al., 2020; Wästlund et al., 2018), no research has examined whether sustainability practices and information on premium brands' packaging may capture more attention in premium red meat. In this research, we test the two competing hypotheses:

H1A: Consumers expect and therefore pay significantly more attention to sustainability claims on premium food products when compared to non-premium food products.

H1B: Consumers do not expect and therefore pay significantly less attention to sustainability claims on premium food products when compared to non-premium food products.

5.2.5 Eye-Tracking

Due to the limitations of self-reported measures in the existing literature, the current research used eye-tracking to measure consumers' attention objectively. Eye-tracking is a sensor technology that can detect where and how long an individual is looking at a specific area in real-time (Ćosić, 2016). In fact, eye-tracking indicates the number of times participants fixate on a particular area and the overall time that area has been fixated (Barakat et al., 2015). Thus, beyond the duration of visual attention, other eye-tracking measures, such as the number of fixations and their specific location, may also identify the locus of attention (Clement et al., 2015).

Eye-tracking is one of the most effective tools for measuring visual attention (Barakat et al., 2015; Orquin & Wedel, 2020) by showing what consumers are actually looking at in product packaging or brand advertisements (Babic-Rosario et al., 2020). The wide application of eye-tracking in previous studies demonstrates that using neuromarketing tools, especially eye-tracking, allows researchers to move beyond self-reported responses and track consumers' unconscious responses to marketing stimuli (Van Loo et al., 2021). While eye-tracking provides valuable insights into consumers' responses to the information and claims on products' packaging (e.g., Ballco et al., 2020; Orquin et al., 2012; Russo, 2011), it has rarely been applied to examine consumers' visual attention to sustainability claims. Specifically, no study examines consumers' visual attention to the sustainability logo on premium red meat using eye-tracking.

5.3 Methods

5.3.1 Participants and Sampling

The current research was conducted in Australia. This study targeted consumers who purchase food and groceries on a regular basis. Specifically, we sampled students and staff from an Australian metropolitan university. The sampling technique for this study was non-probability self-selected and snowball sampling which is suggested for exploratory research (Saunders, 2012). In total, 82 individuals participated in this study. In fact, in each condition (i.e., premium and non-premium products), 41 individuals participated. Participants were recruited based on several inclusion criteria: (1) they must reside in Australia; (2) they should have personally made decisions to purchase food or groceries at least once in the past three months to ensure that they are decision-makers for the research stimulus; and (3) they should not follow any food dietaries (e.g., food allergies or vegetarianism) in order to reduce any biases due to food consumption. In addition, individuals should have normal vision to participate in this study.

5.3.2 Design and Procedure

This study is a biometric experiment manipulating three products from Harvey Beef. These were sausages, mince, and scotch fillets. All the products' packaging features were kept consistent. The only difference was related to their price. We aimed to see whether participants pay greater attention to the sustainability logo on the product packaging when the product is charged at a premium price (i.e., double the market price) vs. non-premium price (i.e., at market price). Thus, the current study followed a simple one-way between-subject experimental design.

For data collection, each participant was tested individually. Before data collection, a trained research assistant elaborated on the study procedure to the participants and asked them to minimize their head movements during data collection. Then, participants were asked to read through the research information sheet and provide consent to participate in this research. Next, a trained research assistant calibrated the eye-tracking for each participant by using Gazepoint's nine-point calibration. The quality of eye-tracking data was also monitored during the study. We recalibrated participants with low-quality eye-tracking data until we obtained an excellent calibration. Participants who had low calibration after five re-calibrations were excluded from the study to improve the quality of the collected data. During the study, a picture of each product was displayed on the testing monitor, and each participant was asked to answer several questions after they saw the research stimuli. The three products were presented in a random order to avoid any sequence bias.

Table 5.1 Self-reported scales used in the study

Construct	Adopted Items	Cronbach's Alpha	Citation
Naturalness	1. Harvey Beef's products are natural. 2. Harvey Beef's products are disrespectful to nature. 3. Harvey Beef's products are made from natural ingredients only. 4. I can tell how Harvey Beef's meats are produced. 5. I know where Harvey Beef's meats come from.	0.80	Lunardo and Saintives (2013)
Eco-friendliness	1. Harvey Beef's products are friendly to environment and harmless for nature. 2. Harvey Beef's products reduce the consumption of energy. 3. Harvey Beef's products are green and harmless to human. 4. Harvey Beef's products will reduce the impact of global warming.	0.87	Chen et al. (2020)
Animal welfare	1. Harvey Beef's products help to improve the quality of life of farmed animals. 2. Harvey Beef's products help to improve the treatment of farm animals. 3. Harvey Beef's products help to reduce animal suffering. 4. Harvey Beef's products are ethical. 5. Harvey Beef's products will improve animal welfare conditions.	0.75	Kendall et al. (2006)
Attitudes	1. "Unfavourable" to "Favourable" 2. "Negative" to "Positive" 3. "Dislike it" to "Like it" 4. "Bad" to "Good"	0.85	Schlosser (2003)
Purchasing intentions	1. Would you be willing to try Harvey Beef's products? 2. Would you be willing to eat Harvey Beef's products regularly? 3. Would you be willing to eat Harvey Beef's products? 4. How likely are you to buy Harvey Beef's products?	0.87	Wilks and Phillips (2007)
Willingness to pay a premium	1. I am willing to pay more for Harvey Beef's products. 2. I am keen to pay a higher price for Harvey Beef's products. 3. Buying Harvey Beef's products seems proper to me even if they cost more.	0.89	Aksoy and Özsönmez (2019)

5.3.3 Manipulation Check and Measurement Scales

We checked the manipulation for this study to ensure that participants can properly and accurately recall the information regarding the "naturalness," "eco-friendliness," and "animal welfare" on each product packaging. Then, participants were asked to respond to questions regarding their attitudes, purchasing intentions, and WTP for premium and non-premium products.

A 7-point Likert scale from strongly disagree (1) to strongly agree (7) was used to measure each item. All measurement scales were adopted from the previous studies with a few changes to align them with this study. Table 5.1 shows the details of each scale. Eye-tracking data were also analysed based on participants' areas of interest. We considered participants' attention to the sustainability logo at the top centre of the product's packaging. Each product packaging contained product information, including the brand, the name of the product, the sustainability logo, the raw food product, and other product information, such as weight (see Figure 5.1). We also added the price of each product at the bottom of their packaging.

5.4 Results

The manipulation check results show that consumers' perception of naturalness ($t(80) = -1.93$, $p = 0.84$), eco-friendliness ($t(76.5) = 0.79$, $p = 0.43$), and animal welfare ($t(80) = 0.00$, $p = 1$) information did not differ significantly between premium vs. non-premium products. This shows that the manipulation of premium vs. non-premium through pricing was robust and did not introduce any other potential confounds (e.g., consumers did not perceive premium products to be more natural). These findings suggest that manipulation was effective.

The eye-tracking results (see Figure 5.1 for an example) indicate that participants paid greater attention to the sustainability information on the premium product's packaging (M = 8.5%, SD = 6.3%) compared to non-premium

(a)   (b)

Figure 5.1 Example of eye-tracking heat map from the study.

product (M = 5.9%, SD = 3.9%), t(67.2) = 2.25, p = 0.02). However, the participants' attention toward the products' prices was not significant, t(66.3) = −1.25, p = 0.21. Therefore, the higher price of premium products may only increase consumers' attention toward the brand's sustainability practices. Apart from attention, our findings show that the changes in the product's price did not significantly affect the consumers' attitudes (t(80) = 0.75, p = 0.45), purchasing intentions (t(80) = 0.63, p = 0.52), and WTP (t(80) = −0.44, p = 0.66) (see Appendix). This suggests that there is no significant relationship between product price (i.e., the manipulation of product premiumness) and consumers' intentions to purchase premium food products. In fact, the higher price of premium food products does not necessarily lead to lower purchasing intentions and WTP.

5.5 Discussion

The food industry is one of the industries that has a significant negative impact on the environment and society (Pullman et al., 2010). Due to these significant effects, many food brands, especially meat producers (Tuomisto, 2019), have reduced their damages by operating their businesses sustainably (Pullman et al., 2010). Despite the significant efforts of food producers in practising sustainability in their businesses, it is still ambiguous how these efforts have influenced consumers' attitudes and attention toward sustainability information in food products, especially premium red meat. The current study examined how consumers perceive sustainability labels on premium vs. non-premium red meat packaging. Based on our findings, consumers expect premium food brands to engage in sustainability practices; therefore, they have paid greater attention to sustainability information on products charging a premium price. In fact, our findings provide robust and empirical eye-tracking data to show that a simple manipulation of the pricing can shift consumers' attention toward the sustainability information on the packaging of red meat products. This finding assists premium food managers and marketers to better understand the psychological mechanism (i.e., visual attention) underlying consumers' responses to sustainability practices in premium food brands. Furthermore, our findings help marketers and food producers to understand how to shift consumers' attention toward sustainability in food products by manipulating their prices.

These findings contrast with previous findings suggesting the concept of premium or luxury and sustainability are incompatible (e.g., Kong et al., 2021; Osburg et al., 2021; Talukdar & Yu, 2020). Based on prior evidence, premium products manifest indulgence, selfishness, and elegance (Osburg et al., 2021), while sustainable products emphasize scarifying and ethics (Talukdar & Yu, 2020). Therefore, luxury consumers may negatively evaluate premium and luxury brands practising sustainability in their businesses (Achabou & Dekhili, 2013). However, our findings indicate that consumers pay greater attention to the sustainability label on premium (vs. non-premium) red meat packaging. This suggests that they expect premium food brands to practice sustainability. Hence, consumers' expectations toward sustainability for premium brands in the food industry differ from premium or luxury brands in other industries. This finding allows marketing managers and sustainability practitioners to better anticipate consumers' responses to sustainability practices in premium food brands. In fact, despite the incompatibility between the concept of sustainability and luxury, our findings suggest that premium food brands need to practise sustainability in their businesses.

Based on previous findings, consumers develop positive attitudes toward sustainable products (Valenzuela et al., 2022). However, our findings indicate that consumers' greater attention to sustainability labels did not result in higher purchasing intentions and WTP for premium food products. This supports the statement that consumers are in a state of psychological imbalance or an attitude-behaviour gap between their sustainability or green concerns and their actual purchasing behaviour (e.g., Han et al., 2017; Keller et al., 2014). This attitude-behaviour paradox is even greater when purchasing food products (Yamoah & Acquaye, 2019). Tosun et al. (2021) postulated that premium food consumers mainly fail to walk their talk regarding sustainability as they perceive sustainable food as unusual or less tasty. Furthermore, even when a product provides additional benefits, such as a sustainability label, the consumers' perceptions of the technology used to produce the product sustainably may negatively affect the acceptance of the product (Lahteenmaki et al., 2007). Therefore, the sustainability attributes of a product may not necessarily lead to higher purchasing intentions.

The current study is not without its limits. For instance, the current research has only focused on beef as other types of red meat, chicken, or seafood were out of the scope of this research. Interestingly, previous studies have reported differences in consumers' attitudes toward different types of meat. For example, McClenachan et al. (2016) have suggested that consumers are willing to pay for all types of sustainability practices (i.e., environmental, social, and economic) in seafood. Therefore, consumers' attention and attitudes toward premium red meat might differ from premium chicken, seafood, or other types of red meat. Accordingly, future studies are recommended to examine consumers' attitudes and attention to sustainability labels on other types of premium meat. This will provide a more robust and generalized examination of how consumers' attention differs between premium vs. non-premium food brands.

Furthermore, another limitation of this study is the narrow focus on the environmental aspect of sustainability. However, previous findings acknowledged that sustainability could also be examined based on different dimensions (i.e., environmental, social, and economic) (see Grunert et al., 2014; Toussaint et al., 2021). For instance, Toussaint et al. (2021) suggested a framework to measure social sustainability and corporate social responsibilities in the food value chain. Lerro et al. (2018) have also examined consumers' preferences for social sustainability in the food industry. Therefore, consumers' preferences for sustainability in premium food products could be examined based on different dimensions of sustainability. Hence, a potential research avenue for future studies is to examine consumers' attitudes toward different dimensions of sustainability (e.g., environmental vs. social) in premium food products, especially red meat.

Sustainability can also be practised at different stages of the value chain (i.e., packaging, ingredients, and manufacturing) (see Jagtap et al., 2019; Seo et al., 2016; Ting et al., 2014). For example, Seo et al. (2016) argued that consumers develop different attitudes toward sustainability practices in products' packaging vs. ingredients. However, the current study has only focused on sustainability labels on products' packaging as other stages of the value chain were out of the scope of this research. Therefore, we recommend that future researchers examine and compare consumers' attitudes and attention to sustainability practices at different value chain stages of premium food products, especially red meat.

5.6 Concluding Remark

- Our findings highlight that consumers' perception of naturalness, eco-friendliness, and animal welfare were not significant between premium vs. non-premium red meat. Hence, consumers did not perceive premium red meat as more natural, eco-friendly, and less cruel to animals than non-premium red meat.
- The current empirical findings highlight that consumers pay more attention to the sustainability label on premium red meat than non-premium red meat. Hence, despite the incompatibility between sustainability and luxury, food consumers expect premium brands to practice sustainability in their businesses.
- The current empirical findings contribute to extending the knowledge of sustainability in premium and luxury literature and assist marketers in understanding consumers' attitudes toward sustainability in premium food brands.
- The current findings postulate an attitude-behaviour gap between premium consumers' sustainability concerns and their actual consumption. In fact, although consumers have paid greater attention to the sustainability logo in premium red meat, they have not shown any interest in purchasing or paying a premium for the product

References

Achabou, M. A., & Dekhili, S. (2013). Luxury and sustainable development: Is there a match? *Journal of Business Research*, *66*(10), 1896–1903.

Aksoy, H., & Özsönmez, C. (2019). How millennials' knowledge, trust, and product involvement affect the willingness to pay a premium price for fairtrade products. *Asian Journal of Business Research*, *9*(2), 95–112.

Allen, D. G., Biggane, J. E., Pitts, M., Otondo, R., & Van Scotter, J. (2013). Reactions to recruitment web sites: Visual and verbal attention, attraction, and intentions to pursue employment. *Journal of Business and Psychology, 28*(3), 263–285.

Al-Qudah, A. A., Al-Okaily, M., & Alqudah, H. (2022). The relationship between social entrepreneurship and sustainable development from economic growth perspective: 15 'RCEP'countries. *Journal of Sustainable Finance & Investment, 12*(1), 44–61.

Al-Odeh, M., Smallwood, J., & Badar, M. A. (2021). A framework for implementing sustainable supply chain management. *International Journal of Advanced Operations Management, 13*(3), 212–233.

Amatulli, C., De Angelis, M., & Stoppani, A. (2021). The appeal of sustainability in luxury hospitality: An investigation on the role of perceived integrity. *Tourism Management, 83*, 104228. https://doi.org/10.1016/ j.tourman.2020.104228.

Axsen, J., Orlebar, C., & Skippon, S. (2013). Social influence and consumer preference formation for pro-environmental technology: The case of a UK workplace electric-vehicle study. *Ecological Economics, 95*, 96–107.

Babic-Rosario, A., de Valck, K., & Sotgiu, F. (2020). Conceptualizing the electronic word-of-mouth process: What we know and need to know about eWOM creation, exposure, and evaluation. *Journal of the Academy of Marketing Science, 48*(3), 422–448. https://doi.org/10.1007/s11747-019-00706-1.

Balconi, M., Sebastiani, R., & Angioletti, L. (2019). A neuroscientific approach to explore consumers' intentions towards sustainability within the luxury fashion industry. *Sustainability, 11*(18), 5105.

Ballco, P., Caputo, V., & de-Magistris, T. (2020). Consumer valuation of European nutritional and health claims: Do taste and attention matter? *Food Quality and Preference, 79* (January, 2020), 103793.

Barakat, B., Crump, C., Cades, D., Rauschenberger, R., Schwark, J., Hildebrand, E., & Young, D. (2015). Eye tracking evaluation of driver visual behavior with a forward collision warning and mitigation system. In *Proceedings of the Human Factors and Ergonomics Society Annual Meeting* (pp. 1321–1325). Sage.

Becker, E. J. (2009). *The Proximity Hotel: A Case Study on Guest Satisfaction of Sustainable Luxury Environments*, Master's Thesis, The University of North Carolina at Greensboro, Greensboro, NC.

Beckham, D., & Voyer, B. G. (2014). Can sustainability be luxurious? A mixed-method investigation of implicit and explicit attitudes towards sustainable luxury consumption. *ACR North American Advances,* 245–250.

Behe, B. K., Bae, M., Huddleston, P. T., & Sage, L. (2015). The effect of involvement on visual attention and product choice. *Journal of Retailing and Consumer Services, 24*, 10–21.

Bendell, J., & Kleanthous, A. (2007). *Deeper Luxury*. Godalming: WWF-UK.

Bialkova, S., & van Trijp, H. (2011). An efficient methodology for assessing attention to and effect of nutrition information displayed front-of-pack. *Food Quality and Preference, 22*, 592–601.

Bloomberg. (2017). The future of whole foods isn't about groceries. Retrieved May 21, 2018, from https://www.bloomberg.com/news/articles/2017-05-23/sushi-lovingwhole-foods-fanatics-are-seen-as-key-to-turnaround.

Bray, J., Johns, N., & Kilburn, D. (2011). An exploratory study into the factors impeding ethical consumption. *Journal of Business Ethics, 98*(4), 597–608.

Brundtland Report. (1987). *Our Common Future*. New York: United Nations World Commission on Environment and Development.

Canavari, M., & Coderoni, S. (2019). Green marketing strategies in the dairy sector: Consumer-stated preferences for carbon footprint labels. *Strategic Change, 28*(4), 233–240. https://doi.org/10.1002/jsc.2264.

Cervellon, M. C., & Shammas, L. (2013). The value of sustainable luxury in mature markets: A customer-based approach. *Journal of Corporate Citizenship, 52* (December, 2013), 90–101.

Chan, T.-Y., & Wong, C. W. Y. (2012). The consumption side of sustainable fashion supply chain: Understanding fashion consumer eco-fashion consumption decision. *Journal of Fashion Marketing & Management, 16*(2), 193–215.

Chen, X., Sun, X., Yan, D., & Wen, D. (2020). Perceived sustainability and customer engagement in the online shopping environment: The rational and emotional perspectives. *Sustainability, 12*(7), 2674.

Clement, J., Aastrup, J., & Forsberg, S. C. (2015). Decisive visual saliency and consumers' in-store decisions. *Journal of Retailing and Consumer Services, 22*, 187–194.

Consumer Report. (2017). Faster, fresher, cheaper: The grocery shopping revolution. Retrieved May 21, 2018, from https://www.consumerreports.org/grocery-storessupermarkets/faster-fresher-cheaper-grocery-shopping-revolution/.

Ćosić, D. (2016). Neuromarketing in market research. *Interdisciplinary Description of Complex Systems: INDECS, 14*(2), 139–147.

Costanza, R., & Patten, B. C. (1995). Defining and predicting sustainability. *Ecological Economics, 15*(3), 193–196.

CPP-Luxury. (2020). Gucci reduces environmental impact by 21% ahead of 2025 targets. CPPLUXURY Business of Luxury, June 9. https://cpp-luxury.com/gucci-reduces-environmental-impact-by-21-aheadof-2025-targets/.

Danner, L., de Antoni, N., Gere, A., Sipos, L., Kovács, S., & Dürrschmid, K. (2016). Make a choice! Visual attention and choice behaviour in multi alternative food choice situations. *Acta Alimentaria, 45*(4), 515–524.

Davies, I. A., Lee, Z., & Ahonkhai, I. (2012). Do consumers care about ethical-luxury? *Journal of Business Ethics, 106*(1), 37–51.

De Angelis, M., Adıgüzel, F., & Amatulli, C. (2017). The role of design similarity in consumers' evaluation of new green products: An investigation of luxury fashion brands. *Journal of Cleaner Production, 141*, 1515–1527.

De Barnier, V., Falcy, S., & Valette-Florence, P. (2012). Do consumers perceive three levels of luxury? A comparison of accessible, intermediate and inaccessible luxury brands. *Journal of Brand Management, 19*(7), 623–636.

Drexler, D., Fiala, J., Havlíčková, A., Potůčková, A., & Souček, M. (2018). The effect of organic food labels on consumer attention. *Journal of Food Products Marketing, 24*(4), 441–455.

Earth.org. (March 2022). https://earth.org/sustainable-food-companies/.

Epicurious. (2017). The 21 best grocery stores in America. Retrieved May 21, 2018, from https://www.epicurious.com/expert-advice/the-21-best-grocery-stores-in-americasupermarketsgallery/list.

Food Business News. (2017). Exclusive: Tapping premium trends to drive growth. Retrieved May 21, 2018, from https://www.foodbusinessnews.net/articles/10684-exclusive-tapping-premium-trends-to-drive-growth.

European Commission. (2006). Environmental impact of products (EIPRO) e analysis of the life cycle environmental impacts related to the final consumption of the EU-25. Main Report. IPTS/ESTO Project. Technical Report EUR 22284 EN.

Franceschelli, M. V., Santoro, G., & Candelo, E. (2018). Business model innovation for sustainability: A food start-up case study. *British Food Journal, 120*(10), 2483–2494. https://doi.org/10.1108/BFJ01-2018-0049.

Garzón-Jiménez, R., & Zorio-Grima, A. (2021). Sustainability in the food and beverage sector and its impact on the cost of equity. *British Food Journal, 124*(8), 2497–2511.

Golini, R., & Gualandris, J. (2018). An empirical examination of the relationship between globalization, integration and sustainable innovation within manufacturing networks. *International Journal of Operations & Production Management, 38*(3), 874–894.

Goodland, R. (1995). The concept of environmental sustainability. *Annual Review of Ecology and Systematics, 26*(1), 1–24.

Graham, D. J., & Jeffery, R. W. (2011). Location, location, location: Eye-tracking evidence that consumers preferentially view prominently positioned nutrition information. *Journal of the American Dietetic Association, 111*(11), 1704–1711.

Grail Research. (2010). Green—The new color of luxury: Moving to a sustainable future. www.grailresearch.com/pdf/ContenPodsPdf/2010-Dec-Grail-Research-Green-The-New-Color-of Luxury.pdf, accessed 25 February 2013.

Grebitus, C., Roosen, J., & Seitz, C. C. (2015). Visual attention and choice: A behavioral economics perspective on food decisions. *Journal of Agricultural & Food Industrial Organization, 13*(1), 73–81.

Grunert, K. G., Hieke, S., & Wills, J. (2014). Sustainability labels on food products: Consumer motivation, understanding and use. *Food Policy, 44*, 177–189.

Han, J., Seo, Y., & Ko, E. (2017). Staging luxury experiences for understanding sustainable fashion consumption: A balance theory application. *Journal of Business Research, 74*, 162–167.

Hartmann, L. H., Nitzko, S., & Spiller, A. (2016). The significance of definitional dimensions of luxury food. *British Food Journal, 118*(8), 1976–1998.

Hartmann, L. H., Nitzko, S., & Spiller, A. (2017). Segmentation of German consumers based on perceived dimensions of luxury food. *Journal of Food Products Marketing, 23*(7), 733–768.

Huddleston, P. T., Behe, B. K., Driesener, C., & Minahan, S. (2018). Inside–outside: Using eye-tracking to investigate search-choice processes in the retail environment. *Journal of Retailing and Consumer Services, 43*, 85–93.

Istenič, S. P., & Bajec, J. F. (2021). Luxury food tour: perspectives and dilemmas on the" luxurification" of local culture in tourism product. *Acta geographica Slovenica, 61*(1), 169–184.

Jagtap, S., Bhatt, C., Thik, J., & Rahimifard, S. (2019). Monitoring potato waste in food manufacturing using image processing and internet of things approach. *Sustainability, 11*(11), 3173.

Janssen, C., Vanhamme, J., & Leblanc, S. (2017). Should luxury brands say it out loud? Brand conspicuousness and consumer perceptions of responsible luxury. *Journal of Business Research, 77*, 167–174.

Janssen, C., Vanhamme, J., Lindgreen, A., & Lefebvre, C. (2013). The catch-22 of responsible luxury: Effects of luxury product characteristics on consumers' perception of fit with corporate social responsibility. *Journal of Business Ethics.* https://doi.org/10.1007/s10551-013-1621-6.

Kahn, B. E. (2017). Using visual design to improve customer perceptions of online assortments. *Journal of Retailing, 93*(1), 29–42.

Kang, E. Y., & Sung, Y. H. (2022). Luxury and sustainability: The role of message appeals and objectivity on luxury brands' green corporate social responsibility. *Journal of Marketing Communications, 28*(3), 291–312.

Kapferer, J. N., & Michaut-Denizeau, A. (2017). Is luxury compatible with sustainability? Luxury consumers' viewpoint. In *Advances in Luxury Brand Management* (pp. 123–156). Palgrave Macmillan.

Keller, C., Magnus, K. H., Hedrich, S., Nava, P., & Tochtermann, T. (2014). *Succeeding in Tomorrow's Global Fashion Market.* McKinsey Global Institute.

Kendall, H. A., Lobao, L. M., & Sharp, J. S. (2006). Public concern with animal well-being: Place, social structural location, and individual experience. *Rural Sociology, 71*(3), 399–428.

Ki, C., & Kim, Y. K. (2016). Sustainable luxury fashion consumption and the moderating role of guilt. *Fashion, Industry and Education, 14*(1), 18–30.

King, A. J., Bol, N., Cummins, R. G., & John, K. K. (2019). Improving visual behavior research in communication science: An overview, review, and reporting recommendations for using eye-tracking methods. *Communication Methods and Measures, 13*(3), 149–177. https://doi.org/10.1080/19312458.2018.1558194.

Ko, E., Costello, J. P., & Taylor, C. R. (2019). What is a luxury brand? A new definition and review of the literature. *Journal of Business Research, 99*, 405–413.

Kong, H. M., Witmaier, A., & Ko, E. (2021). Sustainability and social media communication: How consumers respond to marketing efforts of luxury and non-luxury fashion brands. *Journal of Business Research, 131*, 640–651.

Kücükgül, E., Cerin, P., & Liu, Y. (2022). Enhancing the value of corporate sustainability: An approach for aligning multiple SDGs guides on reporting. *Journal of Cleaner Production, 333*, 130005.

Kumagai, K., & Nagasawa, S. Y. (2017). The effect of selective store location strategy and self-congruity on consumers' apparel brand attitudes toward luxury vs. non-luxury. *Journal of Global Fashion Marketing, 8*(4), 266–282.

Lahteenmaki, L., Lyly, M., & Urala, N. (2007). Consumer attitudes towards functional foods. In *Understanding Consumers of Food Products* (pp. 412–427). Woodhead. https://doi.org/10.1533/9781845692506.4.412.

Lee, H., Jang, Y., Kim, Y., Choi, H. M., & Ham, S. (2019). Consumers' prestige-seeking behavior in premium food markets: Application of the theory of the leisure class. *International Journal of Hospitality Management, 77*, 260–269.

Lee, H., Min, J., & Yuan, J. (2021). The influence of eWOM on intentions for booking luxury hotels by Generation Y. *Journal of Vacation Marketing, 27*(3), 237–251.

Lerro, M., Vecchio, R., Caracciolo, F., Pascucci, S., & Cembalo, L. (2018). Consumers' heterogeneous preferences for corporate social responsibility in the food industry. *Corporate Social Responsibility and Environmental Management, 25*(6), 1050–1061.

Li, H., Ye, Q., & Law, R. (2013). Determinants of customer satisfaction in the hotel industry: An application of online review analysis. *Asia Pacific Journal of Tourism Research, 18*(7), 784–802.

Liu, C. C., Chen, C. W., & Chen, H. S. (2019a). Measuring consumer preferences and willingness to pay for coffee certification labels in Taiwan. *Sustainability, 11*(5), 1297.

Liu, H., Jayawardhena, C., Osburg, V. S., & Babu, M. M. (2019b). Do online reviews still matter post-purchase? *Internet Research, 30*(1), 109–139.

Lunardo, R., & Saintives, C. (2013). The effect of naturalness claims on perceptions of food product naturalness in the point of purchase. *Journal of Retailing and Consumer Services*, *20*(6), 529–537.

Matzembacher, D. E., & Meira, F. B. (2018). Sustainability as business strategy in community supported agriculture: Social, environmental and economic benefits for producers and consumers. *British Food Journal*, *121*(2), 616–632. https://doi.org/10.1108/BFJ-03-2018-0207.

Maughan, L., Gutnikov, S., & Stevens, R. (2007). Like more, look more. Look more, like more: The evidence from eye-tracking. *Journal of Brand Management*, *14*(4), 335–342.

McClenachan, L., Dissanayake, S. T., & Chen, X. (2016). Fair trade fish: Consumer support for broader seafood sustainability. *Fish and Fisheries*, *17*(3), 825–838.

McDonough, W., & Braungart, M. (2010). *Cradle to Cradle: Remaking the Way We Make Things* (pp. 153–154). MacMillan.

Missimer, M., Robèrt, K. H., & Broman, G. (2016). A strategic approach to social sustainability–Part 1: Exploring the social system. *Journal of Cleaner Production*, *140*, 32–41.

Moscovici, D., Gow, J., Ugaglia, A. A., Rezwanul, R., Valenzuela, L., & Mihailescu, R. (2022). Consumer preferences for organic wine-global analysis of people and place. *Journal of Cleaner Production*, *368*, 133215.

Oliveira, D., Machín, L., Deliza, R., Rosenthal, A., Walter, E. H., Giménez, A., & Ares, G. (2016). Consumers' attention to functional food labels: Insights from eye-tracking and change detection in a case study with probiotic milk. *LWT-Food Science and Technology*, *68*, 160–167.

Olofsson, L., & Mark-Herbert, C. (2020). Creating shared values by integrating un sustainable development goals in corporate communication—The case of apparel retail. *Sustainability*, *12*(21), 8806.

Orazalin, N. (2019). Corporate governance and corporate social responsibility (CSR) disclosure in an emerging economy: Evidence from commercial banks of Kazakhstan. *Corporate Governance: The International Journal of Business in Society*, *19*, 490–507.

Orquin, J. L., Bagger, M. P., Lahm, E. S., Grunert, K. G., & Scholderer, J. (2020). The visual ecology of product packaging and its effects on consumer attention. *Journal of Business Research*, *111*, 187–195.

Orquin, J. L., Scholderer, J., & Jeppesen, H. (2012). What you see is what you buy: How saliency and surface size of packaging elements affect attention and choice. Paper presented at the Society for Advancement of Behavioural Economics, Granada, Spain.

Orquin, J. L., & Wedel, M. (2020). Contributions to attention-based marketing: Foundations, insights, and challenges. *Journal of Business Research*, *111*, 85–90. https://doi.org/10.1016/j.jbusres.2020.02.012.

Osburg, V. S., Akhtar, P., Yoganathan, V., & McLeay, F. (2019). The influence of contrasting values on consumer receptiveness to ethical information and ethical choices. *Journal of Business Research*, *104*, 366–379.

Osburg, V. S., Davies, I., Yoganathan, V., & McLeay, F. (2021). Perspectives, opportunities and tensions in ethical and sustainable luxury: Introduction to the thematic symposium. *Journal of Business Ethics*, *169*(2), 201–210.

Pearson, D., & Henryks, J. (2008). Marketing organic products: Exploring some of the pervasive issues. *Journal of Food Products Marketing, 14*, 95–108. https://doi.org/10.1080/10454440801986421.

Peschel, A. O., Orquin, J. L., & Loose, S. M. (2019). Increasing consumers' attention capture and food choice through bottom-up effects. *Appetite, 132*, 1–7.

Pomarici, E., & Vecchio, R. (2014). Millennial generation attitudes to sustainable wine: An exploratory study on Italian consumers. *Journal of Cleaner Production, 66*, 537–545.

Pullman, M. E., Maloni, M. J., & Dillard, J. (2010). Sustainability practices in food supply chains: How is wine different? *Journal of Wine Research, 21*(1), 35–56.

Russo, J. E. (2011). Eye fixations as a process trace. In *Process Tracing Methods for Decision Research* (pp. 43–64). Psychology Press.

Samant, S. S., & Seo, H. S. (2016). Effects of label understanding level on consumers' visual attention toward sustainability and process-related label claims found on chicken meat products. *Food Quality and Preference, 50*, 48–56.

SanMiguel, P., Pérez-Bou, S., Sádaba, T., & Mir-Bernal, P. (2021). How to communicate sustainability: From the corporate web to e-commerce. The case of the fashion industry. *Sustainability, 13*(20), 11363.

Saunders, M. N. (2012). Choosing research participants. *Qualitative Organizational Research: Core Methods and Current Challenges, 35*, 52.

Schlosser, A. E. (2003). Experiencing products in the virtual world: The role of goal and imagery in influencing attitudes versus purchase intentions. *Journal of Consumer Research, 30*(2), 184–198.

Schrobback, P., & Meath, C. (2020). Corporate sustainability governance: Insight from the Australian and New Zealand port industry. *Journal of Cleaner Production, 255*, 120–280.

Sciulli, L. M., Bebko, C. P., & Bhagat, P. (2017). How emotional arousal and attitudes influence ad response: Using eye tracking to gauge nonprofit print advertisement effectiveness. *Journal of Marketing Management, 5*(1), 1–11.

Seo, S., Ahn, H. K., Jeong, J., & Moon, J. (2016). Consumers' attitude toward sustainable food products: Ingredients vs. packaging. *Sustainability, 8*(10), 1073.

Shukla, P., Rosendo-Rios, V., & Khalifa, D. (2022). Is luxury democratization impactful? Its moderating effect between value perceptions and consumer purchase intentions. *Journal of Business Research, 139*, 782–793.

Siano, A., Conte, F., Amabile, S., Vollero, A., & Piciocchi, P. (2016). Communicating sustainability: An operational model for evaluating corporate websites. *Sustainability, 8*(9), 950.

Singh, K., & Misra, M. (2021). Linking corporate social responsibility (CSR) and organizational performance: The moderating effect of corporate reputation. *European Research on Management and Business Economics, 27*(1), 100139.

Sung, B., Butcher, L., & Easton, J. (2021). Elevating food perceptions through luxury verbal cues: An eye-tracking and electrodermal activity experiment. *Australasian Marketing Journal*, 18393349211028676.

Suopajärvi, L., Poelzer, G. A., Ejdemo, T., Klyuchnikova, E., Korchak, E., & Nygaard, V. (2016). Social sustainability in northern mining communities: A study of the European North and Northwest Russia. *Resources Policy, 47*, 61–68.

Statista. (2020). https://www.statista.com/forecasts/1093588/preference-for-premium-products-in-food-categories-in-the-us.

Statista. (2022). https://www.statista.com/forecasts/1298375/volume-food-consumption-worldwide.

Strong, E. K., Jr. (1925). *The Psychology of Selling and Advertising.* McGraw-Hill.

Talukdar, N., & Yu, S. (2020). Do materialists care about sustainable luxury? *Marketing Intelligence & Planning, 38*(4), 465–478.

Tait, P., Saunders, C., Dalziel, P., Rutherford, P., Driver, T., & Guenther, M. (2019). Estimating wine consumer preferences for sustainability attributes: A discrete choice experiment of Californian Sauvignon blanc purchasers. *Journal of Cleaner Production, 233,* 412–420.

Ting, S. L., Tse, Y. K., Ho, G. T. S., Chung, S. H., & Pang, G. (2014). Mining logistics data to assure the quality in a sustainable food supply chain: A case in the red wine industry. *International Journal of Production Economics, 152,* 200–209.

Torkayesh, A. E., Ecer, F., Pamucar, D., & Karamaşa, Ç. (2021). Comparative assessment of social sustainability performance: Integrated data-driven weighting system and CoCoSo model. *Sustainable Cities and Society, 71,* 102975.

Tosun, P., Yanar, M., Sezgin, S., & Uray, N. (2021). Meat substitutes in sustainability context: A content analysis of consumer attitudes. *Journal of International Food & Agribusiness Marketing, 33*(5), 541–563.

Toussaint, M., Cabanelas, P., & Blanco-González, A. (2021). Social sustainability in the food value chain: An integrative approach beyond corporate social responsibility. *Corporate Social Responsibility and Environmental Management, 28*(1), 103–115.

Truong, Y., & McColl, R. (2011). Intrinsic motivations, self-esteem, and luxury goods consumption. *Journal of Retailing and Consumer Services, 18*(6), 555–561.

Tseng, M. L., Lim, M. K., & Wu, K. J. (2018). Corporate sustainability performance improvement using an interrelationship hierarchical model approach. *Business Strategy and the Environment, 27*(8), 1334–1346.

Tuomisto, H. L. (2019). The eco-friendly burger: Could cultured meat improve the environmental sustainability of meat products? *EMBO Reports, 20*(1), e47395.

Valenzuela, L., Ortega, R., Moscovici, D., Gow, J., Alonso Ugaglia, A., & Mihailescu, R. (2022). Consumer willingness to pay for sustainable wine—The Chilean case. *Sustainability, 14*(17), 10910.

Vallance, S., Perkins, H. C., & Dixon, J. E. (2011). What is social sustainability? A clarification of concepts. *Geoforum, 42*(3), 342–348.

Van Loo, E. J., Caputo, V., Nayga, R. M., Jr., Seo, H.-S., Zhang, B., & Verbeke, W. (2015). Sustainability labels on coffee: Consumer preferences, willingness-to-pay and visual attention to attributes. *Ecological Economics, 118,* 215–225.

Van Loo, E. J., Grebitus, C., Nayga, R. M., Verbeke, W., & Roosen, J. (2018). On the measurement of consumer preferences and food choice behavior: The relation between visual attention and choices. *Applied Economic Perspectives and Policy, 40*(4), 538–562.

Van Loo, E. J., Grebitus, C., & Verbeke, W. (2021). Effects of nutrition and sustainability claims on attention and choice: An eye-tracking study in the context of a choice experiment using granola bar concepts. *Food Quality and Preference, 90,* 104100.

Wang, E., Cakmak, Y. O., & Peng, M. (2018). Eating with eyes—Comparing eye movements and food choices between overweight and lean individuals in a real-life buffet setting. *Appetite, 125,* 152–159.

Wang, J., Bai, H., & Han, W. (2017). Is your brain green? An ERP based study of consumers' choice over recycling services. In *International Conference on Service Systems and Service Management* (pp. 1–5). IEEE.

Wästlund, E., Shams, P., & Otterbring, T. (2018). Unsold is unseen… or is it? Examining the role of peripheral vision in the consumer choice process using eye-tracking methodology. *Appetite, 120*, 49–56.

WCED. (1987). *World Commission on Environment and Development: Our Common Future*. University Press.

White, K., Habib, R., & Hardisty, D. J. (2019). How to shift consumer behaviors to be more sustainable: A literature review and guiding framework. *Journal of Marketing, 83*(3), 22–49. https://doi.org/10.1177/0022242919825649.

Wilks, M., & Phillips, C. J. (2017). Attitudes to in vitro meat: A survey of potential consumers in the United States. *PloS One, 12*(2), e0171904.

Winston, A. (2016). Luxury brands can no longer ignore sustainability. *Harvard Business Review*, February 8. https://hbr.org/2016/02/luxury-brands-can-no-longer-ignore-sustainability.

WSSD. (2002). *World Summit on Sustainable Development: Report of the World Summit on Sustainable Development*. Johannesburg, South Africa.

Yamoah, F. A., & Acquaye, A. (2019). Unravelling the attitude-behaviour gap paradox for sustainable food consumption: Insight from the UK apple market. *Journal of Cleaner Production, 217*, 172–184.

Yang, S., Song, Y., & Tong, S. (2017). Sustainable retailing in the fashion industry: A systematic literature review. *Sustainability, 9*(7), 1266.

Yogesh, S. G., & Ravindran, D. S. (2018). Neuromarketing-an emerging trend in business. *International Research Journal of Business and Management, 4*, 82–87.

Appendix

Table A.1 T-Test results

Independent Samples Test

		Levene's Test for Equality of Variances		t-Test for Equality of Means		Significance		Mean Difference	Std. Error Difference	95% Confidence Interval of the Difference	
		F	Sig.	t	Df	One-Sided p	Two-Sided p			Lower	Upper
Efriend	Equal variances assumed	6.055	0.016	0.793	80	0.215	0.430	0.20732	0.26141	−0.31291	0.72754
	Equal variances not assumed			0.793	76.573	0.215	0.430	0.20732	0.26141	−0.31326	0.72790
att_price	Equal variances assumed	6.731	0.011	−1.259	80	0.106	0.212	−1.04764	0.83186	−2.70310	0.60781
	Equal variances not assumed			−1.259	66.356	0.106	0.212	−1.04764	0.83186	−2.70834	0.61305
att_sus	Equal variances assumed	10.388	0.002	−2.257	80	0.013	0.027	−2.64902	1.17352	−4.98440	−0.31365
	Equal variances not assumed			−2.257	67.210	0.014	0.027	−2.64902	1.17352	−4.99124	−0.30681
Cog	Equal variances assumes	2.035	0.158	−2.262	80	0.013	0.026	−0.20416	0.09024	−0.38375	−0.02457
	Equal variances not assumed			−2.262	45.972	0.014	0.028	−0.20416	0.09024	−0.38581	−0.02251

6 Exploring the Role of Sustainable Organic Food Consumption and the Role of Organic Food as a Luxury Product

A Case Study in Nepal

Udgam Mishra, Nirma Sadamali Jayawardena, and Park Thaichon

6.1 Introduction

One of the key drivers of the Anthropocene is the global food production system (Fraundorfer, 2022). Although newer innovations in agriculture have reduced hunger and improved nutrition, there remains a deficiency in one or more important nutrients in billions of people's diets, leading to the spread of infectious diseases (Rohr et al., 2019). Global food production has threatened food security followed by greenhouse gas emissions, water abstraction, soil, water, and air pollution (Berners-Lee et al., 2018; Lavuri et al., 2022). In this connection, there is the rapid emergence of organic food consumption (Berners-Lee et al., 2018).

The term "organic food" refers to food produced naturally without the use of fertilizers or pesticides, making it a healthier choice to consume (Rambabu et al., 2022). According to Halberg et al. (2009), organic farming is an unjustified luxury when the world faces a food shortage. In addition, regular users spend a considerable amount of money purchasing organic food without considering it to be a luxury item, but rather a good and safe food source (Halberg et al., 2009; Jensen et al., 2011). In contrast, organic food is being debated on a variety of platforms since customers with a high disposable income consider organic food to be a luxury product (Poulston et al., 2011). Additionally, the knowledge of its benefits leads to customers not being sensitive to organic food prices (Rambabu et al., 2022). Food is one of many tools for expressing oneself in different settings with different luxury goods (Mori et al., 1987).

6.1.1 The Importance of Organic Food Products

The sales of organic food have witnessed tremendous growth across various political borders (Rambabu et al., 2022). According to the Organic

DOI: 10.4324/9781003321378-6

Trade Association (2022), organic food sales in the United States exceeded $63 billion, an increase of 2% compared to last year, and 90% of total food sales are organic (IFOAM, 2022). In the western part of the world, luxury consumption patterns have changed and are inclined toward organic products (Hartmann et al., 2017) and 81% of organic food production companies are more profitable than conventional food due to luxury beliefs (Rambabu et al., 2022).

When considering the sales of organic food, organic food is willingly purchased by customers if the price is equal to non-organic food, but if the price is double, organic food becomes a luxury item (Hjelmar, 2011; Rana & Paul, 2020). Generally, organic food is best, however, it is an expensive luxury that not everyone can afford (Aschemann-Witzel & Niebuhr Aagaard, 2014; Nosi et al., 2020). Although organic food is expensive, it is a sign of high quality, and it has achieved the status of luxury (Hasimu et al., 2017). Hence, there has been increasing interest from marketers toward the sustainability and luxury of organic food consumption centering on the health impacts of conventional food and organic food consumption and food security (Pachapur et al., 2020). However, the threats to global sustainability that exist in the context of the food industry remain unexplored (Gulaliyev et al., 2019).

As organic food has become more prevalent in consumers' food baskets, frequent buyers are unsure whether their purchases should be considered normal goods or luxury goods (Yiridoe et al., 2005). Lexus and sustainability are pivotal motives for organic purchases, according to these studies (Yiridoe et al., 2005). Other key considerations include social influences, label standards, justifications, social structure, health-related impact, and environmental impact (Hansmann et al., 2020; Yiridoe et al., 2005). Additionally, it was found that organic food consumption is perceived differently (Feil et al., 2020) and that could be due to the reasons such as corporate image, corporate social responsibility, and consumer trust towards organic food (Yu et al., 2022). Although these studies are explanatory, limited study has been explored regarding sustainable organic food and the consideration of organic food consumption as a luxury product (Hasimu et al., 2017). This further emphasizes the need to underpin sustainability and organic food consumption under luxury product categories.

6.1.2 Background of the Study

This study is divided into two key sections. First, this study will explore sustainable organic food consumption, and second, the importance of considering organic food as a luxury item. The rapid spreading of awareness of the environmental impact on the agri-food sector has led to sustainability in the global food system as one of the utmost goals of this century (Rizzo et al., 2020). Following the above discussion, organic food has become the most widespread sustainable substitute for traditional food (Asian et al., 2019; Chowdhury et al., 2021). Luxury foods are those foods that offer refinement in texture, taste, fat content, or another quality (Veen, 2003). Consumers with high discretionary income tend organic food as a luxury food (Chowdhury et al., 2021; Poulston et al., 2011).

This study includes a detailed literature review and in-depth interviews with 25 regular organic food consumers in Nepal. Prior to the collection of data, a pilot study was conducted (Saraiva et al., 2021; Sexton et al., 2022). The pilot study group contained six consumers, who were regular organic food consumers and a sales representative of an organic food store in Nepal. Recently many individuals, institutions, and farmers were engaging in organic agriculture as the total organic land in Nepal has increased from 9,361 ha in 2017 to 11,851 ha in 2020, presenting a 26.6% increase every year contributing 0.0004% share in the global organic market (Nandwani et al., 2021). Nepal is a developing country and has a dynamic market, and the consumers of Nepal can show a greater interest in organic food consumption. This study is conducted using semi-structured interviews with 25 consumers who have consumed organic food and have at least five years of knowledge regarding it. This approach can be further justified based on the precedent of studies such as Guthman (2003); Sexton et al. (2022) and Chowdhury et al. (2021). All the data were collected from the capital city of Province No. 1 of Nepal i.e., Biratnagar from May 2022 to August 2022 (Saraiva et al., 2021). Every participant who participated in this study was interviewed in their convenience locations (Saraiva et al., 2021). All the interviews were recorded digitally and translated later. The interview transcripts were analyzed using SPSS *text analytics.*

Key Takeaways

- Organic food is willingly purchased by customers when the price is equal to non-organic food, but if the price is double, organic food can be considered a luxury item.
- Marketers are increasingly concerned about the health impacts of conventional food consumption, organic food consumption, and food security.
- Food industry threats toward global sustainability remain unexplored.

6.2 Literature Review

The literature review of this study was divided into three main sections: an overview of organic agriculture, the role of organic food as a luxury product, and the role of organic food as a sustainable product. This study aims to bridge the gap between sustainable organic food consumption in Nepal by exploring the perceptions of organic food consumers in Nepal (Chowdhury et al., 2021). For example, Nepalese organic farms are currently practicing ways to minimize wastage in their farms by using several sustainable practices such as crop rotation and embracing diversity; planting perennials and cover

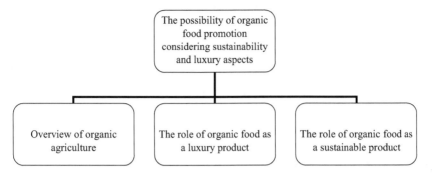

Figure 6.1 The overview of the literature review section of this study.

crops; reducing tillage and by bringing livestock and crops together (Chowdhury et al., 2021; Sekhar et al., 2021; Singh & Verma, 2017).

Furthermore, the concept of organic food as a luxury product evolves based on the tourist attraction in Nepal. In Nepal's rural Tourism sector, representative local associations facilitate innovation through the integration of dynamic capabilities and resources (Sekhar et al., 2021; Shrestha et al., 2023). Although, the study confirms the significant role government plays in facilitating cooperation among stakeholders to legitimize relationships and ensure sustainability, the study further outlines the possibility of organic food promotion as a luxury item. Figure 6.1 further illustrates the overview of the literature review of this section.

Based on the above diagram, this research aims to outline the importance of sustainable organic food consumption and the role of organic food as a luxury product in Nepal.

6.2.1 Brief Introduction to Organic Agriculture

The movement of organic agriculture in developed and industrial countries such as the United States, United Kingdom, Japan, and Germany materialized in the 1930s and 1940s as an alternative to the use of synthetic nitrogen fertilizers (Heckman, 2006). The organic agriculture concept was developed by Sir Albert Howard before 1940 and later his philosophy and research were covered by F. H. King in his book, *Farmers of Forty Centuries* (Heckman, 2006). The philosophy of healthy food consumption and production is not new in the global scenario as a comparison to the conventional farming system, a study conducted by Stanhill (1990) could not show any evidence of organic systems with greater yield (Heckman, 2006). There is a debatable situation wherein some claim organic agriculture is an inefficient approach to food production nonetheless, organic food is an emerging and speedy growing segment in the global food industry (Reganold & Wachter, 2016; Tal, 2018). Conventional agriculture provides a higher yield than organic agriculture and offers sustainability at the global level to meet the needs of the population simultaneously reducing the cumulative environmental impact (Singh & Verma, 2017; Tal, 2018). In the global picture, the demand for organic food has increased principally in Western countries, Australia is among the highest certified organic farmed land with 23 million hectares under cultivation and India is among the most recognized organic farmers (Sexton et al., 2022; Tal, 2018).

Principles of organic agriculture formulated by IFOAM are health, ecology, fairness, and care (Tal, 2018), and the primary goal of organic agriculture is to use ecological processes instead of external inputs to manage crops and livestock (Seufert et al., 2019). Hence, there is a requirement for a holistic method for enhancing soil fertility, water storage, and biological control of crops and disease (Chowdhury et al., 2021). Organic cultivation has a great aid in increasing social welfare and the logical use of natural resources such as water, land, and energy that diminishes greenhouse gases which improves land cultivation (Cidón et al., 2021). Additionally, developed nations have adopted the latest technologies such as biotechnology, artificial intelligence, robotics, nanoscience, nanotechnology, satellite and remote screening, and drones in organic food cultivation (Chowdhury et al., 2021; Solaiman & Salaheen, 2019).

The methods of practicing agriculture have always been the subject of debate, with one highly productive, not ecologically sustainable traditional production systems that are dominated by monoculture, capital, chemical, and energy dependency which is harmful to the environment (Zimdahl, 2022). There will always be a difference between poorly managed conventional farms and organic farms, and the way in which conventional farms are managed is changing as time progresses (Trewavas, 2004). In addition, organic agriculture is not only motivated by the preservation of biodiversity, health protection, and environmental preservation but also perceived profitability (Alotaibi et al., 2021). For example, chemical protection crops have become increasingly popular, which are approved for organic production and promote high yield values and yield stability, but at the same time negatively affect a range of organisms in fields and agricultural landscapes, some of which are currently approved for use in organic agriculture in Sweden (Alotaibi et al., 2021). With the different organisms in the field, organic production isn't the best method for agricultural production (Chowdhury et al., 2021; Solaiman & Salaheen, 2019). Despite its risks, organic production has become a global trend due to its health and environmental benefits (Asian et al., 2019; Singh & Verma, 2017).

Organic farming has emerged to become one of the platforms for job creation over conventional farming (Finley et al., 2018). Organic farming has employed more workers per acre (95% CI: 2–12% more) and a greater fraction (95% CI: 13–43% more) of employed workers in organic farming worked more than 150 days compared to the average farm indicating more workers requirement (Finley et al., 2018). Organic farming is redefining the method of production in the context of agriculture around the communities and has largely contributed to the food security of small landowners that promoted self-reliance on food, protection of natural resources and environment, production management for the sufficient economy by ensuring sustainable food production (Finley et al., 2018). There are various institutions that offer diverse courses related to organic agriculture both physical and online modes as short-term certification courses (Finley et al., 2018; Saraiva et al., 2021).

In summary, organic agriculture is rapidly increasing and taking a definite shape. In addition to providing job opportunities, organic agriculture has contributed to economic development. In terms of sustainability, environmental concerns, and ethical application, it is a major platform for employment and economic contribution. People who consume organic agriculture determine its sustainability. Therefore, interviewing organic food consumers and store representatives is necessary to explore the factors affecting sustainable organic food consumption and the use of organic food as a luxury component in the lifestyle among people in Nepal. The next section discusses the role of organic food as a luxury product.

Key Takeaways

- Organic farming has emerged to become one of the platforms for job creation over conventional farming.
- In addition to providing job opportunities, organic agriculture has contributed to economic development.
- In terms of sustainability, environmental concerns, and ethical application, it is a major platform for employment and economic contribution.

6.2.2 The Role of Organic Food as a Luxury Product

There is a rapid increase in the consumption of organic food (Liu et al., 2022). It is estimated that the global organic food market will reach $320 billion by 2025, up from the current level of $77 billion (Liu et al., 2022; Septianto et al., 2019). Due to its high involvement and longer production time, organic food is more expensive than conventional food (Kautish et al., 2019). Based on the study conducted by Singh and Verma (2017), it was identified that price is considered an explanatory variable in India as the "green revolution" technology adopted by Indian farmers increased production while reducing pesticides and fertilizers ending up bearing higher expenses in farming. Thus, organic food can be considered a luxury item due to the higher expenses in production such as environmental protection techniques, minimum time and labor, lower yields of crops, and due to the maintenance of strict organic certification standards within the farm (Seufert et al., 2019).

The intention of consumers to purchase organic foods may not always translate into actual purchases (Finley et al., 2018; Saraiva et al., 2021). Therefore, it is also necessary to examine how socio-demographic factors affect actual buying behavior (Han, 2021; Singh & Verma, 2017). Consumer attitudes toward organic food products are influenced by four factors (health consciousness, knowledge of organic foods, subjective norms, and perceived price) (Wijekoon & Sabri, 2021). In addition to these four factors, one additional factor (availability) affects purchase intentions toward organic foods. Consumers consider store location when making purchase-related decisions (Kautish et al., 2019; Singh & Verma, 2017).

In addition, previous research has demonstrated that luxury products are perceived by many consumers in a more psychologically distant manner than conventional products, thus resulting in a high construal level (Kautish et al., 2019). Despite being highly desirable, luxury products are only affordable to a limited number of people (Septianto et al., 2019). In fact, some consumers may feel that luxury is foreign to them (Ding & Legendre, 2022). Hence, organic food is perceived to be more exclusive than conventional food, leading consumers to view organic food in a more psychologically distant manner than conventional food (Saraiva et al., 2021) showing that organic (as opposed to conventional) food is associated with a high level of construal by making it a luxury product. Furthermore, the number of consumers of organic food has increased rapidly in recent years (Saraiva et al., 2021). According to the leisure class theory, luxury goods are products whose demand increases in proportion to their price increase (Vernon, 1974) and faster than the increase in incomes of potential buyers (Beierlein et al., 2013). From the perspective of economics, an increase in price increases the demand for the product (Septianto et al., 2019). People are psychologically inclined to buy expensive and rare goods (Septianto et al., 2019). Furthermore, it distinguishes between wealthy and less privileged consumers by using organic food as a symbol of socio-economic value.

According to the Organic Trade Association, demand for organic food is undeniable and sustainable (Organic Trade Association, 2022). As stated by the Italian organic food department, certain foods are consumed as symbols of status (Canavari, 2007) and the production of organic food requires skilled labor (Jansen, 2000). Organic production contributes to economic development in various nations, such as the United States, Canada, and Japan (Rana & Paul, 2017). Its exorbitant price and exclusivity have increased the demand for organic food in elite societies (Rana & Paul, 2017).

Additionally, Polish consumers are convinced of the health benefits of organic food due to its high price (Bryła, 2016). There are several reasons why organic food an absolute luxury is: a significant portion of the world cannot afford organic food because they are striving to meet their living expenses and their only option is starvation (Liu et al., 2022; Septianto et al., 2019). In terms of health, there is no concrete evidence that organic food is more beneficial than non-organic food (Liu et al., 2022). A study conducted by Petrescu and Petrescu-Mag (2015) found that over 33% of Romanians consume organic food as it is a fashionable trend.

Furthermore, research has also demonstrated that organic food consumption is motivated by altruistic motives, including perceived environmental friendliness and improved animal welfare (Soler et al., 2022). The consumption of organic food is also associated with altruistic motives (e.g., universalism, benevolence) (Vardarlıer & Girgin, 2022). The research also indicates that when consumers conceptualize sustainable food and effective strategies for reducing the impact of their food consumption on the environment, organic food is seen as a sustainable source of food over and above other strategies, such as reducing meat consumption (Potter et al., 2023).

Key Takeaways

- Due to its high involvement and longer production time, organic food is more expensive than conventional food.
- The intention of consumers to purchase organic foods may not always translate into actual purchases and it is necessary to examine how socio-demographic factors affect actual buying behavior.
- Consumers perceive organic food as more exclusive than conventional food, resulting in a more psychological distance indicating that organic (as opposed to conventional) food is associated with high levels of connotation since it is viewed as a luxury product.
- Organic production contributes to economic development in various nations, such as the United States, Canada, Japan, and Poland.

6.2.3 The Role of Organic Food as a Sustainable Product

Cultural differences have led to different perceptions of sustainable products (Serravalle et al., 2022; Yu et al., 2022). Sustainable food is discussed in this section in terms of the supply chain, which includes sourcing raw materials and processing organic food. In addition, we discuss the global scenario supporting organic food sustainability. In addition to causing the demand for organic raw materials, there is also increasing competition for organic raw materials, which results in challenges with maintaining stable raw material supplies at times when they are needed at a time when season and storage costs are of the utmost importance (Yu et al., 2022). Organic food production in Poland is highly dependent on raw materials imported from other countries due to the limited availability of raw materials (Górska-Warsewicz et al., 2021; Królak et al., 2022).

The California Organic Food Act of 1979 lists specific raw materials that should not be used in the production of organic food, including lime and sulfur (Stanhill, 1990). Since organic food has become more popular in both industrialized nations, such as the United States and Canada, the price of raw materials has increased (Nosi et al., 2020). Due to the high cost of organic food, measures have been taken to control the supply of raw materials and one of the methods is the integration of conventional and organic agriculture, commonly referred to as sustainable agriculture (Carrié & Smith, 2022; Martínez-Sabater et al., 2022). Sustainable agriculture aims to achieve three principal outcomes: environmental health, economic profitability, and social and economic equality, with an improvement in the food distribution system, a reduction in food waste, and a narrowing of yield gaps (Carrié & Smith, 2022; Martínez-Sabater et al., 2022).

The development of nanotechnology-based sustainable alternatives to plant management is another way to reduce the dangers arising from bacteria, viruses, insects, seeds, and food production (Panzarini et al., 2022; Rasheed et al., 2022). On the other hand, researchers up to date have concluded that the high demand for organic foods is also due to health and environmental concerns (Niggli, 2015; Rasheed et al., 2022). According to a study comparing organically produced vegetables with integrated vegetables (Fjelkner-modig et al., 2000), organically produced vegetables yielded 60–95% less (Fjelkner-modig et al., 2000). As a result of a study conducted in India by Koner and Laha (2021), zero-budget natural farming (ZBNF) and scientific organic farming were not significantly different in yield and production cost, but ZBNF led to an increase in income for farmers, while scientific organic farming led to a substantial reduction in income (Carrié & Smith, 2022; Martínez-Sabater et al., 2022).

The availability and sustainability of organic products have been raised considering the lack of raw materials for organic farming and different platforms (Martínez-Sabater et al., 2022; Moshood et al., 2022). Several government bodies have formulated lists of raw materials that are harmful to use in production based on the nature and superiority of their soil (He et al., 2022; Moshood et al., 2022). Compared to conventional agriculture, this method is time-consuming and yields lower yields (Hazarika et al., 2022). To meet the global food demand, new and innovative farming practices are needed in terms of raw materials, and organic farming differs significantly from conventional farming (Hazarika et al., 2022).

In countries with a high demand for organic products and a limited supply, this factor should be carefully considered (Panzarini et al., 2022; Rasheed et al., 2022). For example, developing countries such as Bangladesh, India, Pakistan, and Sri Lanka is still in the process of exogenous shocks, income growth, relative prices, and environmental consciousness (Fjelkner-modig et al., 2000; Panzarini et al., 2022).

The use of mineral fertilizers and synthetic pesticides is prohibited in organic production enhancing crop rotation, intercropping and biological control (van Bruggen et al., 2016). Many pesticides used in Uganda and Costa Rica are claimed highly hazardous by World Health Organization and maximum farmers know about the negative impact on the health of the consumers (Staudacher et al., 2020). Recently, there are various fertilizers labeled as 'organic fertilizers' and sold freely in the domestic market of developing countries (Fjelkner-modig et al., 2000). Some of the raw materials used in organic farming are animal manure, household garbage, industrial waste, agriculture waste, and municipal sludge (Fjelkner-modig et al., 2000).

Key Takeaways

- A sustainable food supply chain, which includes raw materials and organic food processing, is discussed in this section.
- In sustainable agriculture, there are three principal outcomes: environmental health, economic profitability, and social and economic equality, as well as improved food distribution, reduced food waste, and narrowed yield gaps.
- Developing nanotechnology-based sustainable alternatives to plant management is another way to reduce the dangers associated with bacteria, viruses, insects, seeds, and food production.
- Researchers have concluded, however, that the high demand for organic foods is also due to concerns regarding health and the environment.

6.3 Research Method

This study was conducted by using qualitative interviews. The authors conducted 25 interviews with regular organic food consumers in Nepal. Table 6.1 list the demographic identities of interviewees as follows.

Interviewees with more or the same ideas and opinions are summarized and endorsed together. The order of interview questions followed an order of different levels of sustainability namely investigation of the consumption of organic products, sustainability of the organic market, and sustainable demand for organic food. Table 6.2 shows the interview questions used in the study as follows.

6.4 Thematic Results

The findings of the interviews showed three main factors regarding sustainability and luxury role as (a) investment in an organic product, (b) sustainability of the organic market, and (c) the demand for organic products. These findings explain the behavior of consumers towards organic products as luxury.

6.4.1 Investment in Organic Products

The investment in organic products is concerned with the consumer's intention to consume organic food, which results in health and environmental benefits for them and their family members and friends. Organic food

Table 6.1 Brief profile of participants

Participants	Age	Gender	Job Role
P1	20–29	Male	University student
P2	30–39	Male	Banker
P3	20–29	Male	University student
P4	20–29	Female	Accountant
P5	50–59	Female	Manager
P6	40–49	Male	Chef
P7	30–39	Female	Housewife
P8	30–39	Female	Housewife
P9	30–39	Female	Housewife
P10	20–29	Male	University student
P11	40–49	Female	Hotel Manager
P12	50–59	Male	Officer
P13	20–29	Female	University student
P14	30–39	Female	Housewife
P15	50–59	Male	Director
P16	30–39	Male	Banker
P17	30–39	Female	Housewife
P18	30–39	Female	PhD student
P19	40–49	Male	Manager
P20	40–49	Female	Officer
P21	50–59	Male	Director
P22	20–29	Female	University student
P23	20–29	Female	University student
P24	40–49	Female	Housewife
P25	40–49	Female	Housewife

consumption is chiefly motivated by health benefits and the absence of pesticides and fertilizers (Rizzo et al., 2020). This is further identified using the below thematic concepts:

> Not only my health but the health of my family is concerned with food consumption. You have no idea about the kind of food you are eating but the impact is seen after years. It is good to eat organic food. (Participant 2, Male, 30s). The price of organic food is twice the price of average food but ultimately the expenses are the same if someone is hospitalized. It is an investment in ourselves. (Participant 21, Male, 50s). Though it isn't a habit passed from generation to generation, it has several benefits.
> (Participant 14)

Health benefits, long-term well-being, and future requirements are the primary motives of organic food. Specifically, consumers consider organic food consumption as a long-term investment in their health and the environment. Based on the comment of Participant 22, we have shown that organic food is a symbol of social status (Hansmann et al., 2020). "My family is financially well built [....]. Consumption of organic food gives me a sense of recognition than other benefits" (Participant 22).

Table 6.2 Interview questions

	Interview Questions	Related to Sustainability
1	What role would organic farming play in the future when the entire world is talking about sustainability?	Product
2	How does your consumption pattern of organic food affect conventional food?	Demand
3	Why is organic food considered ecological in the food industry?	Product
4	What activities are adopted by organic agriculture farmers to stay in the competition?	Product
5	How are you comfortable and assured about organic food purchase and consumption?	Product
6	Other than environmental and health benefits, what economic and social benefits does organic consumption provide?	Market
7	Many debates about whether organic food is luxury food. What do you think about it?	Demand
8	How creative are the organic food retailer?	Product
9	Do organic farming results in wastage and harm the environment?	Product
10	Do you think organic food is healthier than conventional food?	Demand, product
11	What role do you think organic farming plays in the sustainable food industry?	Product
12	Have you witnessed any change in consumption patterns in recent years?	Demand
13	Should global farmers opt for organic farming?	Product, market
14	Do people willingly listen to the benefits of organic food?	Demand
15	Where do you see the organic market in ten years?	Product, market

Compared to conventional food, organic food in Nepal is more expensive, indicating that it is of higher quality. Organic food has a greater value when it is consumed over a longer period of time by the consumer. The purchase of organic food is a long-term investment for themselves, especially for their children:

> I feel like, investing in garments and other materialistic items, I invest in food is good. Basically, I want to provide the best for my children and food comes in priority. We don't find the kind of safe and healthy food that we found in the 20s.
>
> (Participant 25)

When people lack knowledge about investment, they do not invest for the long term. In our study, participants were able to describe the benefits of organic food, how it is produced, and chemical-free production. Due to the lack of policy and labeling systems in Nepal, they purchased their food from specific stores that were well-known in the city as organic stores. As a result, it can be concluded that consumers are aware of the difference between organic and non-organic foods. As organic consumers, participants promoted themselves to their neighbors and family members. The number of advertisements for organic food was nil or zero. Word-of-mouth promotion is the only means of promoting a business. Without knowing the benefits of organic food, people are less likely to consider investing in organic food in the long run. Packaging, certification, and labeling play a vital role in encouraging people to invest in organic products.

6.4.2 Sustainability of Organic Food Markets

To adopt sustainability practices that are related to the high quality of organic products, it is crucial to understand the production process of organic products that are less harmful to health and the environment. This is further identified using the below thematic concepts:

> Organic products are more a fashion these days and we buy organic products as it has become a trend rather understating the positive aspect of it. Every new thought and practice is a fashion, be organic or non-organic. If non-organic practices after 10 years come into practice would again be a fashion and signify luxuries like the race of a horse and a car. Few know about the health and environmental value of organic food, but many follow them considering it as a new lifestyle and trend. I am too into fashion and purchase organic products.
>
> (Participant 10)

The sustainability of organic products relies basically on behavioral aspects such as perception, attitude, and motivation (Feil et al., 2020). Similarly, the sustainability of organic food relies on the thought process of individuals (Feil et al., 2020). Our participants linked a sustainable food consumption lifestyle which would adopt non-organic or conventional products if it becomes a trend in the future. Furthermore, retailers sell products that are in demand and in fashion. To locate the items that are in demand, retailers are aware of the perception of the venue. However, it does not indicate the sustainability of organic products but rather signifies social status and class. The comment from Participant 25 further illustrates this viewpoint as follows:

> Mostly people with high income and earnings are into fashion and luxury. But people with certain income level care for benefits than lifestyle. They consume it because of its value and benefits of it. People with high income tend to purchase organic products to stay in fashion than recognizing the benefits of it.
>
> (Participant 25)

Several respondents expressed concern about certification, labeling, and una-wareness as key factors for the sustainability of organic products. Participant 18 defines her value of organic products as: 'I buy organic products because I care about the health and the environment' (Participant 18). Another medium that educates respondents is old, aged citizens as they indicated the health benefits while consuming chemicals, fertilizers, and pesticides free food. Further other forms of information to obtain sustainability-related information are the booklets that are distributed by the retailers at the time of visit to the store.

> Some retailers inform about the health benefits that come from organic food consumption. Retailers in regularly manner share information about the method of production and its long-term benefits of it. At certain times, retailers even gather people and promote organic products. These programs raise the confidence and trust of consumers towards organic food.
>
> (Participant 12)

The practice of communicating sustainability was thus carried out by inform-ing retailers, and elderly citizens regarding the method of production and influencing their behavioral aspects such as perception, attitude, and moti-vation. By implementing such practices, organic products will become more useful. As well as educating consumers about the production method, the outlets that confirm organic products while illustrating the purchasing pat-tern could lead to organic sustainability.

6.4.3 Demand for Organic Products

The consumption and use of organic products will ultimately increase their demand (Cabigiosu, 2020). Research has shown, however, that demand for organic foods is increasing in the global market (Rohr et al., 2019). The demand for organic foods is influenced by perceived risks including una-vailability, performance, and price (Cabigiosu, 2020). If the desired product is not available when it is needed, people substitute purchases. As high-lighted by participant 5, organic food in Nepal is not readily available:

> In Nepal, people tend to switch purchases if the products aren't avail-able at the times required. People don't enjoy waiting for organic food because there is a number of alternatives at a lower price. I think people must order in advance or order from different locations to fulfill their desire.
>
> (Participant 5)

As a result of its low price and easy availability, conventional food has remained in fashion in Nepal. Today, health–conscious consumers are linking organic food to health benefits, environmental benefits, and sustainable alternatives. There is a growing demand for healthy eating habits today. Participants 17 describe the different factors, freshness, and taste of organic food, similar to Martindale's (2021) study as follows.

> The taste and freshness that I get while eating organic food are different. While the packed and stored food does not have a freshness and lose its taste day after day. I started cooking organic food soon after my husband came from Dubai. He told me about the taste and freshness of organic food. I only look for organic food and inform my relatives about its taste and freshness.
>
> (Participant 17)

Our participants also exhibited a high level of disbelief when purchasing regular items. The participants did not purchase organic food for a period of time because they did not believe that organic food offered health and environmental benefits. In each of the food stores they visited, organic food was not properly regarded, creating a sense of uncertainty. One of the reasons for skepticism was that department stores did not sell organic products:

> I couldn't believe it the first time when I heard about organic food. To some extent, I could adjust to the health impact but could believe in the environmental impact because the retailer never sold organic food. Even when I asked about organic food, they often ignored it and said these are new ways to sell food, don't believe it.
>
> (Participant 11)

The participants all connected symbolic meanings to their consumption of organic food. The purchase of organic products was not accompanied by any additional materials or knowledge to help the customer understand it. Most participants knew the production system and standards of organic farming and were aware of the price difference between organic and non–organic food. Materials used in the practice include organic foods, retail stores, labeling packaging of the products, and posters used in marketing.

Key Takeaways

- Organic products are purchased by consumers who intend to consume organic food, which benefits their health and the environment.
- Organic food in Nepal is more expensive than conventional food, indicating that it is of higher quality. Health benefits, long-term well-being, and future requirements are the primary motivators.
- Due to the lack of policy and labeling systems in Nepal, they purchased their food from specific stores that were well-known in the city as organic stores.

- Understanding how organic products are produced that are less harmful to health and the environment is crucial to adopting sustainable practices related to high-quality organic products.
- The demand for organic foods is influenced by perceived risks including unavailability, performance, and price.

6.5 Discussion of the Findings

This study proposed several new insights into the current organic food consumption in Nepal through two ways of sustainability and luxury markets (Sapkota et al., 2021; Suman, 2021). Today, decisions are influenced more by social and cultural factors than by individual factors (Dahal & Dhakal, 2016). Organic food and luxury have attracted the attention of researchers as a result of the shift in decision-making, which is still unrecognized in many nations (Hazarika et al., 2022). Based on the findings of this study, organic food consumption is not only about health and the environment, but also about perception, attitude, and motivation (Hazarika et al., 2022; Nandwani et al., 2021). This illustrates how organic food can be considered an additional form of luxury fashion (Hazarika et al., 2022; Nandwani et al., 2021).

Luxury has evolved from garments, cosmetics, and similar products (Christodoulides & Wiedmann, 2022). Consumers are willing to pay a premium, pay in advance, and visit different locations for purchases based on their attitudes and perception toward organic food (Lang & Rodrigues, 2022). This has inbuilt a different ambiance of organic food creating a logic of luxury and fashion (Nosi et al., 2020). This has led to a debate about what constitutes an authentic luxury (Nosi et al., 2020). Our study of organic food consumption revealed the same results. There has been a change in the way people consume organic food (Nosi et al., 2020). People who can afford organic food consume it, regardless of whether it provides health benefits or other benefits associated with luxury or fashion (Nafees et al., 2022). Hence, our study contributes to the literature about organic food signifying luxury or a symbol of fashion.

Marketers and policymakers can gain crucial insight into the kinds of marketing policies that can be used to promote organic foods based on the results of this study (Harris-Fry et al., 2022). It is important to realize that different consumer perceptions can arise based on socio-economic status (Harris-Fry et al., 2022). By connecting organic food with luxury, food production houses can capture mileage and create a different market proposition (Adhikari et al., 2021). Moreover, positioning organic food based on health and environmental benefits and incorporating luxury into it can be a powerful marketing strategy (Adhikari et al., 2021). The "green" aspect of organic food has been exploited by marketers, but our findings strongly suggest promoting organic food as a luxury product (Makaju & Kurunju, 2021).

Organic food has long been promoted as a luxury product (Harris-Fry et al., 2022; Makaju & Kurunju, 2021). It has been demonstrated in various studies that promoting organic food as a luxury will enhance the quality of life of consumers and the living standards of food producers at the same time (Adhikari et al., 2021). Numerous studies have demonstrated the negative effects of conventional food; therefore, marketers should create awareness regarding the benefits of organic food (Harris-Fry et al., 2022; Malla et al., 2021). In turn, this will result in the formulation of potential market segments. The policies must be a win-win situation for both the consumer and the seller (Malla et al., 2021).

Thus, small, and rural farmers will be encouraged and motivated to engage in organic farming, thereby increasing the supply of organic food (Joshi et al., 2021). Organic farming should be understood by universities, and they should establish syllabuses that teach the method and its benefits (Joshi et al., 2021). Politicians should rethink organic farming's prospects and contribution to economic development in the future (Harris-Fry et al., 2022; Makaju & Kurunju, 2021). Organic farming is a small part of economic policy and as a luxury product, organic farming has potential on both a national and international scale (Harris-Fry et al., 2022; Malla et al., 2021).

Key Takeaways

- Organic food and luxury have attracted the attention of researchers as a result of the shift in decision-making, which is still unrecognized in many nations
- Consumers are willing to pay a premium, pay in advance, and visit different locations for purchases based on their attitudes and perception toward organic food
- Marketers and policymakers can gain crucial insight into the types of marketing policies that can be used to promote organic foods based on the results of this study

6.6 Implications for Marketers and Policymakers on Sustainable and Luxury Organic Food Consumption

Researchers, policymakers, and administration bodies can benefit from three broad practical implications identified by the authors (Adhikari et al., 2021; Lamichhane, 2022). First, food security needs to focus on the investment in organic products which results in health and environmental benefits for consumers (Lamichhane, 2022). Agricultural output and job creation have become hot topics in Nepal as a result of foreign investment in the agricultural sector (Harris-Fry et al., 2022; Nafees et al., 2022). A major problem in the Nepalese agricultural sector is the difficulty in selling products (Makaju & Kurunju, 2021). International access to domestic products is provided by foreign direct investment approaches (Makaju & Kurunju, 2021). The presence of many economic sectors on international markets is usually necessary to ensure sales (Makaju & Kurunju, 2021) as agricultural techniques on organic food production aspects become easier through higher capital via foreign direct investment.

Second, when considering the sustainability of organic food markets, a major challenge facing developing countries such as Nepal is food security, which is closely related to social stability as poverty in these countries can reach very high levels (Finley et al., 2018; Saraiva et al., 2021). Hence, this fact further ensures the need for more food safety standards to be implemented in the agricultural sector through the construction of micro-hydropower plants, solar plants, and wind energy systems at a variety of scales (Lamichhane, 2022).

Third, the policymakers should be enlightened about the fact regarding the demand for organic products (Harris-Fry et al., 2022; Malla et al., 2021). In the long run, organic products will become more and more popular (Cabigiosu, 2020). There is, however, growing demand for organic foods on the global market (Rohr et al., 2019). As organic products are not available in every grocery store, which made it is considered luxury items (Cabigiosu, 2020). To update the energy situation in Nepal, the government needs to compile a comprehensive report (Lamichhane, 2022). There are several ministries and departments involved in the energy sector; however, clear data on all energy systems and open-access databases regarding the energy systems should be created and updated regularly (Cabigiosu, 2020).

Key Takeaways

- Food security needs to focus on investment in organic products which results in health and environmental benefits for consumers.
- The sustainability of organic food markets is also strongly related to food security, which is closely related to social stability, as poverty in these countries can reach very high levels.
- The policymakers should be enlightened about the fact regarding the demand for organic products.

6.7 Summary

The purpose of this chapter is to provide insights based on the findings of a qualitative case study conducted in Nepal which explores the factors affecting sustainable organic food consumption and the use of organic food as a luxury component in the lifestyle among people. This study provided marketers and policymakers with some key insights into various marketing policies that may be used to promote organic foods. The importance of understanding the various perceptions of consumers that can arise due to their socio-economic status plays a vital role in luxury marketing related to food. The study indicated that organic food consumption should be marketed as a luxury lifestyle component, despite attempts to exploit the "green" aspect of organic food items.

References

Adhikari, J., Shrestha, M., & Paudel, D. (2021). Nepal's growing dependency on food imports: a threat to national sovereignty and ways forward. *Nepal Public Policy Review*, 1, 68–86.

Alotaibi, B. A., Yoder, E., Brennan, M. A., & Kassem, H. S. (2021). Perception of organic farmers towards organic agriculture and role of extension. *Saudi Journal of Biological Sciences*, 28(5), 2980–2986.

Aschemann-Witzel, J., & Niebuhr Aagaard, E. M. (2014). Elaborating on the attitude–behaviour gap regarding organic products: young Danish consumers and in-store food choice. *International Journal of Consumer Studies*, 38(5), 550–558.

Asian, S., Hafezalkotob, A., & John, J. J. (2019). Sharing economy in organic food supply chains: a pathway to sustainable development. *International Journal of Production Economics*, 218, 322–338.

Beierlein, J. G., Schneeberger, K. C., & Osburn, D. D. (2013). *Principles of agribusiness management* (pp. 1–371). Waveland Press.

Berners-Lee, M., Kennelly, C., Watson, R., & Hewitt, C. N. (2018). Current global food production is sufficient to meet human nutritional needs in 2050 provided there is radical societal adaptation. *Elementa: Science of the Anthropocene*, 6(52), 1–14.

Bryła, P. (2016). Organic food consumption in Poland: motives and barriers. *Appetite*, 105, 737–746.

Cabigiosu, A. (2020). An overview of the luxury fashion industry. In *Digitalization in the luxury fashion industry. Palgrave advances in luxury* (pp. 9–31). Palgrave Macmillan.

Canavari, M. (2007). Current issues in organic food: Italy. In *Organic food* (pp. 171–183). Springer.

Carrié, R., Ekroos, J., & Smith, H. G. (2022). Turnover and nestedness drive plant diversity benefits of organic farming from local to landscape scales. *Ecological Applications*, 32(4), 1–15.

Chowdhury, S., Meero, A., Rahman, A. A. A., Islam, K. A., Zayed, N. M., & Hasan, K. R. (2021). An empirical study on the factors affecting organic food purchasing behavior in Bangladesh: analyzing a few factors. *Academy of Strategic Management Journal*, 20(4), 1–12.

Christodoulides, G., & Wiedmann, K. P. (2022). Guest editorial: a roadmap and future research agenda for luxury marketing and branding research. *Journal of Product & Brand Management*, 31(3), 341–350.

Cidón, C. F., Figueiró, P. S., & Schreiber, D. (2021). Benefits of organic agriculture under the perspective of the bioeconomy: a systematic review. *Sustainability (Switzerland)*, 13(12), 1–19.

Dahal, K. R., & Dhakal, S. C. (2016). The relative efficiency of organic farming in Nepal. *Working Paper-South Asian Network for Development and Environmental Economics*, 107(16), 1–18.

Ding, A., & Legendre, T. S. (2022). Managing luxury brand creation, communication and sustainability: evidence from the four seasons hotels and resorts case. In *The Emerald handbook of luxury management for hospitality and tourism* (pp. 337–352). Emerald Publishing Limited.

Feil, A. A., Candido, C., & Wiebusch, F. C. (2020). Profiles of sustainable food consumption: consumer behavior toward organic food in southern region of Brazil. *Journal of Cleaner Production*, 258, 1–11.

Finley, L., Chappell, M. J., Thiers, P., & Moore, J. R. (2018). Does organic farming present greater opportunities for employment and community development than conventional farming? A survey-based investigation in California and Washington. *Agroecology and Sustainable Food Systems*, 42(5), 552–572.

Fjelkner-Modig, S., Bengtsson, H., Nyström, S., & Stegmark, R. (2000). The influence of organic and integrated production on nutritional, sensory and agricultural aspects of vegetable raw materials for food production. *Acta Agriculturae Scandinavica, Section B-Plant Soil Science*, 50(3), 102–113.

Fraundorfer, M. (2022). Global governance and the anthropocene: an entangled history. In *Global governance in the age of the anthropocene* (pp. 23–76). Palgrave Macmillan.

Górska-Warsewicz, H., Żakowska-Biemans, S., Stangierska, D., Światkowska, M., Bobola, A., Szlachciuk, J., Czeczotko, M., Krajewski, K., & Świstak, E. (2021). Factors limiting the development of the organic food sector—perspective of processors, distributors, and retailers. *Agriculture (Switzerland)*, 11(9), 1–21.

Gulaliyev, M. G., Abasova, S. T., Samedova, E. R., Hamidova, L. A., Valiyeva, S. I., & Serttash, L. R. (2019). Assessment of agricultural sustainability (Azerbaijan case). *Bulgarian Journal of Agricultural Science*, 25(2), 1–80.

Guthman, J. (2003). Fast food/organic food: reflexive tastes and the making of 'yuppie chow'. *Social & Cultural Geography*, 4(1), 45–58.

Halberg, N., Peramaiyan, P., & Walaga, C. (2009). Is organic farming an unjustified luxury in a world with too many hungry people? In *The world of organic agriculture. Statistics & emerging trends 2009* (pp. 95–100). FiBL and IFOAM.

Han, H. (2021). Consumer behavior and environmental sustainability in tourism and hospitality: a review of theories, concepts, and latest research. *Journal of Sustainable Tourism*, 29(7), 1021–1042.

Hansmann, R., Baur, I., & Binder, C. R. (2020). Increasing organic food consumption: an integrating model of drivers and barriers. *Journal of Cleaner Production*, 275, 123058.

Harris-Fry, H., Saville, N. M., Paudel, P., Manandhar, D. S., Cortina-Borja, M., & Skordis, J. (2022). Relative power: explaining the effects of food and cash transfers on allocative behaviour in rural Nepalese households. *Journal of Development Economics*, 154, 102784.

Hartmann, L. H., Nitzko, S., & Spiller, A. (2017). Segmentation of German consumers based on perceived dimensions of luxury food. *Journal of Food Products Marketing*, 23(7), 733–768.

Hasimu, H., Marchesini, S., & Canavari, M. (2017). A concept mapping study on organic food consumers in Shanghai, China. *Appetite*, 108, 191–202.

Hazarika, A., Yadav, M., Yadav, D. K., & Yadav, H. S. (2022). An overview of the role of nanoparticles in sustainable agriculture. *Biocatalysis and Agricultural Biotechnology*, 43, 102399.

He, L., Fang, W., Zhao, G., Wu, Z., Fu, L., Li, R.,... & Dhupia, J. (2022). Fruit yield prediction and estimation in orchards: a state-of-the-art comprehensive review for both direct and indirect methods. *Computers and Electronics in Agriculture*, 195, 106812.

Heckman, J. (2006). A history of organic farming: transitions from Sir Albert Howard's "War in the Soil" to USDA National Organic Program. *Renewable Agriculture and Food Systems*, 21(3), 143–150.

Hjelmar, U. (2011). Consumers' purchase of organic food products. A matter of convenience and. *Appetite*, 56(2), 336–344.

IFOAM, (2022). 20 years of making Europe more organic. Retrieved from https://www.organicseurope.bio. Accessed on 19th of November 2022.

Jansen, K. (2000). Labour, livelihoods and the quality of life in organic agriculture in Europe. *Biological Agriculture and Horticulture*, 17(3), 247–278.

Jensen, K. O. D., Denver, S., & Zanoli, R. (2011). Actual and potential development of consumer demand on the organic food market in Europe. *NJAS - Wageningen Journal of Life Sciences*, 58(3–4), 79–84.

Joshi, D. R., Ghimire, R., Kharel, T., Mishra, U., & Clay, S. A. (2021). Conservation agriculture for food security and climate resilience in Nepal. *Agronomy Journal*, 113(6), 4484–4493.

Kautish, P., Paul, J., & Sharma, R. (2019). The moderating influence of environmental consciousness and recycling intentions on green purchase behavior. *Journal of Cleaner Production*, 228, 1425–1436.

Koner, N., & Laha, A. (2021). Economics of alternative models of organic farming: empirical evidences from zero budget natural farming and scientific organic farming in West Bengal, India. *International Journal of Agricultural Sustainability*, 19(3–4), 255–268.

Królak, M., Górska-Warsewicz, H., Mądra-Sawicka, M., Rejman, K., Żakowska-Biemans, S., Szlachciuk, J.,... & Wojtaszek, M. (2022). Towards sustainable innovation in the bakery sector—an example of fibre-enriched bread. *Sustainability*, 14(5), 2743.

Lamichhane, B. D. (2022). Agricultural development, commercialization, and job creation: does foreign investment matters in Nepal? Retrieved from https://saraswaticampus.edu.np. Accessed on 19th of November 2022.

Lang, M., & Rodrigues, A. C. (2022). A comparison of organic-certified versus non-certified natural foods: perceptions and motives and their influence on purchase behaviors. *Appetite*, 168, 105698.

Lavuri, R., Jabbour, C. J. C., Grebinevych, O., & Roubaud, D. (2022). Green factors stimulating the purchase intention of innovative luxury organic beauty products: implications for sustainable development. *Journal of Environmental Management*, 301, 113899.

Liu, S. Q., Wu, L. L., Yu, X., & Huang, H. (2022). Marketing online food images via color saturation: a sensory imagery perspective. *Journal of Business Research*, 151, 366–378.

Makaju, S., & Kurunju, K. (2021). A review on use of agrochemical in agriculture and need of organic farming in Nepal. *Archives of Agriculture and Environmental Science*, 6(3), 367–372.

Malla, S., Rosyara, U., Neupane, B., & Sapkota, B. (2021). Feasibility study of organic vegetable farming in Baitadi district. *Food and Agri Economics Review (FAER)*, 1(2), 88–92.

Martindale, L. (2021). 'I will know it when I taste it': trust, food materialities and social media in Chinese alternative food networks. *Agriculture and Human Values*, 38(2), 365–380.

Martínez-Sabater, E., Pérez-Murcia, M. D., Andreu-Rodríguez, F. J., Orden, L., Agulló, E., Sáez-Tovar, J.,... & Moral, R. (2022). Enhancing sustainability in intensive dill cropping: comparative effects of biobased fertilizers vs. inorganic commodities on greenhouse gas emissions, crop yield, and soil properties. *Agronomy*, 12(9), 2124.

Mori, D., Chaiken, S., & Pliner, P. (1987). "Eating lightly" and the self-presentation of femininity. *Journal of Personality and Social Psychology*, 53(4), 693–702.

Moshood, T. D., Nawanir, G., Mahmud, F., Mohamad, F., Ahmad, M. H., AbdulGhani, A., & Kumar, S. (2022). Green product innovation: a means towards achieving global sustainable product within biodegradable plastic industry. *Journal of Cleaner Production*, 363, 132506.

Nafees, L., Hyatt, E. M., Garber Jr, L. L., Das, N., & Boya, Ü. Ö. (2022). Motivations to buy organic food in emerging markets: an exploratory study of urban Indian millennials. *Food Quality and Preference*, 96, 104375.

Nandwani, D., Jamarkattel, D., Dahal, K. R., Poudel, R., Giri, S., & Joshi, T. N. (2021). Attitudes of fruit and vegetable farmers towards organic farming in Kathmandu Valley, Nepal. *Sustainability*, 13(7), 3888.

Niggli, U. (2015). Sustainability of organic food production: challenges and innovations. *Proceedings of the Nutrition Society*, 74(1), 83–88.

Nosi, C., Zollo, L., Rialti, R., & Ciappei, C. (2020). Sustainable consumption in organic food buying behavior: the case of quinoa. *British Food Journal*, 122(3), 976–994.

Organic Trade Association, (2022). Organic industry survey shows steady growth, stabilizing purchasing patterns. Retrieved from https://ota.com/news/press-releases/22284. Accessed on 19th of November 2022.

Pachapur, P. K., Pachapur, V. L., Brar, S. K., Galvez, R., Le Bihan, Y., & Surampalli, R. Y. (2020). Food security and sustainability. In: Surampalli, R. Y., Zhang, T. C., Goyal, M. K., Brar, S. K., & Tyagi, R. D. (eds.), *Sustainability: Fundamentals and Applications* (pp. 357–374). Wiley.

Panzarini, E., Carata, E., Mariano, S., Tenuzzo, B. A., Tacconi, S., Fidaleo, M., & Dini, L. (2022). Plant and human health: the new era of biobased nanoscale systems. In *Nanotechnology-based sustainable alternatives for the management of plant diseases* (pp. 301–322). Elsevier.

Petrescu, D. C., & Petrescu-Mag, R. M. (2015). Organic food perception: fad, or healthy and environmentally friendly? A case on Romanian consumers. *Sustainability (Switzerland)*, 7(9), 12017–12031.

Potter, C., Pechey, R., Cook, B., Bateman, P., Stewart, C., Frie, K.,... & Jebb, S. A. (2023). Effects of environmental impact and nutrition labelling on food purchasing: an experimental online supermarket study. *Appetite*, 180, 106312.

Poulston, J., Yau, A., & Yiu, K. (2011). Profit or principles: why do restaurants serve organic food? *International Journal of Hospitality Management*, 30(1), 184–191.

Rana, J., & Paul, J. (2017). Consumer behavior and purchase intention for organic food: a review and research agenda. *Journal of Retailing and Consumer Services*, 38(2), 157–165.

Rambabu, K., Avornyo, A., Gomathi, T., Thanigaivelan, A., Show, P. L., & Banat, F. (2022). Phycoremediation for carbon neutrality and circular economy: potential, trends, and challenges. *Bioresource Technology*, 367, 128257.

Rana, J., & Paul, J. (2020). Health motive and the purchase of organic food: a meta-analytic review. *International Journal of Consumer Studies*, 44(2), 162–171.

Rasheed, S., Begum, R., Amirullah, Rasheed, A., Khan, A. A., & Zubair, A. (2022). Optimised biodiesel production from waste vegetable cooking oil catalysed by green synthesised calcium oxide nanoparticles. *International Journal of Renewable Energy Technology*, 13(4), 377–395.

Reganold, J. P., & Wachter, J. M. (2016). Organic agriculture in the twenty-first century. *Nature Plants*, 2(2), 1–8.

Rizzo, G., Borrello, M., Dara Guccione, G., Schifani, G., & Cembalo, L. (2020). Organic food consumption: the relevance of the health attribute. *Sustainability*, 12(2), 595.

Rohr, J. R., Barrett, C. B., Civitello, D. J., Craft, M. E., Delius, B., DeLeo, G. A.& Tilman, D. (2019). Emerging human infectious diseases and the links to global food production. *Nature Sustainability*, 2(6), 445–456.

Saraiva, A., Fernandes, E., & von Schwedler, M. (2021). The pro-environmental consumer discourse: a political perspective on organic food consumption. *International Journal of Consumer Studies*, 45(2), 188–204.

Sekhar, C., Krishna, S., Kayal, G. G., & Rana, N. P. (2021). Does brand credibility matter? The case of organic food products. *British Food Journal*, 124(3), 987–1008.

Septianto, F., Kemper, J., & Paramita, W. (2019). The role of imagery in promoting organic food. *Journal of Business Research*, 101, 104–115.

Sapkota, B. K., Subedi, A. P., Tripathi, K. M., & Dhakal, S. C. (2021). Economics of organic vs inorganic rice production: a case of Chitwan district of Nepal. *Journal of Nepal Agricultural Research Council*, 7, 109–121.

Serravalle, F., Vannucci, V., & Pantano, E. (2022). "Take it or leave it?": evidence on cultural differences affecting return behaviour for Gen Z. *Journal of Retailing and Consumer Services*, 66, 102942.

Seufert, V., Mehrabi, Z., Gabriel, D., & Benton, T. G. (2019). Current and potential contributions of organic agriculture to diversification of the food production system. In *Agroecosystem diversity* (pp. 435–452). Academic Press.

Sexton, A. E., Garnett, T., & Lorimer, J. (2022). Vegan food geographies and the rise of Big Veganism. *Progress in Human Geography*, 46(2), 605–628.

Shrestha, R. K., & L'Espoir Decosta, P. (2023). Developing dynamic capabilities for community collaboration and tourism product innovation in response to crisis: Nepal and COVID-19. *Journal of Sustainable Tourism*, 31(1), 168–186.

Singh, A., & Verma, P. (2017). Factors influencing Indian consumers' actual buying behaviour towards organic food products. *Journal of Cleaner Production*, 167, 473–483.

Solaiman, S., & Salaheen, S. (2019). Future of organic farming: bringing technological marvels to the field. In *Safety and practice for organic food* (pp. 291–303). Academic Press.

Soler, M., Ruiz-Raya, F., Sánchez-Pérez, L., & Ibáñez-Álamo, J. D. (2022). Parents preferentially feed larger offspring in asynchronously hatched broods irrespective of scramble competition. *Animal Behaviour*, 194, 193–198.

Stanhill, G. (1990). The comparative productivity of organic agriculture. *Agriculture, Ecosystems and Environment*, 30(2), 1–26.

Staudacher, P., Fuhrimann, S., Farnham, A., Mora, A. M., Atuhaire, A., Niwagaba, C.,... & Winkler, M. S. (2020). Comparative analysis of pesticide use determinants among smallholder farmers from Costa Rica and Uganda. *Environmental Health Insights*, 14, 1–15.

Suman, A. (2021). Role of renewable energy technologies in climate change adaptation and mitigation: a brief review from Nepal. *Renewable and Sustainable Energy Reviews*, 151, 111524.

Tal, A. (2018). Making conventional agriculture environmentally friendly: moving beyond the glorification of organic agriculture and the demonization of conventional agriculture. *Sustainability*, 10(4), 1078.

Trewavas, A. (2004). A critical assessment of organic farming-and-food assertions with particular respect to the UK and the potential environmental benefits of no-till agriculture. *Crop Protection*, 23(9), 757–781.

van Bruggen, A. H., Gamliel, A., & Finckh, M. R. (2016). Plant disease management in organic farming systems. *Pest Management Science*, 72(1), 30–44.

Vardarlıer, P., & Girgin, N. (2022). The role of organic products in preventing the climate crisis. In *Clean energy investments for zero emission projects* (pp. 65–75). Springer.

Veen, M. (2003). When is food a luxury? *World Archaeology*, 34(3), 405–427.

Vernon, R. (1974). "The theory of the leisure class" by Thorstein Veblen. *Daedalus*, 103(1), 53–57.

Wijekoon, R., & Tandon, M. F. (2021). Determinants that influence green product purchase intention and behavior: a literature review and guiding framework. *Sustainability*, 13(11), 6219.

Yiridoe, E. K., Bonti-ankomah, S., & Martin, R. C. (2005). Comparison of consumer perceptions and preference toward organic versus conventionally produced foods: a review and update of the literature. *Renewable Agriculture and Food Systems*, 20(4), 193–205.

Yu, Z., Waqas, M., Tabish, M., Tanveer, M., Haq, I. U., & Khan, S. A. R. (2022). Sustainable supply chain management and green technologies: a bibliometric review of literature. *Environmental Science and Pollution Research*, 29 (39), 1–17.

Zimdahl, R. L. (2022). Alternative/organic agricultural systems. In *Agriculture's ethical horizon* (Third Edition) (pp. 227–245). Elsevier.

7 Assessing the Impact of Sustainability News Clips on Fast-Fashion Brands Purchase Intention

A Neuromarketing Study

Nicolas Hamelin and Monica Chaudhary

7.1 Introduction

Sustainability has become a growing concern in the fashion industry over the last three decades (Brydges et al., 2022). The fashion industry is regarded as one of the most polluting industries with its emission of 1.2 billion tonnes of CO_2 equivalent per year throughout its lifecycle (Ellen MacArthur Foundation, 2017). Almost 73% of the produced clothes end up in a landfill/burned and only a small percentage (15%) are recycled or downcycled into other clothing materials (Ellen MacArthur Foundation, 2017).

To encourage the sustainability of the fashion industry, changing consumer behaviour towards more sustainability is a pre-requisite. Consumers in a way influence the industry through their choices; what they buy, how much they buy, maintenance preferences and how and when they discard clothes (Soyer & Dittrich, 2021). Consumers' preferences and choices about sustainable products vary vividly based on the importance that consumers attach to sustainable consumption of fashion products. Consumers' knowledge about the environment and climate change and also their willingness to change behaviour impacts their choices (Soyer & Dittrich, 2021). Another important element that influences consumer's sustainable product decision is the emotions associated with it. Though important, very little research on sustainable consumption has explored the impact of various emotions on sustainable consumption behaviour (Wang & Wu, 2016).

This is not a study that explores sustainable fashion. Instead, this study uncovers a more specific area of consumer's perception of brands in light of all this buzz about sustainability. Even if the brands in question may not promote it, still any news about sustainability impact's consumer's association with the brands. Knowledge and awareness are essential factors in transforming the behaviour and attitude of consumers towards any brands/products.

With this base, the current study focuses on understanding the impact of any environmental or sustainable products news/information on consumer knowledge and emotions about their consumer decisions. More concretely, following objectives are framed for this chapter:

DOI: 10.4324/9781003321378-7

1 To find the impact of environment/sustainability news on the perceived quality of fast-fashion brands.
2 To measure the impact of environment/sustainability news on the buying intention of fast-fashion brands.
3 To measure the impact of environment/sustainability news on the consumer's emotions towards fast-fashion brands.

7.2 Literature Review

7.2.1 Sustainability

Sustainability is increasingly drawing the attention of scholars, policymakers and companies (Kumar & Christodoulopoulou, 2014). The startlingly rising levels of climate failures have intensified the worldwide interest and pressure on corporations to introduce/manage sustainability with a long-term generational perspective (Sheth et al., 2011). As a result, there is a trend toward environmental sustainability, which has resulted in changes in consumer demand and behaviour (Mendelson & Polonsky, 1995).

The concept of sustainability has a rather long history, and it has evolved over time (Kidd, 1992). Varied "intellectual and political streams of thought" have moulded the concepts of sustainability (Kidd, 1992). In 1972 in Stockholm, UN Conference on Human Environment became the cradle that led to the creation of the UN Environmental Programme (UNEP) and many environmental protection agencies. Organization for Economic Co-operation and Development (OECD, 2002) broadly defined sustainable consumption as the "consumption of goods and services that meet basic needs and quality of life without jeopardizing the needs of future generations". It has been argued in previous studies that luxury products and sustainability are incompatible with each other. But in recent times, a paradigm shift has been observed as customers are looking for sustainability in terms of luxury products (Gupta & Wadera, 2020). On account of the latest studies, from the marketers' point of view, sustainability is the new normal (Gauthier, 2017; Leclair, 2017)

7.3 Fast-Fashion Brands

In common language, "fast fashion" describes clothes that are economically priced and casually mimic contemporary luxury fashion trends. According to Fletcher (2008), "Fast fashion—low-cost clothing collections based on current, high-cost luxury fashion trends—is, by its very nature, a fast-response system that encourages disposability". High-end luxury fashion brands are not very affordable to a large section of society.

Accessibility is another reason why fast fashion is becoming quite popular in today's generation. These new-age brands have quick turnaround time. The standard turnaround time from fashion shows to end user used to be around six months; this has been reduced and is compressed to just a few weeks by fast-fashion brands like Zara and H&M (Tokatli, 2008). These fast-fashion brands flourish on rapid production cycles; this involves quick prototyping, modest production consignments, greater assortment, economical shipping and delivery, and "floor ready" merchandize (Skov, 2002). Interestingly these fast-fashion brands also provide "mass exclusivity" to the consumers (Schrank, 2004). Though it sounds like an oxymoron, it is true. Lower production costs lead to lower product prices, which leads to volume sales and higher revenue. For example, many such brands have their manufacturing outsourced to cost-effective countries like China, Turkey, Bangladesh and India. For example, Zara now outsourced almost 13% of their manufacturing to China and Turkey (Tokatli, 2008).

7.4 Sustainability and Brands

Sustainability has become a growing concern in the fashion industry over the last three decades (Brydges et al., 2022). Many brand manufacturers and retailers are increasingly focusing on sustainability (Vadakkepatt et al., 2021). Sustainability is an important issue for consumers (Martins, 2019, Reints, 2019). Sustainability has come out to be a successful strategy that mitigates high failure rates (Van Doorn et al., 2021). Studies reported that sustainable strategies can be very beneficial for brand manufacturers (Sustainable Brands, 2018). There are globally many research that have explored the diverse relationship between sustainability and brands; Singapore (Loh & Tan, 2020), Sweden (Brydges et al., 2022), Spain (Bañares et al., 2021), Indonesia (Ramli et al., 2020), Netherlands (Soyer & Dittrich, 2021).

Different dimension has been explored when sustainability and brands have been discussed together. Studies advocate organizations to integrate sustainability into their marketing communication as a tool for brand differentiation (Chabowski et al., 2011). Sustainability and brand value both are categorized as intangible company assets that are tough to quantify or to assign a fair worth (Oliveira & Sullivan, 2008). This helps brands in building good-will and as a result enhances the company's reputation (Farooq, 2015). Though sustainability is not a regular company asset as it cannot be purchased or sold in the market, still it has developed into a central philosophy of corporations (Sheth et al., 2011). Reports show that more than 90% of the top management feels that sustainability is an important fundamental in their company (Hoffman, 2018). Sustainable brands exhibit a sense to the environment and society (Montiel & Delgado-Ceballos, 2014). They are believed to be more responsible and hence could be the reason why these brands have high levels of employee satisfaction and considerably low turnover rates (Turban & Greening, 1997).

Consumers have begun to show concern for the environment and prefer environmentally friendly products and services (Nimse et al., 2007). There is a need for the study to explore the "intersection of brand-sustainability" and its communication with consumers (Brydges et al., 2022).

7.5 Consumer Knowledge and Buying Intention

Based on their concern for environment, there are three categories of consumers (McNeil & Moore, 2015). First are those consumers who regard fashion as a representative of their individual expression and place a huge weight on newness; more often they see sustainable fashion with uncomfortable material and smell. The second category is of those consumers who place huge importance on their social image and are more willing to integrate sustainable practices, but not at all cost. The third category of consumers are those who wish to reduce their ecological footprint and work actively towards it.

Knowledge about climate change may not cause consumers to change their behaviour (Hofstede, 2018; Kang et al., 2013). Research also found that young respondents in the age group (18–29 years) are more unaware and hence unwilling to change behaviour when compared to their older counterparts (Park & Lin, 2020). As a result, younger individuals are more susceptible to influencers in sustainable decision-making (Johnstone & Lindh, 2018).

Communicating sustainability refers to "brands seeking to raise awareness about how their products and/or services align with social, economic, and environmental sustainability" (Brydges et al., 2022). Henninger and Oates (2018) understood sustainability communication (news) is to broadcast targeted, one-way messages, and also to encourage dialogic communication between brands and their consumers. With such news related to sustainability, brands provide environmental and social cues to consumers that their brands are successful in reducing negative impacts on the environment (Brydges et al., 2022). The brands that communicate such news to consumers are seeking to alter their consumers' consumption patterns to be more environmentally and socially conscious (Henninger et al., 2017).

On the other side, brands that involve themselves in actions/strategies that are against the sustainability goals are criticized too. To cite an example, a particular brand was under consumer's lens when it decided to burn its unsold products (Shannon, 2020). Also, there was some news related to unethical production practices (like employing underage children) (Duncan, 2020). Such news articles stir the consumer's trust (Brydges et al., 2022).

Another term that must be discussed and understood is "Greenwashing". Greenwashing could be defined as the "act of misleading consumers regarding the environmental practices of a company (firm-level greenwashing) or the environmental benefits of a product or service (product-level greenwashing)" (From, 2011). In simpler terms, Greenwashing is when a company claims to be environmentally mindful for only branding and marketing purposes but in reality, isn't producing any significant sustainability attempts.

The theory of planned behaviour (TPB) (Ajzen, 1991) is used most often to explain the buying intention of consumers in the light of sustainable products (Bagher et al., 2018; Kapferer & Michaut-Denizeau, 2020; Laureti & Benedetti, 2018, Maichum et al., 2016; Paul et al., 2016; Wang et al., 2019). According to TPB, human's behaviour intentions are most accurately projected by three factors – personal attitude towards that behaviour, subjective norms and perceived behavioural control. Health consciousness and environmental concern were analysed most frequently in combination with the TPB (Fleșeriu et al., 2020).

7.6 Sustainability and Perceived Quality

"Perceived product quality is the perceived ability of a product to provide satisfaction relative to the available alternatives" (Dodds & Monroe, 1985). One simple way to analyse the quality of a product is to recognize its different dimensions such as performance, features, reliability, conformance, durability, serviceability, aesthetics and perceived quality, and rank them individually (Garvin, 1988). Previous studies found that consumers' perceptions of product properties and product quality were significantly affected by information (Verbeke & Ward, 2006). Studying more about sustainability and product quality, mixed results were found. Some studies argued about the positive impact of product sustainability on perceived quality (Haglund et al., 1998; Lee et al., 2013; Lee & Yun, 2015), while others rejected this claim (Luchs et al., 2010; Newman et al., 2014). Instead, few studies found that sustainable products may be perceived to be of lower quality compared to conventional products (Van Doorn et al., 2020). Low-quality arguments seem to be stronger for vice products (products that consumers are likely to over-consume at the consumption stage (Jain, 2012)). Green or environmentally friendly products are less effective, and therefore consumers' usage of these products is higher (Lin & Chang, 2012). With regards to fast fashion, acceptable quality seems to be enough as long as it allows achieving a desired style for an affordable price (Gabrielli et al., 2013; Joy et al., 2012).

There was no such study that discusses the impact of any sustainability or environmental news on the perceived quality of fast-fashion products. And hence make the current study important to conduct.

7.7 Role of Emotions in Sustainable Fashion Choices

Consumer emotions are an important factor in making sustainable fashion choices. Previous studies found that emotions play important roles when consumers are involved in sustainable consumption behaviours (Carrus et al., 2008; Swim et al., 2011). Sustainability is a "behavioural issue, and not one simply of technology, production, and volume" (Chapman, 2012). Emotions directly influence consumer's participation in environmental protection (Kollmuss & Agyeman, 2002). Very little research on sustainable consumption has explored the impact of various emotions on sustainable consumption behaviour (Wang & Wu, 2016). Sustainable consumption is correlated more with emotion than with cognition (Kanchanapibul et al., 2014). These emotions are pride (Onwezen et al., 2014), anger (Van Zomeren et al., 2010), guilt (Kaiser, 2006), regret (Kim et al., 2013), fear (Van Zomeren et al., 2010), distress (Lee & Holden, 1999) and sadness (Nerb & Spada, 2001). One particular study found that certain human emotions have certain effects on particular types of sustainable behaviour (Harth et al., 2013). Pride for example predicts intentions of in-groups to favour environmental protection, on the other hand, anger influences intentions to punish those who have damaged the environment.

7.8 Methods

7.8.1 *Testing the Impact of Negative News: The Experiment*

A total of 25 participants – international MBA students – (60% male and 40% female) were submitted to a series of negative news – about the negative impact of fast fashion on the environment. At the same time, monitor their subconscious emotional state. The total duration of the experiment was two weeks. The respondents were asked to answer a survey about their perception of quality and buying intention, before and after being exposed to the news slides. Each slide was displayed for five seconds before moving on to the next slide. The respondents were then asked to provide another approval rating of the brands after being exposed to the news slides. While conducting the experiment, participants' autonomic body reactions using galvanic skin response and the participant's facial expressions were monitored. iMotions

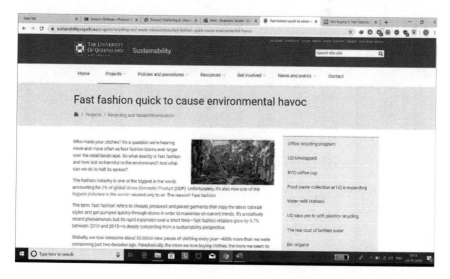

Figure 7.1 Fast fashion quick to cause environmental havoc (Sustainability, 2018).

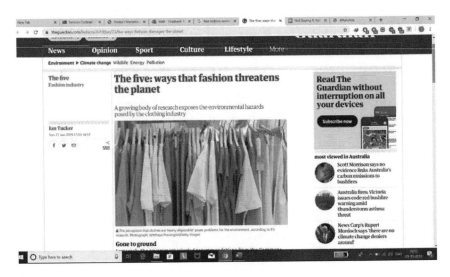

Figure 7.2 The five: ways that fashion threatens the planet (Tucker, 2019).

Figure 7.3 The fashion industry is the second largest polluter in the world (Charpail, 2017).

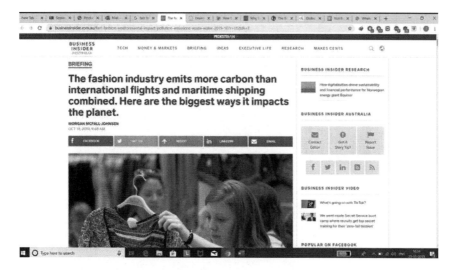

Figure 7.4 The fashion industry emits more carbon than international flights and maritime shipping combined here are the biggest ways it impacts the planet (McFall-Johnsen, 2019).

Figure 7.5 Why fast fashion is bad for people and planet (www.ETRetail.com, 2019).

Figure 7.6 How fast fashion hurts environment, works and society (Schoenherr, 2019).

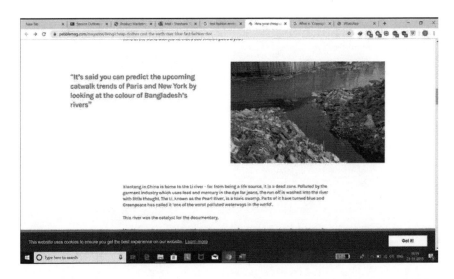

Figure 7.7 How your cheap clothes are costing the Earth (Pebble Magazine, 2022).

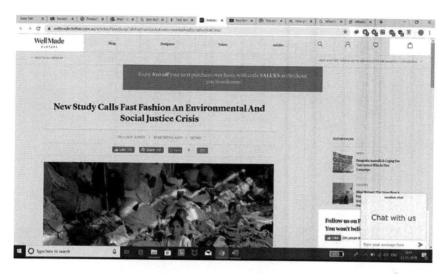

Figure 7.8 New study calls fast fashion an environmental and social justice crisis (Well Made Clothes, 2022).

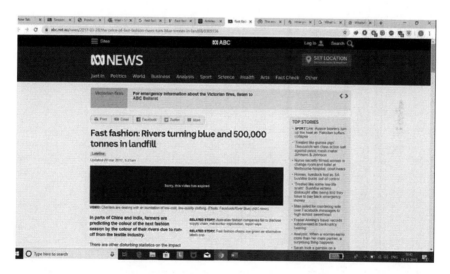

Figure 7.9 Fast fashion: rivers turning blue and 500,000 tonnes in landfill (ABC News, 2017).

Figure 7.10 The environmental costs of fast fashion (Perry et al., 2018).

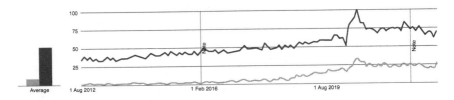

Figure 7.11 Google Trends of sustainable clothes and organic cotton.

biometric platform was used to measure changes in galvanic skin response as well as facial expression. Autonomic body reaction gives great insight into people's emotional state. Emotions influence both individual's attitudes and judgements and subsequently the decision-making process (Figures 7.1–7.10).

7.9 Results

It is clear from Google trends in Figure 7.1 that there has been a healthy increase in interest globally in sustainable clothes and organic cotton. In the past ten years, searches for organic cotton increased twofold, while online searches for sustainable clothing increased 27 times (Figures 7.11).

7.10 The Survey

Respondents were requested to answer a survey before visioning the news about the negative impact of fast fashion on the environment and the same survey after having read the news. The survey was made of three questions: Rate the quality of the following brands Zara, H&M and Forever 21, on a 5 pts Likert scale, with 1 being the lowest quality and five the highest. The second question measured respondents buying intention, yes or no, attributed 1 or 2 values respectively.

7.11 Results: Buying Intention per Brand

There was a significant effect of the brand prior to reading the news on purchase intention at the $p < 0.05$ level for the three conditions [$F_{(2, 57)} = 5.97$, $p = 0.004$]. With most respondent stated their preference for Zara (Table 7.1).

After reading the news clips the preference for Zara still dominates significantly [$F_{(2, 56)} = 6.87$, $p = 0.0021$], however, the average buying intention score has decreased substantially (Table 7.2).

Following a t-test, a significant difference was found with respondents less likely to buy the three brands after reading the news clip. The results showed that participants reading the negative news clips had statistically significantly lower purchase intention for the three brands 1.3, 1.55 and 1.84 respectively after reading the news clip than before 1.05, 1.25, 1.5 respectively, $t_{(33)} = -2.0851$, $p = 0.0447$, $t_{(45.9)} = -1.84$, $p = 0.07$ and $t_{(46.55)} = -1.98$, $p = 0.0534$ respectively. Following the news clips, respondents were less likely to buy the three brands.

Regarding quality perception findings, no difference was recorded before and after reading the news for both H&M and Forever 21; however, Zara's perception of quality decreased after reading the news. The results showed that participants reading the negative news clips had statistically significantly lower perception of quality for Zara 3.48 respectively after reading the news clip than before 4.08 respectively, $t_{(43.6)} = 1.928$, $p = 0.0603$.

Table 7.1 Buying intention – prior to reading the news clip

Buying Intention – Prior to Reading the News Clip	Count	Sum	Average (1 Will Buy – 2 Will Not Buy)	Variance
Zara	20	21	1.05	0.05
H&M	20	25	1.25	0.1973
Forever 21	20	30	1.5	0.2631

Table 7.2 Buying intention – after reading the news clip

Buying Intention – After Reading the News Clip	Count	Sum	Average (1 Will Buy – 2 Will Not Buy)	Variance
Zara	20	26	1.3	0.2210
H&M	20	31	1.55	0.2605
Forever 21	19	35	1.84	0.1403

Table 7.3 Impact of emotions

Delta Buying Intention for Zara	Mean of Anger	Std. Dev.	Freq.
No change	0.04558797	0.10657553	16
Will not buy	0.56208226	0.83553284	5
Total	0.1685628	0.44604307	21

7.12 Impact of Emotions

Respondents' emotional reactions to the news clip were recorded using the iMotions biometric platform. The human face is one of the strongest indicators of emotions. The iMotion biometric platform uses facial expression analysis to capture raw emotional responses toward news clips. Respondent's emotional states are detected in real-time via webcam. Seven core emotions (joy/happiness, confusion/anger, fear, disgust, contempt, sadness and surprise) were recorded and correlated with the results of the surveys.

An ANOVA test was carried out to assess the impact of each core emotion on the change in buying intention. The only significant difference was reported for Zara, with an adverse change in purchase intention being associated with a high level of respondents' anger. Hence there was a significant and negative effect of anger on purchase intention at the $p < 0.05$ level for the three conditions [$F(1, 19) = 6.52$, $p = 0.0194$]. No other significant effect on the recorded emotions was recorded on purchase intention or quality perception for the three brands (Table 7.3).

7.13 Conclusion & Implications

The three major takeaways from this empirical study are

1 Consumer's buying intention decreases substantially when they are made aware of the negative impact of fashion industry on environment.
2 Perceived quality of fashion clothes might fall when consumers are made aware of the negative impact of the fashion industry on the environment.
3 Awareness about fashion sustainability does not have much impact on core human emotions related to their fashion product choices
4 Out of the three selected brands, Zara is the only brand for which consumers are reported to be more engaged through their emotions and hence might be more reactive.

These findings have important implications for fashion-industry practitioners, especially for fast-fashion brands. The obvious finding to emerge from this current study is that environmental concerns and perceptions are important elements in explaining consumer sustainable fashion products purchase intentions. This study provides a reference to various themes that need to be explored further. This research area would benefit from studies that investigate the relationship between sustainability, perceived quality and consumer awareness.

This study has four main practical contributions. Firstly, it can be a guide for retailers and marketers in the fast-fashion industry to explore the factors to be considered in promoting sustainable fashion clothing. The average buying intention has decreased substantially once the consumer gets to know the negative impact of the fashion industry on the environment. It is promising to boost buying intention of sustainable clothing by making consumers' aware of the impact of the fashion industry on the environment. This calls for a collective effort from all the stakeholders to put the highest amount of thrust into making consumers aware of the environmental concerns related to the fashion industry.

Secondly, this study also found empirical implications about the perception of quality. Consumers do not find any difference in the quality of fast-fashion products even after reading the news about sustainability. This could be explained in a way that people perceive quality in general for any product. "Perceived quality" is understood as a consumer's subjective judgement about the product quality, and it depends on the individual context (Zeithaml, 1988). As for managerial implications, the study may paper serves as an attempt to understand some elements of quality to be considered in the fast-fashion industry and also throw light to inspire to develop ways of communicating quality to consumers.

Thirdly, this study explored the impact of sustainability awareness on consumer's emotions about fashion clothing. Though more in-depth studies are needed to dig deep into the consumer psychic to understand the emotions they associate with their fashion product choices, still few implications can be drawn. Negative emotions (for example, anger) toward sustainable concerns, directly and indirectly, do impact consumer's buying intentions.

Lastly, the study also has impactful implication for experimental research method. Experimental research methods are often criticized on the grounds that they rely too heavily on artificial settings. This is high time for the researchers to understand that it is very challenging to learn in-depth about specific cause-effect relations in a natural setting without the benefit of a controlled artificial research setting.

References

ABC News. (2017, March 28). The price of fast fashion: rivers turn blue and 500,000 tonnes in landfill. *ABC News*. Retrieved November 21, 2022, from https://www.abc.net.au/news/2017-03-28/the-price-of-fast-fashion-rivers-turn-blue-tonnes-in-landfill/8389156.

Ajzen, I. (1991). The theory of planned behavior. *Organizational Behavior and Human Decision Processes, 50*(2), 179–211.

Bagher, A. N., Salati, F., & Ghaffari, M. (2018). Factors affecting intention to purchase organic food products among Iranian consumers. *Academy of Marketing Studies Journal, 22*(3), 1–23.

Bañares, A. B., Silva, M. F. S., & Rodríguez, S. R. (2021). Green but ignored? The irrelevance of television advertisements on energy sustainability in Spain and its impact on consumer perceptions. *Energy Research & Social Science, 73*, 101835.

Brands, S. (2018). B Corp analysis reveals purpose-led businesses grow 28 times faster than national average. Accessed on March 20, 2018.

Brydges, T., Henninger, C. E., & Hanlon, M. (2022). Selling sustainability: investigating how Swedish fashion brands communicate sustainability to consumers. *Sustainability: Science, Practice and Policy, 18*(1), 357–370.

Carrus, G., Passafaro, P., & Bonnes, M. (2008). Emotions, habits and rational choices in ecological behaviours: the case of recycling and use of public transportation. *Journal of Environmental Psychology, 28*(1), 51–62.

Chabowski, B. R., Mena, J. A., & Gonzalez-Padron, T. L. (2011). The structure of sustainability research in marketing, 1958–2008: a basis for future research opportunities. *Journal of the Academy of Marketing Science, 39*(1), 55–70.

Chapman, J. (2012). *Emotionally durable design: objects, experiences and empathy.* Routledge.

Charpail, M. (2017). Fashion & environment. SustainYourStyle. Retrieved November 21, 2022, from https://www.sustainyourstyle.org/en/whats-wrong-with-the-fashion-industry#:~:text=The%20fashion%20industry%20is%20the, awareness%20and%20willingness%20to%20change.

Dodds, W. B., & Monroe, K. B. (1985). The effect of brand and price information on subjective product evaluations. *ACR North American Advances, 12,* 85–90.

Duncan, T. (2020). Principles *of advertising and IMC.* Cengage Learning.

Ellen MacArthur Foundation. (2017). *A new textiles economy: redesigning fashion's future.* Ellen MacArthur Foundation.

From, C. Q. (2010). When Karen Larson, a mother of two in Madbury, NH, took the "New Hampshire Carbon Challenge" she couldn't believe the results. *Issues for Debate in Environmental Management: Selections from CQ Researcher, 73.*

Farooq, O. (2015). Financial centers and the relationship between ESG disclosure and firm performance: evidence from an emerging market. *Journal of Applied Business Research (JABR), 31*(4), 1239–1244.

Fletcher, K. (2008). *Sustainable fashion and textiles: design journeys.* Earthscan.

Fleşeriu, C., Cosma, S. A., & Bocăneţ, V. (2020). Values and planned behaviour of the Romanian organic food consumer. *Sustainability, 12*(5), 1722.

Gabrielli, V., Baghi, I., & Codeluppi, V. (2013). Consumption practices of fast fashion products: a consumer-based approach. *Journal of Fashion Marketing and Management: An International Journal, 17*(2), 249–262.

Garvin, D. A. (1988). *Managing quality: the strategic and competitive edge.* Simon and Schuster.

Gauthier, J. (2017). Sustainable business strategies: typologies and future directions. *Society and Business Review, 12*(3), 245–270.

Gupta, S. S., & Wadera, D. (2020). Impact of cause-affinity and CSR fit on consumer purchase intention. *Society and Business Review, 15*(1), 69–88.

Haglund, Å., Johansson, L., Berglund, L., & Dahlstedt, L. (1998). Sensory evaluation of carrots from ecological and conventional growing systems. *Food Quality and Preference, 10*(1), 23–29.

Harth, N. S., Leach, C. W., & Kessler, T. (2013). Guilt, anger, and pride about in-group environmental behaviour: different emotions predict distinct intentions. *Journal of Environmental Psychology, 34*, 18–26.

Henninger, C. E., Kim, Y., & Park, H. J. (2017). Design for sustainable fashion. In *Fashion and Textile Design: Theory and Practice* (pp. 145–169). Springer.

Henninger, C. E., & Oates, C. (2018). Designing fashion for social change. *Fashion Practice, 10*(1), 83–106.

Hoffman, A. J. (2018). The next phase of business sustainability. *Stanford Social Innovation Review, 16*(2), 34–39.

Hofstede, H. (2018). *Circulariteit in retail [circularity in the retail sector].* ABN AMRO.

Jain, S. (2012). Marketing of vice goods: a strategic analysis of the package size decision. *Marketing Science, 31*(1), 36–51.

Johnstone, L., & Lindh, C. (2018). The sustainability-age dilemma: a theory of (un)planned behaviour via influencers. *Journal of Consumer Behaviour, 17*(1), e127–e139.

Joy, A., Sherry Jr, J. F., Venkatesh, A., Wang, J., & Chan, R. (2012). Fast fashion, sustainability, and the ethical appeal of luxury brands. *Fashion Theory, 16*(3), 273–295.

Kaiser, F. G. (2006). A moral extension of the theory of planned behavior: norms and anticipated feelings of regret in conservationism. *Personality and Individual Differences, 41*(1), 71–81.

Kanchanapibul, M., Lacka, E., Wang, X., & Chan, H. K. (2014). An empirical investigation of green purchase behaviour among the young generation. *Journal of Cleaner Production, 66*, 528–536.

Kang, J., Liu, C., & Kim, S. H. (2013). Environmentally sustainable textile and apparel consumption: the role of consumer knowledge, perceived consumer effectiveness and perceived personal relevance. *International Journal of Consumer Studies, 37*(4), 442–452.

Kapferer, J. N., & Michaut-Denizeau, A. (2020). Are millennials really more sensitive to sustainable luxury? A cross-generational international comparison of sustainability consciousness when buying luxury. *Journal of Brand Management, 27*(1), 35–47.

Kidd, T. (1992). Green marketing: a global legal perspective. *Journal of International Consumer Marketing, 4*(2), 77–100.

Kim, Y. J., Njite, D., & Hancer, M. (2013). Anticipated emotion in consumers' intentions to select eco-friendly restaurants: augmenting the theory of planned behavior. *International Journal of Hospitality Management, 34*, 255–262.

Kollmuss, A., & Agyeman, J. (2002). Mind the gap: why do people act environmentally and what are the barriers to pro-environmental behavior? *Environmental Education Research, 8*(3), 239–260.

Kumar, V., & Christodoulopoulou, A. (2014). Sustainability and branding: an integrated perspective. *Industrial Marketing Management, 43*(1), 6–15.

Laureti, T., & Benedetti, I. (2018). Exploring pro-environmental food purchasing behaviour: an empirical analysis of Italian consumers. *Journal of Cleaner Production, 172*, 3367–3378.

Leclair, M. (2017). "Dior and I": understanding the combination of creativity and economy in fashion industry. *Society and Business Review, 12*(3), 353–376.

Lee, J. A., & Holden, S. J. (1999). Understanding the determinants of environmentally conscious behavior. *Psychology & Marketing, 16*(5), 373–392.

Lee, H. J., & Yun, Z. S. (2015). Consumers' perceptions of organic food attributes and cognitive and affective attitudes as determinants of their purchase intentions toward organic food. *Food Quality and Preference, 39*, 259–267.

Lee, W. C. J., Shimizu, M., Kniffin, K. M., & Wansink, B. (2013). You taste what you see: do organic labels bias taste perceptions? *Food Quality and Preference, 29*(1), 33–39.

Lin, Y. C., & Chang, C. C. A. (2012). Double standard: the role of environmental consciousness in green product usage. *Journal of Marketing, 76*(5), 125–134.

Loh, L., & Tan, S. (2020). Impact of sustainability reporting on brand value: an examination of 100 leading brands in Singapore. *Sustainability, 12*(18), 7392.

Luchs, M. G., Naylor, R. W., Irwin, J. R., & Raghunathan, R. (2010). The sustainability liability: potential negative effects of ethicality on product preference. *Journal of Marketing, 74*(5), 18–31.

Maichum, K., Parichatnon, S., & Peng, K. C. (2016). Application of the extended theory of planned behavior model to investigate purchase intention of green products among Thai consumers. *Sustainability, 8*(10), 1077.

Mendelson, R., & Polonsky, M. (1995). Using strategic alliances to develop credible green marketing. *Journal of Consumer Marketing, 12*(2), 4–18.

McFall-Johnsen, M. (2019, October 17). The fashion industry emits more carbon than international flights and maritime shipping combined. Here are the biggest ways it impacts the planet. Business Insider. Retrieved November 21, 2022, from https://www.businessinsider.in/science/news/the-fashion-industry-emits-more-carbon-than-international-flights-and-maritime-shipping-combined-here-are-the-biggest-ways-it-impacts-the-planet-/articleshow/71640863.cms.

McNeill, L., & Moore, R. (2015). Sustainable fashion consumption and the fast fashion conundrum: fashionable consumers and attitudes to sustainability in clothing choice. *International Journal of Consumer Studies, 39*(3), 212–222.

Martins, A. (2019). Most consumers want sustainable products and packaging. Businessnewsdaily.com.

Montiel, I., & Delgado-Ceballos, J. (2014). Defining and measuring corporate sustainability: are we there yet? *Organization & Environment, 27*(2), 113–139. Nerb, J., & Spada, H. (2001). Evaluation of environmental problems: a coherence model of cognition and emotion. *Cognition & Emotion, 15*(4), 521–551.

Newman, G. E., Gorlin, M., & Dhar, R. (2014). When going green backfires: how firm intentions shape the evaluation of socially beneficial product enhancements. *Journal of Consumer Research, 41*(3), 823–839.

Nimse, S. B., Pal, D., & Kalyane, V. L. (2007). Ethical issues and challenges in contemporary human resource management: a conceptual analysis. *Journal of Management and Social Sciences, 3*(1), 47–56.

OECD. (2002). Glossary of statistical terms. Retrieved from https://stats.oecd.org/glossary/detail.asp?ID=2256.

Oliveira, P., & Sullivan, A. (2008). *Sustainability and its impact on brand value. Creating and managing brand value.* Interbrand.

Onwezen, M. C., Bartels, J., & Antonides, G. (2014). Environmentally friendly consumer choices: cultural differences in the self-regulatory function of anticipated pride and guilt. *Journal of Environmental Psychology, 40*, 239–248.

Park, H. J., & Lin, L. M. (2020). Exploring attitude–behavior gap in sustainable consumption: comparison of recycled and upcycled fashion products. *Journal of Business Research, 117*, 623–628.

Paul, J., Modi, A., & Patel, J. (2016). Predicting green product consumption using theory of planned behavior and reasoned action. *Journal of Retailing and Consumer Services, 29*, 123–134.

Perry, P., Hui-Miller, J.-A., Enerva, K., Prabha, A., Spencer, M., & Sharuddin, S. (2018, January 3). The environmental costs of Fast Fashion. Inside Retail. Retrieved November 21, 2022, from https://insideretail.com.au/news/the-environmental-costs-of-fast-fashion-201801.

Pebble Magazine. (2022) How your cheap clothes are costing the Earth. Pebble Magazine. Retrieved November 21, 2022, from https://pebblemag.com/magazine/living/cheap-clothes-cost-the-earth-river-blue-fast-fashion-doc.

Ramli, Y., Permana, D., Soelton, M., Hariani, S., & Yanuar, T. (2020). The implication of green marketing that influence the customer awareness towards their purchase decision. *Mix Jurnal Ilmiah Manajemen, 10*(3), 385–399.

Reints, R. (2019). Consumers say they want more sustainable products. Now they have the receipts to prove it. Fortune, November 5.

Shannon, L. (2020). Consumer culture and the fashion industry: the power of marketing communications. In: Vecchi, A. (ed.), *Handbook of Research on Global Fashion Management and Merchandising* (pp. 26–46). IGI Global.

Sheth, J. N., Sethia, N. K., & Srinivas, S. (2011). Mindful consumption: a customer-centric approach to sustainability. *Journal of the Academy of Marketing Science, 39*(1), 21–39.

Schoenherr, N. (2019, January 10). How fast fashion hurts environment, workers, society. Phys.org. Retrieved November 21, 2022, from https://phys.org/news/2019-01-fast-fashion-environment-workers-society.html.

Schrank, H. (2004). Organic cotton moving into the mainstream. *Ecological Agriculture Projects, Sustainable Cotton Project, 4*, 2–4.

Skov, L. (2002). A review of sustainability principles in the clothing sector. *Journal of Fashion Marketing and Management, 6*(3), 259–271.

Soyer, M., & Dittrich, K. (2021). Sustainable consumer behavior in purchasing, using and disposing of clothes. *Sustainability, 13*, 8333.

Sustainability. (2018). Fast fashion quick to cause environmental havoc. Retrieved November 21, 2022, from https://sustainability.uq.edu.au/projects/recycling-and-waste-minimisation/fast-fashion-quick-cause-environmental-havoc.

Swim, J. K., Stern, P. C., Doherty, T. J., Clayton, S., Reser, J. P., Weber, E. U.,... & Howard, G. S. (2011). Psychology's contributions to understanding and addressing global climate change. *American Psychologist, 66*(4), 241.

Tokatli, N. (2008). Global sourcing: insights from the global clothing industry—the case of Zara, a fast fashion retailer. *Journal of Economic Geography, 8*(1), 21–38.

Tucker, I. (2019, June 23). The five: ways that fashion threatens the planet. The Guardian. Retrieved November 21, 2022, from https://www.theguardian.com/fashion/2019/jun/23/five-ways-fashion-damages-the-planet.

Turban, D. B., & Greening, D. W. (1997). Corporate social performance and organizational attractiveness to prospective employees. *Academy of Management Journal, 40*(3), 658–672.

Vadakkepatt, G. G., Winterich, K. P., Mittal, V., Zinn, W., Beitelspacher, L., Aloysius, J.,... & Reilman, J. (2021). Sustainable retailing. *Journal of Retailing, 97*(1), 62–80.

Van Doorn, J., Risselada, H., & Verhoef, P. C. (2021). Does sustainability sell? The impact of sustainability claims on the success of national brands' new product introductions. *Journal of Business Research, 137*, 182–193.

Van Doorn, J., Verhoef, P. C., & Risselada, H. (2020). Sustainability claims and perceived product quality: the moderating role of brand CSR. *Sustainability, 12*(9), 3711.

Van Zomeren, M., Spears, R., & Leach, C. W. (2010). Experimental evidence for a dual pathway model analysis of coping with the climate crisis. *Journal of Environmental Psychology, 30*(4), 339–346.

Verbeke, W., & Ward, P. (2006). A fresh look at the strategic use of corporate social responsibility. *Academy of Management Perspectives, 20*(1), 5–19.

Wang, X., Pacho, F., Liu, J., & Kajungiro, R. (2019). Factors influencing organic food purchase intention in developing countries and the moderating role of knowledge. *Sustainability, 11*(1), 209.

Wang, J., & Wu, L. (2016). The impact of emotions on the intention of sustainable consumption choices: evidence from a big city in an emerging country. *Journal of Cleaner Production, 126*, 325–336.

Well Made Clothes. (2022, October 14). Retrieved November 21, 2022, from https://www.wellmadeclothes.com.au/.

www.ETRetail.com. (2019, January 12). Why fast fashion is bad for people and planet - et retail. ETRetail.com. Retrieved November 21, 2022, from https://retail.economictimes.indiatimes.com/news/apparel-fashion/apparel/why-fast-fashion-is-bad-for-people-and-planet/67499987.

Zeithaml, V. A. (1988). Consumer perceptions of price, quality, and value: a means-end model and synthesis of evidence. *Journal of Marketing, 52*(3), 2–22.

8 The Present and Future of the Luxury-Sustainability Paradox

Kevin Teah, Isaac Cheah and, Anwar Sadat Shimul

8.1 Introduction

Luxury and sustainability have long been seen as mutually incompatible concepts. According to research (Freire & Loussaïef, 2018; Kim et al., 2022; Teah et al., 2021), maintaining an elite market presence and exclusive branding while staying socially and environmentally responsible creates uncomfortable tensions for luxury brands. However, the past decade has seen luxury businesses change their standpoint and make sustainability, environmental responsibility, and corporate social responsibility (CSR) central to their value propositions (Cavender, 2018; Freire & Loussaïef, 2018; Rapp & Mikeska, 2014). Luxury customers' and investors' awareness of environmental, social, and governance (ESG) concepts has increased significantly over the past year (DiPasquantonio et al., 2021). Luxury firms will have to produce less, avoid waste, and build products that (theoretically) a lifetime and this shift has forced some introspection over an existential question: Is the definition of luxury in tune with today's customers?

Frequently, what some consumers consider to be a luxury, others may view as a fundamental necessity. Additionally, the idea of luxury can take on a completely different meaning in a future society with diminishing resources (Cavender, 2018; Rapp & Mikeska, 2014). The widespread belief that sustainable behaviour is expensive, unnecessary, or unpleasant to daily living is one that changes regularly. However, although sharing many of the same "negative" characteristics as luxury goods, such as being pricey, unnecessary, and usually inconvenient, owning them is seen as a privilege rather than a hassle (Rapp & Mikeska, 2014). Sustainable products typically have "fundamental" traits to luxury goods: they need exceptional innovation and design, excellent materials, high quality, and uniqueness (Kunz et al., 2020; Peng & Chen, 2019). Thus, buying luxury goods does not necessarily mean conspicuous consumption; rather it is also perceived as an investment in quality and sustainability (Cheah et al., 2022; Janssen et al., 2014; Kumagai & Nagasawa, 2020). Arguably, both concepts do not differ all that much from one another.

While research examining sustainable luxury exists, current knowledge lacks agreement and structure. To move the debate forward, this chapter

DOI: 10.4324/9781003321378-8

intends to explore issues related to luxury brands and sustainability, with two main objectives: (i) to explore the extent of the perceived contradiction between their luxury consumption and sustainability in the eye of the luxury consumer and (ii) to understand the drivers of this perceived contradiction.

8.2 Luxury-Sustainability Paradox: Can Luxury and Sustainability Stay Together?

8.2.1 Binomial Identity of Luxury Brands

Luxury purchases are, by definition, "irrational" (Kapferer, 2012). For instance, a non-luxury handbag is a fraction of the cost of a luxury handbag, but the functional values of both handbags are the same. "Irrationality", in this case, can be seen as buying a product not for its function but for other reasons that are symbolic and hedonistic (Davies et al., 2012). Thus, luxury is bought out of emotions, not rationality. Paradoxically, the notion of luxury also means excess, whereas the notion of sustainability invites us to meet the needs of the current generation without compromising the future generation's ability to meet theirs (Janssen et al., 2014). Furthermore, luxury exhibits social distinction (Kapferer, 1998) and is magnified as an exclusive consumption (Muniz & Guzmán, 2021). However, CSR and sustainability focus on the planet and people and not only on profit (Peng & Chen, 2019). The binomial values of luxury versus CSR are summarised in Table 8.1.

Sustainable luxury was long considered an oxymoron until recent shifts in the industry responding to trends in luxury took sustainability from niche to necessary. Until now, luxury has been linked to wealth, status, and possessions (Kapferer, 2012); however, luxury expectations are changing, especially for the young affluent and socially conscious luxury consumer. These consumers not only indulge in extravagant luxury experiences but also aspire to be associated with brands that espouse values such as moderation and sustainable consumption (Cavender, 2018; Freire & Loussaïef, 2018; Rapp & Mikeska, 2014). As a result, "status has become less about 'what I have' and much more about 'who I am'." According to research (Davies et al., 2012; Janssen et al., 2014), maintaining an elite market presence and exclusive branding while staying

Table 8.1 Binomial Values of Luxury versus CSR

Luxury	CSR
i) Hedonism	Altruism
Superficiality	Responsibility
Wants	Needs
Ostentation	Moderation
Self-enhancing	Self-transcendence
Social distinction	Equality
Excess	Frugality
Emotions	Rationality

socially and environmentally responsible creates uncomfortable tensions for luxury brands and businesses. This is because CSR entails self-transcendent values such as equality, moderation, and universalism, while luxury brands relate to self-enhancement values such as elitism, hedonism, and extravagance (see Table 8.1, for example, of binomial values). Recent studies and media coverage reveal that luxury brands are frequently implicated in environmental scandals, including those involving the burning of out-of-season clothing (Paton, 2018), resource-intensive fast fashion (Brooks, 2019), violations of animal and human rights (Mueller-Hirth, 2017), mink farming (Donato et al., 2019), and slave/child labour (Thevenon & Edmonds, 2019). Instead of the stakeholder idea that is depicted, these activities demonstrate that businesses are maximising profits at any cost, as mentioned in the shareholder theory (Rugimbana et al., 2008). As a result, consumers' scepticism about luxury businesses grows as they are forced to contend with beliefs that clash with their commitment to CSR (Teah et al., 2021). More specifically, consumers are finding it difficult to discern between ethical and unethical businesses as a result of the recent media stories of corporations engaged in corporate malpractice despite promoting themselves as having strong corporate citizenship (Muniz & Guzmán, 2021; Wong & Dhanesh, 2017).

8.3 Factors Influencing Consumers' Preference for Sustainable Luxury

8.3.1 Consumer Value Perception of Sustainable Luxury Brands

Many people who buy luxury goods typically exhibit consumption goals that combine personal and social objectives (Freire & Loussaïef, 2018). By introducing two key dimensions – personal perceptions, which include perceived hedonic value and perceived extended self, and non-personal perceptions, which include perceived conspicuousness, perceived uniqueness, and perceived quality – Vigneron and Johnson (2004) distinguished between luxury and non-luxury brands. To enlarge these categories, Wiedmann et al. (2009) used four latent dimensions of value: social (including prestige and noticeable), functional (including usability, quality, and originality), individual (including self-identity, material, and hedonic), and financial (e.g., price). Customers' impressions of "sustainable luxury" are impacted more by the concept of sustainability than by the concept of luxury, according to a recent study by Wang et al. (2021). When a luxury commodity is linked to sustainability, for instance, the perceived value connected to scarcity may be reduced. For example, the average luxury buyer is hesitant to purchase a Hermès product manufactured with recycled cotton, according to Achabou and Dekhili's (2013) study, because they believe recycling diminishes the item's worth and originality, which, in turn, diminishes its status. Another similar example is Italian luxury fashion house Prada's "fur-free" policy, which demonstrates a commitment to innovation and social responsibility;

however, the environmental impact of sourcing alternatives such as synthetic faux fur is now in the spotlight (Bramley, 2019). This implies that when the sustainable idea for a premium product is advocated, some commonly held values or needs linked with luxury purchasing are challenged. The research on how hedonism and sustainable luxury fit together has been inconsistent, according to Athwal et al. (2019), which is another illustration of a change in value perception. On the one hand, a consumer can consider sustainability to be purely practical and luxury to be hedonistic (Steinhart et al., 2013). However, Cervellon and Shammas (2013) assert that hedonism is a crucial element of sustainable luxury and a significant advantage of eco-friendly products. Increasingly, the purchase intents of luxury consumers are frequently motivated by hedonic necessity and sustainable luxury (Wang et al., 2021). As such, luxury manufacturers must find a method to market their products as something more than symbols of consumers' wealth and social standing in order to fulfil the rising need for businesses to develop items that adhere to high ESG standards.

8.3.2 Consumers' Sociodemographic Characteristics

Environmentally conscious consumers are becoming more prevalent, and they look for businesses that operate ethically and sustainably (Janssen et al., 2014). According to research, between 30% and 40% of consumers of luxury items, according to research, might be categorised as sustainable luxury customers (Quach et al., 2022). Sociodemographic characteristics, for example, including gender, income, occupation, and product familiarity, influence how often people buy green products (Kim et al., 2022). Studies reveal that younger women are the group most worried about environmental and ethical problems in the case of textile items (Niinimäki & Hassi, 2011). Furthermore, low childhood socioeconomic status increases consumer preference for sustainable luxury brands and products (Kim et al., 2022). It would seem that the younger luxury consumer segments are increasingly attempting to fit their purchases with freshly discovered ethical principles and ecological lifestyles in addition to feeling conflicted about what they truly need (Davies et al., 2012; Wong & Dhanesh, 2017).

Younger customers are flooding the luxury market; in 2025, it's predicted that demand will be made up of 50% of those aged 45 and under (DiPasquantonio et al., 2021). Younger millennials and Generation Z, for instance, have completely distinct sets of beliefs and are only starting to enter the workforce. These young customers express new ideals when they purchase; they are more deliberate in their decision-making and want to buy less and buy better (Kim et al., 2022). They search for specific products that correspond to what they value or consider important and demand more luxury companies in terms of everything from equality to the environment (Quach et al., 2022). To purchase products that are environmentally friendly products, this new generation of consumers who are responsible and concerned with the environment (Bianchi & Birtwistle, 2012) research the use of recycled materials or organic labelling in the products that they purchase. Additionally, they frequently understand and are even willing to pay more for green products than they would for conventional ones (DiPasquantonio et al., 2021; Gam et al., 2010). As a result, this is timely evidence that consumers of luxury goods are altering their behaviour.

8.3.3   Communicating Social Changes

While prosocial actions like recycling and reusing products can be highly beneficial, encouraging sustainable consumer behaviour can have a greater positive influence on the environment (Bianchi & Birtwistle, 2012; Gam et al., 2010; Paton, 2018). The concept of subjective happiness may be applied in the context of sustainable consumption (Xiao & Li, 2011). The survey, which was conducted in 14 locations, identified a brand-new pattern: customers who indicated green purchasing intents and sustainable behaviour started receiving higher ratings for life satisfaction than purchasers of more traditional, "unsustainable" goods. The study also revealed that consumers were willing to engage in "prosocial spending", giving up their individual interests in favour of collective interests and short-term losses in favour of long-term gains (e.g., purchasing greener items) (Xiao & Li, 2011). This shows that people are beginning to value sustainable consumption more than non-sustainable consumption, beyond only the cost (Janssen et al., 2014; Kim et al., 2022).

On the basis of this, we may assert that encouraging sustainable consumption is a feasible self-fulfilling action (e.g., subjective happiness). Due to this cultural transition, ideas like voluntary simplicity, ecological living, ethical consumerism, and consumption reduction must be promoted and accepted globally (Bianchi & Birtwistle, 2012; Cervellon & Shammas, 2013). Using luxury brands as agents of social change is one approach to do this. Progressiveness, timelessness, resiliency, originality, craftsmanship, and a positive customer experience are the guiding characteristics of luxury businesses (Wang et al., 2021), and the ideals of luxury, sustainability, and social responsibility are all based on these traits. Luxury businesses are also well-positioned to lead by example and influence social change since they are frequently recognised as admired, copied, or emulated aspirational brands (DiPasquantonio et al., 2021; Freire & Loussaïef, 2018). Given the aforementioned discussions, critics should focus on bringing about social change through consumer-driven strategies rather than resisting consumerism (Janssen et al., 2014). This might be done using luxury brands directly or aspirational advertising or marketing similar to that used in luxury branding. In the end, people cannot be asked to change their behaviour if they are not given new goals to strive towards.

8.4 Barriers to Consumers' Preference for Sustainable Luxury

To meet consumer demand for ethical consumption, many luxury brands have incorporated sustainability as a principal direction for branding (e.g., Han et al., 2017, Jang et al., 2012; Quach et al., 2022). However, luxury brand CSR is not without its challenges. Luxury brands have to contest with conflicting values between CSR and luxury (see CSR-luxury paradox in Muniz & Guzmán, 2021; Wong & Dhanesh, 2017), logistic and supply chain issues (Fernie & Sparks, 2018; Towers et al., 2013), and consumer scepticism (Osburg et al., 2021; Teah et al., 2021). In particular, the debate over whether luxury and sustainability coexist has been evident in current literature. Although the arguments regarding the binomial identity of luxury brands and sustainability (Feng et al., 2020; Freire & Loussa, 2018) have gained academic attention, scholars agree by large that luxury brands should mitigate the contradictory factors in their CSR practices (Davies et al., 2012). The current body of research has uncovered several factors that act as barriers to consumers' preference for sustainable luxury products.

8.4.1 Perceived Risks and Benefits

The additional costs associated with sustainable brands have been identified as one of the key factors that result in negative consumer evaluation (Grasso et al., 2000). However, consumers' higher level of interest and involvement in luxury branding reduces the adverse effect of a higher price on purchase intention (Kapferer, 2012). Studies show that consumers not only feel a sense of risk toward "the sustainable" products (e.g., sustainable plastic clothing) but also develop scepticism regarding the quality of the product (e.g., Kumagai & Nagasawa, 2020). The perceived functional, financial, emotional, and self-image risks prevent consumers from adopting luxury products and services (Kunz et al., 2020; Peng & Chen, 2019). Studies report that consumers' perceived risks and scepticism (i.e., potential greenwashing) are associated with green product knowledge (Peng & Chen, 2019). Studies also note that a lack of information, availability of goods/services, and the irregularity of the purchase could influence luxury consumers' negative attitude toward sustainability (Davies et al. 2012). Therefore, providing relevant CSR information could not only increase consumer awareness but also positively influence luxury buying decisions (Bray et al., 2011). For instance, Stella McCartney, through its Cares Green platform, attempts to influence policymakers to take action and to empower students, professionals, and businesses to embrace sustainability and ethical practices (O'Connor, 2018). Taken together, building consumer knowledge, educating consumers about sustainability practices, and nurturing eco-conscious consumer groups may dilute the impact of the aforementioned risk and scepticism (Petersen & Wilcox, 2016). Such risk and scepticisms are also relevant to the consumers' understanding of the luxury value and related alignment with sustainability practices (Septianto et al., 2021).

8.4.2 Consumer, Culture, and Conspicuousness

The impact of consumers' demographic and cultural factors on their evaluation of sustainable luxury brands has been examined as well. For example, consumers in a collectivist society (vs. individualistic society) tend to share more negative word-of-mouth regarding the price of sustainable luxury products (Amatulli et al., 2017). Notwithstanding, brand positioning also plays a role in constituting consumers' preference for sustainable luxury brands. For instance, a higher level of perceived conspicuousness in luxury branding negatively impacts consumers' perception of sustainability practices in the luxury sector (Janssen et al., 2017). This can also be relevant to the specific product characteristics – as such, consumers of luxury brands consider durable products (e.g., jewellery or cars) more sustainable than less enduring purchases (Janssen et al., 2014).

Another stream of research upholds the question of whether sustainability practices in luxury branding match or conflict with the consumer's self-identity (Athwal et al., 2019). Due to the distinct characteristics of luxury brands (e.g., exclusivity and rarity), the perceived benefits are different from their non-luxury counterparts. One can argue that ultra-high net worth (UHNW) consumers' desired luxury (e.g., products made from crocodile skins) does not fit within the sustainability practices of the brand (Beckham & Voyer, 2014; Line & Hanks, 2016). The simultaneous presence of sustainability practices and environmental misconduct (e.g., burning unsold products) may result in brand hypocrisy, whereby consumers' desire for exclusivity may reduce the perceived hypocrisy (Cheah et al., 2022). Furthermore, the production exploitation with manufacture in luxury industries may have a mixed impact on consumer evaluation (Eisenberg, 2016). However, the changes in luxury branding strategy in relation to sustainability practices have been evident with the notion that sustainable luxury brands should embrace the consumers' culture and community to enhance the new worldview (DeLeon, 2019).

8.4.3 Consumer-Brand Identification

There are counterintuitive arguments regarding whether the up-class and sophisticated personalities of luxury brands are affected by their CSR initiatives, whereas sophisticated brands are perceived to be less ethical than sincere brands (Pinto et al., 2019). Also, to some extent, consumers' "dream for exclusive luxury" and "parenthesis of pleasure" are not expected to be reduced by sustainability guidelines and principles (Kapferer & Michaut-Denizeau, 2020). Notwithstanding, a group of consumers also feel that the global luxury manufacturing industry is too small to have a significant impact on the future of the planet; consequently, sustainability in luxury branding does not seem desired by these consumers (Ehrich & Irwin, 2005). Studies suggest that luxury brands need to show strong links between sustainability practices and the inherent traits of the brands (Kapferer & Michaut-Denizeau, 2014; Seng-abira et al., 2020). For example, Hermès emphasised the human touch in their branding strategy to communicate the authenticity of sustainable luxury (de Kerviler et al., 2021). Such a link is important for both maintaining the brand identity at the consumer level and financial stability at the macro-level (i.e., the stock market) (Feng et al., 2020). As a result, the interplay of perceived luxury, perceived sustainability, and CSR scepticism result in the attitude–behaviour gap (de Klerk et al., 2018).

8.5 Moving Ahead: How to Mitigate the Paradox?

To navigate the paradox, brands have endeavoured in various initiatives to build consumer confidence and evaluation. The principles of "stakeholder marketing" and "cause-related" activities have been proven to be effective strategies when building consumer trust and engagement in the short term (Janssen et al., 2014; Teah et al., 2021). For example, through a charitable endeavour (such as MasterCard and the United Nations World Food Programme for the Brazil World Cup), customer relationship management activities enable companies to experiment with CSR and philanthropy. This endeavour is carried out with the assistance of a third-party charity that may convey ideas of CSR through association. Another short-term opportunity lies in leveraging existing environmentally friendly knowledge and behaviours. Recycling waste products and refuse has been a long staple of sustainability initiatives employed and mandated by governments, households, and businesses (Bianchi & Birtwistle, 2012; Gam et al., 2010). However, scepticism among recyclers has raised questions regarding the efficacy of recycling. Reports have shown that recycling may not be beneficial for the environment – labour, carbon footprint, and the fact that items collected are not actually recycled.

Luxury brands have showcased their support towards green initiatives like recycling through 100% recyclable packaging and embedding their supply chain with the sustainable sourcing of raw materials (Kunz et al., 2020; Peng & Chen, 2019). Some examples of luxury brands that implement green practices include the InterContinental Hotels Group with its Green EngageTM System to measure energy, waste, and water use (IHG, 2015); Stella McCartney has used eco-friendly materials for its products, including vegan leather, recycled synthetic fabrics, organic cotton, and faux fur (Wolfe, 2018); Versace, Burberry, and Furla have also committed to stopping using real fur for their products (Jones, 2018), and Gucci has used eco-friendly materials for its eyewear since 2011 as well as a new environmentally friendly production process (Heerde, 2018). More recently, sustainable social movements have focused on upcycling: giving materials a second life and new function. This involves repurposing wasted or broken materials: furniture and plastics for form or function. Luxury brands, in addition to shifting production closer to end consumers and adopting technologies like blockchain to increase traceability and transparency, are looking to create products that theoretically last forever; refreshing and repairing products when required (DiPasquantonio et al., 2021). In the same vein, second-hand designer websites such as Vestiaire Collective, Farfetch, and Purse Affair sell certified pre-loved/owned items. Brands like Hermès, Chanel, and Coach have repair services to

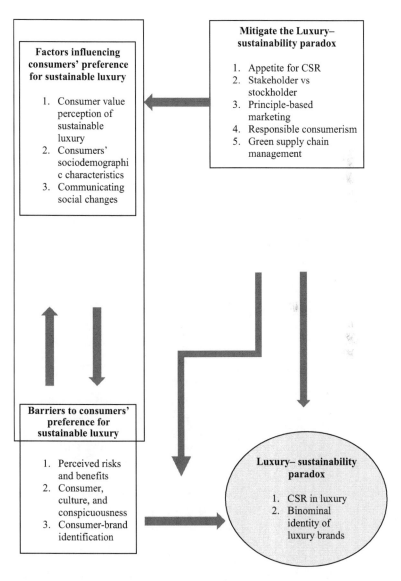

Figure 8.1 Framework for mitigating luxury-sustainability paradox.

freshen up jewellery, leather goods, and watches. Luxury cars such as BMW, Audi, Porsche, and Mercedes Benz have certified pre-owned vehicles in their showrooms. However, companies' business model of planned obsolescence requires the constant purchase of new releases. The secondary market prevents new purchases.

Unless companies have a financial incentive to operate in a secondary market, they may not do so. More significantly, is a purchase from a secondary market a real luxury experience? Luxury brands would require a retail environment they can control to reflect the brand experience. In the longer term, for luxury companies and brands to buy into ethical consumerism, they should enlist a financial imperative to do so. To bridge the gap between binomial identity values and the advent of CSR and the rise of ethical consumerism has given birth to companies with an agenda to help parts of society from its moment of inception (Janssen et al., 2014; Kim et al., 2022; Teah et al., 2021). These companies are thus "born and bred" to do CSR; unlikely to be seen by some as "jumping onto the CSR bandwagon" or "greenwashing" (Bianchi & Birtwistle, 2012; Cervellon & Shammas, 2013). Furthermore, these "Principle-based Entities" have principles to help parts of society as part of their brand DNA (Janssen et al., 2014). For instance, Patagonia, an apparel company born and bred in CSR principles, has higher consumer evaluations when engaging in CSR compared to companies that are not born and bred in CSR principles, such as North Face, Columbia Sportswear, Puma, and GAP (Rapp & Mikeska, 2014). Similarly, luxury brands have had success with repositioning to better adhere to CSR obligations. For instance, the LVMH group of companies has conducted a company-wide shift towards CSR as its core principle leading to changes in infrastructure, supply chain, staff KPIs, and marketing communications (Freire & Loussaïef, 2018). This was achieved through the prioritised allocation of resources and management attention. However, some brands within the umbrella have a deeply entrenched image of traditional luxury that will benefit more from brand extension simply because changing public perception and attitudes towards the brand is too far-fetched. For example, Hermès is deeply rooted in traditional luxury due to its vintage and heritage, while Petite H was born as a brand extension to pursue more CSR-related endeavours. Overall, in order to move forward, luxury companies will have to embrace a paradigm shift in business models to address the challenges faced in stakeholder versus shareholder theories and perspectives (Rugimbana et al., 2008; Teah et al., 2021). Luxury companies must also consider the economic viability and take years to have these changes cascade to parts of the business. As a result, many luxury companies have started initiatives like ethical sourcing as well as employing traditional artisans and incorporating their designs into artworks and motifs (Cavender, 2018). Based on the foregoing, a framework for mitigating the luxury-sustainability paradox is presented in Figure 8.1.

8.6 Conclusion

Ethical consumerism is here to stay. Certain consumer groups realise their power over companies and will punish brands that do not fall within their ethical requirements. To coexist, luxury brands must find ways to navigate the landscape of luxury and CSR. Scholars have sought to understand the drivers and barriers behind sustainable luxury consumption. While the collective consumer has yet to come to a consensus, considerable headway has been made towards bridging the gap between binomial identity values. Brands have also embarked on various CSR initiatives to foster positive consumer evaluations and prevent negative consequences. Some of these solutions are labelled "band-aid"; these are short-term methods such as stakeholder marketing, cause-related marketing, and other efforts such as recyclable packaging, upcycling, and developing secondary markets for pre-owned/loved items. Standalone, these efforts have been shown to diminish in their return towards maintaining positive consumer evaluations once the novelty wears off and eventually serve little purpose but to be seen as greenwashing. However, a long-term solution may exist in the form of principle-based marketing – principles and values that form the DNA of the brand that aligns with CSR values which cascade into all aspects of the company, such as infrastructure, supply chain, sourcing of raw materials, and staff KPIs. This endeavour requires a concerted effort company-wide and requires resources and time to shift brand perceptions and image, particularly in brands that have a long-established image of traditional luxury entrenched in consumer perception.

Taken together, the key takeaways from this book chapter are as follows:

1 Ethical consumerism, green consumption, and social responsibility is a prioritised agenda on the list of many stakeholders including luxury brands.
2 Luxury brands face challenges when communicating CSR initiatives due to binomial identity values.
3 Understanding barriers and drivers behind the consumption of luxury brands from an ethical perspective allows luxury brands to further understand the attitude–behaviour gap.
4 There are ways luxury brands can try to reconcile the attitude–behaviour gap, some shorter term, while some endeavours are more permanent but more resource intensive.

References

Achabou, M. A., & Dekhili, S. (2013). Luxury and sustainable development: Is there a match? *Journal of Business Research, 66*(10), 1896–1903.

Amatulli, C., De Angelis, M., Pino, G., & Guido, G. (2017). Unsustainable luxury and negative word-of mouth: The role of shame and consumers' cultural orientation. *Advances in Consumer Research, 45*, 498.

Athwal, N., Wells, V. K., Carrigan, M., & Henninger, C. E. (2019). Sustainable luxury marketing: A synthesis and research agenda. *International Journal of Management Reviews, 21*(4), 405–426.

Beckham, D., & Voyer, B. G. (2014). Can sustainability be luxurious? A mixed-method investigation of implicit and explicit attitudes towards sustainable luxury consumption. In *NA – Advances in consumer research volume 42*, eds. J. Cotte, & S. Wood. Association for Consumer Research, Duluth, MN, pp. 245–250.

Bianchi, C., & Birtwistle, G. (2012). Consumer clothing disposal behaviour: A comparative study. *International Journal of Consumer Studies, 36*(3), 335–341.

Bramley, E. V. (2019, May 23). Prada announces it is to go fur-free. *The Guardian*, https://www.theguardian.com/fashion/2019/may/23/prada-announces-it-is-to-go-fur-free.

Bray, J., Johns, N., & Kilburn, D. (2011). An exploratory study into the factors impeding ethical consumption. *Journal of Business Ethics, 98*(4), 597–608.

Brooks, A. (2019). *Clothing poverty: The hidden world of fast fashion and second-hand clothes*. Zed Books, London.

Cavender, R. (2018). The marketing of sustainability and CSR initiatives by luxury brands: Cultural indicators, call to action, and framework. In *Sustainability in luxury fashion business*, eds. C. K. Lo, & J. Ha-Brookshire. Springer, Singapore, pp. 29–49.

Cervellon, M. C., & Shammas, L. (2013). The value of sustainable luxury in mature markets: A customer-based approach. *Journal of Corporate Citizenship, 52*, 90–101.

Cheah, I., Shimul, A. S., & Teah, M. (2022). Sustainability claim, environmental misconduct and perceived hypocrisy in luxury branding. *Spanish Journal of Marketing-ESIC* (ahead-of-print). https://doi.org/10.1108/SJME-02-2022-0012.

Davies, I. A., Lee, Z., & Ahonkhai, I. (2012). Do consumers care about ethical-luxury? *Journal of Business Ethics, 106*(1), 37–51.

de Kerviler, G., Gentina, E., & Heuvinck, N. (2021). Research: How to position a luxury brand as sustainable. *Harvard Business Review*. https://hbr.org/2021/09/research-how-to-position-a-luxury-brand-as-sustainable.

De Klerk, H. M., Kearns, M., & Redwood, M. (2018). Controversial fashion, ethical concerns and environmentally significant behaviour: The case of the leather industry. *International Journal of Retail & Distribution Management, 47*(1), 19–38.

DeLeon, J. (2019). *The new luxury: Defining the aspirational in the age of hype*. Gestalten, Berlin.

DiPasquantonio, F., Jones, D., & Gianera, D. (2021, August). *Sustainability as the ultimate luxury: How realistic?* Deutsche Bank Research. https://www.dbresearch.com/PROD/RPS_EN-PROD/PROD0000000000519692/Q%26A_series%3A_Sustainability_as_the_ultimate_luxury%3A.pdf?undefined&realload=uQk5Qmpj4YeykNBKuajEWlc4gdbbTuzzy8G0pqRe4wbVpV5xf9Vn2xSmeVXOc40U.

Donato, C., Amatulli, C., & De Angelis, M. (2019). Responsible luxury development: A study on luxury companies' CSR, circular economy, and entrepreneurship. In Gardetti, M. & Muthu, S. (Eds.), *Sustainable luxury. Environmental footprints and eco-design of products and processes*, Springer, Singapore, pp. 21-–38.

Ehrich, K. R., & Irwin, J. R. (2005). Willful ignorance in the request for product attribute information. *Journal of Marketing Research, 42*(3), 266–277.

Eisenberg, M. (2016). The luxury brand-building canvas. *Proceedings of the Global Marketing Conference*, Hong Kong, 21–24 July.

Feng, Y., Tong, X., & Zhu, Q. (2020). The market value of sustainable practices in the luxury industry: An identity mismatch and institutional theoretical perspective. *Transportation Research Part E: Logistics and Transportation Review, 137*, 101919.

Fernie, J., & Sparks, L. (Eds.). (2018). *Logistics and retail management: Emerging issues and new challenges in the retail supply chain*. Kogan page publishers, London.

Freire, A. N., & Loussaïef, L. (2018). When advertising highlights the binomial identity values of luxury and CSR principles: The examples of Louis Vuitton and Hermès. *Corporate Social Responsibility and Environmental Management, 25*(4), 565–582.

Gam, H. J., Cao, H., Farr, C., & Kang, M. (2010). Quest for the eco-apparel market: A study of mothers' willingness to purchase organic cotton clothing for their children. *International Journal of Consumer Studies, 34*(6), 648–656.

Grasso, M. M., McEnally, M., Widdows, R., & Herr, D. G. (2000). Consumer behavior toward recycled textile products. *Journal of the Textile Institute, 91*(2), 94–106.

Han, J., Seo, Y., & Ko, E. (2017). Staging luxury experiences for understanding sustainable fashion consumption: A balance theory application. *Journal of Business Research, 74*, 162–167.

Heerde, L. V. (2018). Luxury brands moving to sustainability. *Luxiders.* https://luxiders.com/luxury-brands-moving-sustainability/.

IHG (2015). IHG Green Engage™ system, available at: www.ihgplc.com/index.asp?pageid_742 (accessed 28 September 2019).

Jang, J., Ko, E., Chun, E., & Lee, E. (2012). A study of a social content model for sustainable development in the fast fashion industry. *Journal of Global Fashion Marketing, 3*(2), 61–70.

Janssen, C., Vanhamme, J., & Leblanc, S. (2017). Should luxury brands say it out loud? Brand conspicuousness and consumer perceptions of responsible luxury. *Journal of Business Research, 77*, 167–174.

Janssen, C., Vanhamme, J., Lindgreen, A., & Lefebvre, C. (2014). The Catch-22 of responsible luxury: Effects of luxury product characteristics on consumers' perception of fit with corporate social responsibility. *Journal of Business Ethics, 119*(1), 45–57.

Jones, C. (2018). Coach follows Burberry, Versace, Gucci and Hugo Boss, pledging to go fur-free. *USA Today*, October 23. https://www.usatoday.com/story/money/2018/10/23/coach-follows-burberry-versace-gucci-saying-go-fur-free/1743788002/.

Kapferer, J. N. (1998). Why are we seduced by luxury brands? *Journal of Brand Management, 6*(1), 44–49.

Kapferer, J.-N. (2012). *The new strategic brand management: Advanced insights and strategic thinking.* Kogan Page Publishers, London.

Kapferer, J. N., & Michaut-Denizeau, A. (2014). Is luxury compatible with sustainability? Luxury consumers' viewpoint. *Journal of Brand Management, 21*(1), 1–22.

Kapferer, J. N., & Michaut-Denizeau, A. (2020). Are millennials really more sensitive to sustainable luxury? A cross-generational international comparison of sustainability consciousness when buying luxury. *Journal of Brand Management, 27*(1), 35–47.

Kim, J., Park, J., & Septianto, F. (2022). The impact of socioeconomic status on preferences for sustainable luxury brands. *Psychology & Marketing, 39*(8), 1563–1578.

Kumagai, K., & Nagasawa, N. (2020). Brand evaluation based on sustainable products: The effect of perceived risk, brand trust, and luxury. *Proceedings of the 33th*

Biannual Meeting of the Association of Product Development and Management, Article No. 3.

Kunz, J., May, S., & Schmidt, H. J. (2020). Sustainable luxury: Current status and perspectives for future research. *Business Research, 13*(2), 541–601.

Line, N. D., & Hanks, L. (2016). The effects of environmental and luxury beliefs on intention to patronize green hotels: the moderating effect of destination image. *Journal of Sustainable Tourism, 24*(6), 904–925.

Mueller-Hirth, N. (2017). Business and social peace processes: How can insights from post-conflict studies help CSR to address peace and reconciliation? In Vertigans, S. & Idowu, S. (Eds.), *Corporate social responsibility.* Springer, Cham, pp. 137–153.

Muniz, F., & Guzmán, F. (2021). Overcoming the conflicting values of luxury branding and CSR by leveraging celebrity endorsements to build brand equity. *Journal of Brand Management, 28*(3), 347–358.

Niinimäki, K., & Hassi, L. (2011). Emerging design strategies in sustainable production and consumption of textiles and clothing. *Journal of Cleaner Production, 19*(16), 1876–1883.

O'Connor, T. (2018). Stella McCartney announces UN charter for sustainable fashion. *Business of Fashion.* https://www.businessoffashion.com/articles/sustainability/stella-mccartney-announces-un-charter-for-sustainable-fashion/.

Osburg, V. S., Davies, I., Yoganathan, V., & McLeay, F. (2021). Perspectives, opportunities and tensions in ethical and sustainable luxury: Introduction to the thematic symposium. *Journal of Business Ethics, 169*(2), 201–210.

Paton, E. (2018). Burberry to stop burning clothes and other goods it can't sell. *New York Times.*

Peng, N., & Chen, A. (2019). Luxury hotels going green–the antecedents and consequences of consumer hesitation. *Journal of Sustainable Tourism, 27*(9), 1374–1392.

Petersen, F. E., & Wilcox, K. (2016). Education, liberalism and consumers' response to luxury brands. *Advances in Consumer Research, 44,* 589.

Pinto, D. C., Herter, M. M., Gonçalves, D., & Sayin, E. (2019). Can luxury brands be ethical? Reducing the sophistication liability of luxury brands. *Journal of Cleaner Production, 233,* 1366–1376.

Quach, S., Septianto, F., Thaichon, P., & Nasution, R. A. (2022). The role of art infusion in enhancing pro-environmental luxury brand advertising. *Journal of Retailing and Consumer Services, 64,* 102780.

Rapp, J. M., & Mikeska, J. G. (2014). Doing harm while attempting good: A critical eye on corporate social responsibility. In Hill, R.P. & Langan, R. (Eds.), *Handbook of research on marketing and corporate social responsibility.* Edward Elgar Publishing, pp. 381–396.

Rugimbana, R., Quazi, A., & Keating, B. (2008). Applying a consumer perceptual measure of corporate social responsibility: A regional Australian perspective. *Journal of Corporate Citizenship, 29,* 61–74.

Sengabira, C. N., Septianto, F., & Northey, G. (2020). Committed to help: The effects of frequency of corporate donations on luxury brand evaluations. *Asia Pacific Journal of Marketing and Logistics, 32*(3), 681–694.

Septianto, F., Kemper, J., & Northey, G. (2021). Slogans with negations' effect on sustainable luxury brand. *Australasian Marketing Journal.* https://doi.org/10.1177/18393349211046633.

Steinhart, Y., Ayalon, O., & Puterman, H. (2013). The effect of an environmental claim on consumers' perceptions about luxury and utilitarian products. *Journal of Cleaner Production, 53*, 277–286.

Teah, K., Sung, B., & Phau, I. (2021). CSR motives on situational scepticism towards luxury brands. *Marketing Intelligence & Planning, 40*(1), 1–17.

Thevenon, O., & Edmonds, E. (2019). *Child labour: Causes, consequences and policies to tackle it.* OECD Social, Employment and Migration Working Papers No. 235. www.oecd.org/els/workingpapers. Accessed 16 December 2022.

Towers, N., Perry, P., & Chen, R. (2013). Corporate social responsibility in luxury manufacturer supply chains: An exploratory investigation of a Scottish cashmere garment manufacturer. *International Journal of Retail & Distribution Management, 41*(11/12), 961–972.

Vigneron, F., & Johnson, L. W. (2004). Measuring perceptions of brand luxury. *Journal of Brand Management, 11*(6), 484–506.

Wang, P., Kuah, A. T., Lu, Q., Wong, C., Thirumaran, K., Adegbite, E., & Kendall, W. (2021). The impact of value perceptions on purchase intention of sustainable luxury brands in China and the UK. *Journal of Brand Management, 28*(3), 325–346.

Wiedmann, K. P., Hennigs, N., & Siebels, A. (2009). Value-based segmentation of luxury consumption behavior. *Psychology & Marketing, 26*(7), 625–651.

Wolfe, I. (2018). How ethical is Stella McCartney? *Good on You*, July 23. https://goodonyou.eco/how-ethical-is-stella-mccartney/.

Wong, J. Y., & Dhanesh, G. S. (2017). Corporate social responsibility (CSR) for ethical corporate identity management: Framing CSR as a tool for managing the CSR-luxury paradox online. *Corporate Communications: An International Journal, 22*(4), 420–439.

Xiao, J. J., & Li, H. (2011). Sustainable consumption and life satisfaction. *Social Indicators Research, 104*(2), 323–329.

9 Localized Luxury and Luxury Marketing

Meaning Makings of Chinese Luxury Brand

Ting Jin, Wei Shao, and Park Thaichon

9.1 Introduction

While many Western luxury brands have achieved success in the Asian market (Butt & Roberts, 2014), Chinese consumers have been predicted to be the strongest purchasing group of consumers in the global luxury goods market (Danziger, 2020), spending $73.6 billion on luxury goods in 2021, up 36% from 2020 (CNBC, 2022). Previous studies on Chinese consumers have mainly focused on how Chinese consumers are willing to purchase global luxury brands such as Hermes, Chanel, and Prada as status symbols (Li et al., 2012; Wu et al., 2017). Researchers such as Wang et al. (2011) and Zhang and Kim (2013) argue that Chinese consumers are similar to luxury consumers in other countries/cultures in their way to seek worldly possessions and to use well-known global luxury brands as a symbol of wealth and social status. By contrast, there is little in the literature examining why Chinese consumers purchase Chinese luxury brands.

A closer look at the literature reveals several gaps. Kuang-peng et al. (2011) suggest that more research is needed to understand symbolic consumption in an Asian context. According to Ko et al. (2019), there is still a great deal of work to be done in the field of luxury consumption. For instance, a deeper understanding of how culture (i.e. Chinese culture) influences the purchasing behavior of luxury goods is needed (Wiedmann et al., 2007). In addition, research is needed to examine whether cultural factors are essential to luxury consumers, and what type of consumer values or motivations have the biggest impact on luxury consumption (De Barnier et al., 2006; Walley & Li, 2015).

To respond to the calls for future research, this research provides an initial understanding of luxury branding in China. In light of China's long history of producing luxury products such as silk and tea, this research examines the social and cultural meanings of Chinese luxury brands. More recently, Chinese consumers are showing increasing preferences for Chinese luxury brands due to a rise in national loyalty (Danziger, 2020). There has been renewed interest in domestic (Chinese) luxury brands, and many Chinese luxury brands have become highly profitable on a global scale. One good example is Lao Feng Xiang 老鳳祥, a luxury brand from mainland China,

DOI: 10.4324/9781003321378-9

ranked number 15 on the Global Powers of Luxury Goods Top 100, FY 2020 (Deloitte Consulting, 2021). Another jewelry brand Chow Tai Fook 周大福 (Hong Kong and mainland) was ranked number 10 on the list, reporting double-digit sales growth in 2019. This significant market potential is contrasted by a dearth of knowledge of Chinese luxury brands. Researchers and managers have little understanding of why Chinese consumers will purchase Chinese luxury brands, because previous research has mainly focused on examining the relationship between Chinese consumers and global luxury brands, using decision-making rules and scales developed in Western countries rather than focusing on understanding Chinese consumers from an endogenous point of view (e.g. Christodoulides et al., 2009; Li et al., 2012). Furthermore, much of the evolvement of the luxury brand concept has arisen from the notion of consumer desire to achieve social status by signaling wealth through conspicuous luxury consumption (e.g. Han et al., 2010; Pino et al., 2019).

The following research questions are presented: (a) How do Chinese consumers view Chinese luxury brands and what socio-cultural meanings are attached to Chinese luxury brands? (b) How do Chinese consumers use, consume, or experience Chinese luxury brands?; and (c) Why Chinese consumers' preference for Chinese luxury brands might be different from their preferences for global/foreign luxury brands? This research draws on the Consumer Culture Theory (CCT), focusing on the sociocultural, experiential, symbolic, and ideological aspects of consumption (Arnould & Thompson, 2005), using three Chinese luxury brands as illustrative cases, Lao Feng Xiang 老鳳祥 (jewelry), Maotai 茅臺 (liquor), and Shang Hai Tang 上海灘 (fashion). The findings will provide implications for brand managers as to how to distinguish between Chinese and Western/global luxury brands for the Chinese market.

9.2 Literature Review

9.2.1 Theoretical Background

It is the aim of the research to develop a greater understanding of Chinese luxury brands relative to the global luxury brand, using a case study approach. The best context for studying luxury consumers in China is the local or domestic luxury brand market where "particular manifestations of consumer culture are constituted, sustained, transformed, and shaped by broader historical forces" (Arnould & Thompson, 2005). According to the CCT, a greater understanding is required of the distribution of meanings (Waltersdorfer et al., 2015) and the cultural dimensions of consumption in a specific field or context (Algharabat et al., 2020; Arnould & Thompson, 2005). Kuang-peng et al. (2011) suggest that more research is needed to understand symbolic consumption in an Asian context. Ko et al. (2019) also argue that there is still a great deal of work to be done in the field of luxury consumption. To the best of our knowledge, this study is the first to explore the meanings of Chinese luxury brands.

9.2.1 Global vs. Local Luxury Brand

China has shown an increasing demand for luxury in the global market (Yu & Hu, 2020), and many global luxury brands, such as Louise Vuitton, Dior, Prada, and Gucci, are used as social label that contributes to the recognition of individual social standing and position (Zhan & He, 2012). The symbolic value of status and prestige is important for Chinese consumers, which explains why Chinese consumers hold preferences for well-known foreign luxury brands with popular logos (Wang et al., 2011).

Even though the emergence of global consumer culture has been an important force in the luxury markets (Steenkamp, 2019), global luxury brands do not necessarily design their products to cater to consumers with a particular nationality. By contrast, Chinese luxury brands may be perceived as localized luxury brands designed to cater to Chinese consumers' tastes and preferences. Heine and Gutsatz (2015) argue that there are challenges facing Western luxury brands expanding in China due to a lack of understanding of Chinese luxury consumers. Traditional research examined Chinese luxury consumers using Western theoretical paradigms (Liang et al., 2017). Hence, there is a need for understanding Chinese consumers from a localized perspective.

There's been renewed research interest in local consumer culture in recent years due to powerful political and economic forces, which provides new opportunities for local luxury brands to differentiate themselves based on unique local consumer culture (Schuiling & Kapferer, 2004; Steenkamp et al., 2003; Steenkamp, 2019). Many local Chinese luxury brands have developed (Schroeder et al., 2017) that combine distinct aspects of Chinese aesthetics, culture, and values with the notion of luxury of Western culture (Eckhardt et al., 2015). For example, high-end fashion brands such as Shang Xia (上下) and Shanghai Tang (上海滩) are popular among Chinese consumers (Vogue, 2022). By contrast, previous research has largely ignored the Chinese luxury market for Chinese luxury brands. In this research, we propose that Chinese consumers are still keen to discover or rediscover 5,000 years of history and art and their national identity through their consumption of Chinese luxury brands. The aim of the research is to examine the distinctiveness of Chinese luxury brands, and to explore the underpinning social and cultural meanings of Chinese luxury brands, using three Chinese luxury brands as illustrative cases.

9.2.2 Chinese Luxury Brand

Due to the lack of research on Chinese luxury brands, we discuss four unique aspects that could be attributed to Chinese luxury brands: (1) luxury consumption in a highly collectivist culture, (2) the influence of Guanxi or relationship on luxury consumption, (3) self-brand image congruity, and (4) meaning-making as part of cultural experience.

To the extent that China is a highly collectivist society, it is expected that individuals conform to groups and society and individual attitudes and tastes should be replaced by social norms (Wang & Lin, 2009). Hence, we aim to prove that Chinese luxury brands may be purchased to conform to social norms rather than a display of wealth, status, and success. For example, during special events and occasions, a public display of using or wearing only Chinese, not global, luxury brands may be seen as necessary and conforming to a group or social norms. Previous literature focused on conspicuous consumption and exclusively on the global luxury brand (Jinkins, 2016; Hamelin & Thaichon, 2016), assuming it all to be the same for the public display of wealth for all consumers. However, we argue that there are different types of conspicuous consumption and there will be specific social gathering occasions in the Chinese market that focus only on the use of Chinese luxury brands, excluding global luxury brands, as this is determined by Chinese culture.

9.2.3 Conceptual Model

Guanxi is the process of social interactions and another significant cultural factor for Chinese consumers (Hyun et al., 2021; Wang et al., 2011). Yet, past research has largely ignored the role of Guanxi in examining Chinese consumers purchasing luxury brands (Li et al., 2014). Limited research examined luxury brands purchased as a gift by Chinese consumers to develop Guanxi (Hyun et al., 2021; Wang et al., 2011). By contrast, we argue that Guanxi is another key driver for luxury consumption in China and Chinese luxury brand plays an important role in developing Guanxi or relationship-building as it would be considered as culturally meaningful consumption.

The third unique dimension of Chinese luxury brands for Chinese consumers is self-brand image congruity. Luxury brands could be viewed as a signal that transfers meaning to both the consumer and others (Schmitt, 2012). Empirical research by Seo et al. (2015) shows that there are individual differences among consumers concerning their use of luxury brands to signal their identity to others depending on the specific social and cultural context of brand consumption. As a luxury brand can be used to express the self regardless of social status (Pino et al., 2019). It is important for researchers not to equate luxury consumption as simply a display of wealth or social status, but to start exploring the meanings that individual consumers attach to luxury brand consumption (Thaichon & Quach, 2016). Furthermore, one of the theoretical orientations of the CCT research has been to explore luxury consumption that can contribute in many ways to the construction of a coherent self-identity (Arnould & Thompson, 2005). We argue that compared to the global or international luxury brand, a Chinese luxury brand may be considered a better fit with the self-concept of a Chinese consumer due to cultural proximity and congruency between Chinese luxury brands and Chinese consumers.

Lastly, few previous research examined luxury brands as symbols of consumer culture. Schmitt (2012, p. 12) argues that

> brands may be used to signify not only individual selves; they may also be used to represent a group, a society, or culture. As cultural symbols, they can stand for nations (e.g., McDonald's), generations (e.g., Gap), and cultural values (e.g., Harley Davidson).

In the current luxury brand literature, little is known about luxury brands that have been endowed with distinct social and cultural meanings. It is even less clear whether or not Chinese consumers experience Chinese culture through the consumption of Chinese luxury brands. Thus, this research helps

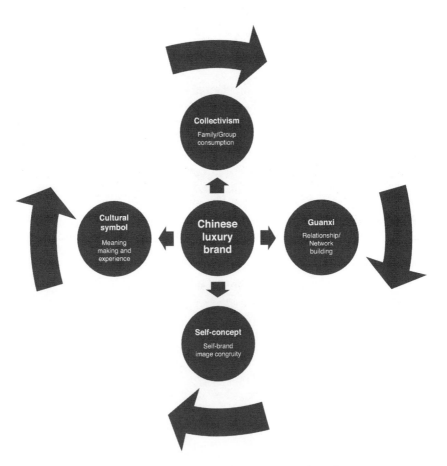

Figure 9.1 Social and cultural meanings of Chinese luxury brands.

to illuminate the meaning-making aspect of Chinese consumers purchasing Chinese luxury brands.

Overall, we present a conceptual model (Figure 9.1) regarding Chinese luxury brands, including the luxury value perception dimensions as commonly discussed in the literature, as well as highlighting the uniqueness of Chinese luxury brand consumption in relation to (1) collectivism, (2) Guanxi or relationship, (3) self-brand image congruity, and (4) cultural symbols.

9.3 Methodology

The purpose of the research is to explore the meanings of Chinese luxury brands from a Chinese consumers' perspective (see Figure 9.1), using three Chinese luxury brands as illustrative cases. The case study methodology is generally utilized in exploratory research or where a phenomenon seems to be inseparable from its context (Yin, 2003). This methodology provides rich qualitative information, allowing a researcher to investigate a topic in greater detail (Farquhar, 2012; Zaidah, 2007).

9.3.1 Selection of Cases

From all of the Chinese luxury brands that were identified by respondents who completed the survey in Study 1 for Chinese luxury brand, we selected three Chinese luxury brands that Chinese consumers are familiar with: Lao Feng Xiang 老鳳祥 (jewelry), Maotai 茅臺 (liquor), and Shanghai Tang 上海灘 (fashion). These three brands not only represent three different product categories but also satisfy the following selection criteria:

1 Lao Feng Xiang 老鳳祥, Maotai 茅臺 are homegrown brands that have a long history and were established prior to the communist takeover of China and have managed to survive the Cultural Revolution in the 1970s, and they continue to continue to thrive until now.
2 Shanghai Tang 上海灘 was chosen because it was originally established in Hong Kong, and has both a domestic and international appeal. Shanghai Tang 上海灘 provides a contrast to Lao Feng Xiang and Maotai, which were originated from mainland China and have mainly a domestic appeal.

9.3.2 Research Participants and Procedure

Twenty in-depth interviews were conducted with Chinese participants. Table 9.1 shows the characteristics of the interviewees. Interviewees were asked to discuss each of the Chinese luxury brands which were identified during the preliminary interviews stage, including Lao Feng Xiang 老鳳祥, Maotai 茅臺, and Shang Hai Tang 上海灘, regarding their thoughts, ideas, feelings, and experiences. The interviews were semi-structured in order to

Table 9.1 Demographic profile of the interviewees

Participant	Gender	Age	Occupation	Level of Education	Yearly Income (RMB)
AW	Female	36	Self-employed	Bachelor	400,001–600,000
JZ	Female	34	Real estate seller	Bachelor	Over 600,000
NW	Male	31	Senior accountant	Master	Over 600,000
KT	Female	21	Student	Bachelor	0–20,000[a]
PQ	Male	29	Project manager	Bachelor	Over 600,000
NW	Male	34	Senior accountant	Bachelor	Over 600,000
MB	Female	28	Self-employed	Bachelor	400,001–600,000
MW	Male	30	College manager	Bachelor	Over 600,000
SN	Female	32	Researcher	Master	400,001–600,000
NZ	Male	32	Pest manager	Master	400,001–600,000
SM	Female	38	Tourism manager	Master	400,001–600,000
ST	Female	35	Self-employed	Bachelor	Over 600,000
AC	Female	28	Logistic manager	Bachelor	400,001–600,000
SP	Male	34	Marketing manager	Master	400,001–600,000
NL	Female	26	Marketing manager	Master	Over 600,000
SA	Male	40	Policy adviser	Bachelor	400,001–600,000
KX	Male	24	Self-employed	Bachelor	Over 600,000
AG	Male	32	Student	College	0–20,000[a]
BY	Male	40	Managing director	Master	Over 600,000
CH	Female	27	Nurse	Bachelor	400,001–600,000

[a] Note: Full-time students are supported financially by their parents.

allow a detailed discussion of each of the luxury brands in a way that is unobtrusive as semi-structured interviews afford the interviewer more opportunity to probe for a deeper explanation (Kajornboon, 2005). The interviewees were free to express their opinions in depth. Interviews were initially transcribed in Chinese, professionally translated into English, and then back-translated into Chinese.

9.4 Results

Content analysis was used concerning each of the three Chinese luxury brands (cases). Table 9.2 provides some illustrative quotes from the interviews relating to the four unique aspects of Chinese luxury brands (Figure 9.1). We then discuss the findings for each of the three Chinese brands, which can provide some insights into reasons why Chinese consumers would purchase Chinese luxury brand and sometimes prefer it to global luxury brands.

9.4.1 Case Study 1: Lao Feng Xiang (老鳳祥)

Lao Feng Xiang (LFX Jewelry) was established in 1848 and is currently the second-largest jewelry retailer in China (Hsu et al., 2014). The company is based in Shanghai and has an extensive retailing network in 27 provinces in China. Lao Feng Xiang is not only a famous jewelry trademark in China but is also China's oldest jewelry company (Lao Feng Xiang, 2017).

Table 9.2 Illustrative quotes (Study 1)

Chinese Luxury Brand	Illustrative Quotes
Collectivism Family/group consumption	• "Even today, premium liquor is still expensive. However, during festivals, especially the Spring Festival, Chinese people have the tradition of treating families and guests with premium liquor (Maotai)" (NZ, Male, 32). • "It (Maotai) is a symbol of unity, the unity of a group of people after a whole year of hardworking" (SM, Female, 38).
Guanxi Relationship/ network building	• "Chinese people think there is a type of friendship maintained by sharing food and liquor (Maotai)" (NW, Male, 34). • In my view, it (Maotai) reflects the role played by liquor in the Chinese culture where liquor is related to making friends and developing Guanxi" (KX, Male, 24).
Self-Concept Self-brand image congruity	• "This (Shanghai Tang) is a local brand in China, everyone as a Chinese loves their local industry and national brands" (BY, Male, 40). • "At weddings, including my personal wedding, the Chinese generally prefer using products from traditional Chinese brands, starting with the taking of the wedding photos, then the whole process of the wedding ceremony, everyone chooses to wear products from Chinese brands. The gentlemen will wear Tang suits, and the ladies will wear cheongsam. It's part of our identity as a Chinese" (CH, Female, 27).
Cultural symbols Chinese culture and experience	• "If I go to Cartier or Bulgari and buy a product, can they convey the meaning…? I don't think there is any way to find the products I want from others (global luxury) brands. Western or international brands are unable to pass on this kind of blessing from me" (SN, Female, 32). • there was one big luxury brand (from overseas) using the drawing of a tiger on their clothes and bags. The truth is that no drawing of the tiger can be used on the clothes. …, a tiger image is not suitable for clothing, according to the Chinese tradition to use tiger mainly in prison where criminals are trialed" (AG, Male, 32). • "Sometimes brands from overseas fail to understand China very well… But for Shanghai Tang, the designers come from China, and they are able to express the feelings that we have for these Chinese traditional elements in the drawings, pictures, and product design" (SA, Male, 40).

9.4.1.1 A Symbol of Rebirth

Lao Feng Xiang has a brand logo of a phoenix, which is a mythological bird in Chinese history. According to Chinese folk stories, the phoenix is an immortal bird that has the magical power to be reborn from its ashes after succumbing to a fiery death (Vogel, 2014). The appearance of the phoenix (or Feng Huang in Chinese) represents an omen foretelling harmony at the ascent to the throne of a new emperor or empress, thus conveying the meaning of power sent from the heavens to the royals (Vogel, 2014). Lao Feng Xiang incorporated these cultural meanings into the design of contemporary jewelry products.

> Phoenix has always been a symbol of rebirth in ancient Chinese history. It represents good fortune, happiness, and wealth, which are components of the concept of luxury.
>
> (NW, Male, 31)

> This brand has as its logo, a phoenix, and phoenix has been exemplary of Chinese culture and other related elements. This is because the Phoenix has always been a symbol of luck in ancient Chinese history.
>
> (AW, Female, 36)

9.4.1.2 Weight in Gold

Chinese consumers favor pure gold when they consider purchasing jewelry (Yiu, 2017). Participants indicated it is a luxury due to the value of the gold associated with this brand.

> The brand's products are either pure gold or pure silver. Gold and silver were used as currency in ancient China, thus the material is highly valuable. From an investment point of view, I will choose Lao Feng Xiang in China because it is made of pure gold and pure silver.
>
> (KX, Male, 24)

> Why would we like to call Lao Feng Xiang a luxury brand? This is because it is a gold jewelry brand.
>
> (CH, Female, 27)

9.4.1.3 Blessing Others the Chinese Way

For Lao Feng Xiang, a considerable market share is acquired through the need for gift giving on important life events such as weddings, birthdays, and Chinese New Year. Participants commented that in comparison to global luxury brands, only Chinese luxury jewelry brands could be used in order to pass on blessings to friends and families on important occasions.

> China has seen changes in dynasties and rulers, such as that of Han and Manchurian. Phoenix, remains a symbol of peace, joy, and wealth throughout the history of China. This (meaning) also extends to the concept of nobility, including the royal family, who used Phoenix like mascots and symbols of well-wishing.
>
> (BY, Male, 40)

Because there is an implicit meaning to the brand, it is ideal to use the brand to pass my blessings to others using messages like "fortune and prosperity brought to you by the dragon and phoenix (extremely good fortune)" and "may you give birth to a child soon". ... If I go to Cartier or Bulgari and buy a product, can they convey the meaning...? I don't think there is any way to find the products I want from other (global luxury) brands. Western or international brands are unable to pass on this kind of blessing from me.

(SN, Female, 32)

9.4.1.4 Carrying on the Tradition

Luxury brands play an important role in the celebration of important life events for Chinese people (Lin, 2011). Participants commented that the use of a Chinese luxury brand is the most appropriate way to pass on blessings and carry on traditions.

When marriages take place in China, we would wish the newlyweds a heavenly match as that of the dragon and phoenix up in heaven. .... These are ancient Chinese values and traditions that we are still keeping through the use of Chinese luxury brand such as Lao Feng Xiang.

(PQ, Male, 29)

It is a cultural heritage that when a daughter is married off, she must have a three-piece set (of gold jewelry). This is a tradition. ... We are talking about the passing down of history ... as well as the inheritance of the culture.

(AC, Female, 28)

9.4.1.5 Beauty in the Eye of the Beholder

The visual attractiveness of product design is a key reason why Chinese consumers favor Chinese luxury brands. Participants commented that local (Chinese) designers seem to have a greater understanding of how to balance trends and traditions in product design. Thus, the Chinese luxury brand is more appealing in art and beauty to Chinese consumers.

It all comes down to the designer's understanding of China's tradition and culture .... If a foreign brand uses an image of a pig (2019 is the year of the pig), the design is often a little bit awkward, or a bit "off" shall we say. It would not be what we are looking for in China.

(AW, Female, 36)

The concept of personal customization of luxury brands was raised by participants who commented on the need for Chinese luxury brands to focus on personal customization in that each piece of jewelry should be customized depending on who is wearing it and the specific social event.

> There's a high demand for the designer's abilities when it comes to designing with traditional Chinese cultural elements. Not only must the designer need to get the aesthetics right (according to Chinese culture), they need to know who will be wearing it and what kind of product would be suitable for a specific event. It wouldn't be as simple as drawing the image of a pig (because it's the year of the pig) … you have to have ways to express the social and cultural meaning behind it.
>
> (JZ, Female, 34)

9.4.2 Case Study 2: Mao Tai (茅臺)

The first formal liquor production site in the town of Maotai was established during the Ming Dynasty (1368–1644) when China was an agricultural society. Made from red sorghum, Maotai, with a 53% alcohol rate is known as China's "National liquor". Culturally, Baijiu (Chinese spirits) has deep historical roots in China and Moutai is the undisputed top brand in China (Baptista, 2018). For example, a 1950s vintage Maotai bottle had an estimated price of USD $14,500–$43,600 (Christies, 2018).

9.4.2.1 Chinese Baijiu Culture

The success of Moutai lies in its popularity in the local market (Wang, 2017). Even though Moutai is considered a luxury product and is one of the most expensive liquors produced in China, Chinese Baijiu culture has humble roots in peasant society.

> It is made from grain. This indicates that Maotai was first made and drunk by farmers before it was consumed by governmental officials. In ancient times, liquor (Baijiu) was a common alcoholic beverage, because Sorghum was widely grown across China, which made liquor easy to get and affordable for everybody, especially farmers. As a result, the Chinese wine culture was inherited through generations.
>
> (KT, Female, 21)

Additionally, Baijiu plays an important part in developing relationships or Guanxi in Chinese culture. Baijiu is served at family dinners and special occasions. Mai Tai, for example, is served at Chinese state banquets. Interviewees also expressed a similar opinion regarding their personal experience in developing Guanxi through drinking Baijiu.

> Chinese people think there is a type of friendship maintained by sharing food and liquor (Maotai).
>
> (NW, Male, 34)

It (Maotai) reflects the role played by liquor in the Chinese culture where liquor is related to making friends and developing Guanxi.

(KX, Male, 24)

9.4.2.2 History in a Bottle

Maotai has a distinctive package design using a white earthenware bottle. The trademark of the brand describes a scene in which two Buddhist angels are offering wine as a blessing to human beings down below on earth. The illustration is typical of that found in Mogao Grottoes where many caves were painted with religious (Buddhist) pictures from ancient Chinese dynasties (Reed, 2016). A less conspicuous component in the trademark is the cup of wine carried by the two angels. The bronze Jue Cup (Chinese wine cup) is a symbol of wine drinking from the Qin dynasty (221 to 206 BC) (Sun et al., 2017).

> China's flying apsaras feature beautiful female spirits and their attire, musical instrument and other social artifacts of their times. …, the liquor cup held by the Flying Apsaras is also a typical traditional Chinese element. This type of drinking vessel was used as early as the Qin Dynasty.
> (MB, Female, 28)

Maotai is also well known for using a white non-transparent earthenware bottle. Perhaps the original intention was to avoid light thus making it more conducive to the storage of liquor. However, for Chinese consumers, it sets Maotai apart from other expensive clear glass bottles of alcohol in the world.

> About the bottle, many famous foreign alcohol drinks, such as XO brandy, are contained in glass bottles, but Maotai uses ceramic bottles. Porcelain is a part of China's history or culture. Many Chinese antiques, as well as vases and ornamental bottles that we use now, are all-porcelain wares. Using a ceramic bottle indicates the inseparable relationship between Maotai and China's culture and history.
> (MW, Male, 30)

9.4.2.3 A Taste of Luxury

In Chinese Baijiu culture, luxury is for everybody when it comes to celebrating important social occasions. Even though Maotai is expensive, everyone can get a taste of luxury in small glasses. It is common for people to consume Maotai to celebrate events such as the Chinese New Year. Participants commented that Maotai is also used for increasing family bonding where the younger generation is paying respect to the older generation (i.e. parents and grandparents). As such, the Chinese luxury liquor brand represents family gatherings, harmony, and paying respects to elders.

… during festivals, especially the Spring Festival, Chinese people have the tradition of treating families and guests with premium liquor. … When I was a child, my family only drank Maotai during the Spring Festival, since it's really expensive.

(NZ, Male, 32)

It is a symbol of unity. The unity of a group of people after a whole year of hardworking.

(SM, Female, 38)

Some people of my age chose to leave home after growing up and drinking it (Maotai) makes us think of our elders, like grandparents.

(ST, Female, 35)

9.4.3 Case Study 3: Shanghai Tang (上海灘)

Shanghai Tang has been a unique Chinese luxury lifestyle brand in both domestic and international high-end fashion markets (Rovai, 2016). Unlike Lao Feng Xiang and Maotai which are Chinese domestic brands with long histories, Shanghai Tang was established in Hong Kong in 1994 by the late Sir David Tang (Schroeder et al., 2017). The brand draws upon Chinese culture and history in its design and has created a unique identity as a Chinese luxury fashion brand.

9.4.3.1 In the Mood for Love

The brand name Shanghai Tang evokes the imagery of the city of Shanghai in the late nineteenth century and the early twentieth century when China was under the government of the Republic of China (中華民國) (Schroeder et al., 2017). At the time, Shanghai was a global hub of cultural interaction and famous for its architecture, fashion, music, and commercial activities (Fogel, 2010). In 2000, the Hong Kong movie In the Mood for Love revived interest in a lifestyle that belongs to the 1930s Shanghai. Shanghai Tang became more popular after the actress Maggie Cheung wore the brand's signature qipao (旗袍) in the movie. Thus, the brand name evokes nostalgia for the "golden days" of Shanghai during the 1920s/30s when it was called the "Paris of the Orient".

At weddings, including my wedding, the Chinese generally prefer using products from traditional Chinese brands, … The gentlemen will wear Tang suits, and the ladies will wear cheongsam. It's part of our identity as a Chinese.

(CH, Female, 27)

This (Shanghai Tang) is a local brand in China, everyone loves their local industry and national brands.

(BY, Male, 40)

9.4.3.2 Silk Is the New Gold

Silk production has a long and colorful history in China and has long been a precious commodity in the luxury market (Boado, 2012). At Shanghai Tang, such luxury materials are used in products such as clothes, scarves, and silk accessories. Respondents commented that wearing silk as compared to wearing gold is a less conspicuous way to consume luxury and is becoming more popular among Chinese consumers.

… these traditional styles, whether the cheongsams or Tang suits, are only affordable by the patricians or the rich in the early days… luxurious pieces of clothes crafted with silk and features traditional Chinese imagery are elegant and classy and a good reflection of the upper class.

(NL, Female, 26)

silk … represents China. So, this is why I think the Shanghai Tang brand can reflect the Chinese culture.

(BY, Male, 40)

9.4.3.3 Authentic Chinese Luxury Experience

Shanghai Tang features Chinese elements and symbols in product design for qipao (also known as cheongsam) and dresses, jewelry, and fragrances (Schroeder et al., 2017). Various aspects of Chinese culture are incorporated into the product design such as chrysanthemum flowers (菊), lotus flowers (荷), bamboo (竹), the dragon (龍), the phoenix (鳳), the auspicious Shou symbol (壽). For participants, the use of traditional Chinese aesthetics is considered to be important in creating an authentic Chinese luxury experience. In contrast, simply adding a Chinese element to an existing foreign luxury brand is not considered sufficient to create an authentic Chinese luxury experience.

Sometimes brands from overseas fail to understand China very well. Perhaps they know the basic stuff such as the dragon and the phoenix, and they can apply these two patterns to their products or brands. But for Shanghai Tang, the designers … can express the feelings that we have for these Chinese traditional elements in the drawings, pictures, and product design.

(SA, Male, 40)

Respondents were also able to provide examples whereby failure to understand Chinese culture can damage the efforts made by foreign brands to enter the Chinese luxury brand market.

> … there was one big luxury brand (from overseas) using the drawing of a tiger on their clothes and bags. The truth is that no drawing of the tiger can be used on the clothes. …, a tiger image is not suitable for clothing, according to the Chinese tradition to use tiger mainly in prison where criminals are trialed.
>
> (AG, Male, 32)

9.5 Discussion

From the above findings from the three illustrative cases, we have identified some unique and distinct aspects of Chinese luxury brands in relation to the conceptual model (Figure 9.1).

9.5.1 Cultural Symbols

Even though previous research (e.g. Zhou & Hui, 2003) argues that Chinese consumers have a negative view of locally produced products, this is not found to be the case for Chinese luxury brands. Chinese consumers are found to have a positive attitude toward Chinese luxury brands and appreciate the cultural elements embedded in these brands. Prior research shows that aesthetics plays an important role in preserving the luxury brand (Berthon et al., 2009). Our study indicates that Chinese consumers are "in the mood for love" and pay tribute to the ancient history of China, manifested in product design, brand name, brand logo, and brand history and reputation. As commented by participants, ancient traditions are still closely followed through the consumption of Chinese luxury brands and cannot be replaced by the consumption of global luxury brands. For example, one interviewee (SN, Female, 32) mentioned that Lao Feng Xiang (老鳳祥) jewelry, which has a traditional symbol of phoenix and is made of pure gold, could not be replaced by a global brand such as Tiffany when a piece of jewelry is to be purchased and used as a gift and a symbol of a blessing she would like to pass on to others (i.e. friends and relatives). For Shang Hai Tang (上海灘), our findings show that the authentic Chinese luxury experience firmly embeds with this brand using traditional drawings, pictures, and product designs. By comparison, the global luxury brand could have missed the mark in terms of creating an authentic Chinese appeal. For example, one interviewee (AG, Male, 32) mentioned that he noticed that tiger print was used by a foreign luxury brand, which could be highly culturally inappropriate, as the tiger image is used in China mainly as a symbol of justice.

9.5.2 Guanxi

This research also shows that Chinese luxury brands play an important role in terms of Chinese consumers building personal relationship with others (i.e. family members and friends). These findings suggest that relationship building, which is expressed in Chinese as Guanxi, is a crucial reason for purchasing Chinese luxury brands as compared to consuming the global luxury brand. Wong and Ahuvia (1998) argue that Chinese consumers are driven by social status and position when it comes to purchasing luxury brands. We agree with Wong and Ahuvia (1998), but we argue that this is perhaps a finding that applies to global luxury brands, it might necessarily be the case for Chinese luxury brands. Interviewees commented that Maotai (茅臺), which is the most premium liquor in China, is associated with making friends and developing Guanxi (NW, Male, 34), and friendship is maintained by sharing the consumption of luxury brands such as Maotai (茅臺) (NW, Male, 34). The consumption of Maotai (茅臺) has become a social activity, and it is related to the fact that China has a highly collectivist culture, where people are expected to be acting in the interests of the group and not necessarily of themselves (Hofstede, 2001).

9.5.3 Collectivism

Collectivism is at the heart of Chinese culture (Hofstede, 2001). It permeates all aspects of day-to-day living including purchasing and using luxury brands for celebrations and special occasions. Previous research argued that elite Chinese consumers tend to purchase more luxury goods for special occasions, festivals, birthdays, holidays, or anniversaries (Wang et al., 2011; Yu, 2016), however, no previous research explored the importance of purchasing Chinese luxury brand for special Chinese occasions and celebrations. This study shows that Chinese luxury brands tend to be consumed less for personal use and more for others in order to create a luxury experience in a social context. For example, drinking Maotai (茅臺) is part of a family celebration during Spring Festival (NZ, Male, 32) (SM, Female, 38), presenting Lao Feng Xiang (老鳳祥) jewelry at a wedding is a way to honor the Chinese tradition and to pass good wishes to the couple (PQ, Male, 29) (AC, Female, 28), and taking a family wedding photo wearing Shanghai Tang (上海灘) clothing is to pay respect to cultural traditions and family traditions (CH, Female, 27) (BY, Male, 40). The findings indicate that the Chinese luxury brand has become part of Chinese culture, an element that is shared by a group of people, and an indispensable part of celebration according to Chinese culture.

9.5.4 Self-Concept (Self-Brand Image Congruity)

As mentioned earlier, in this research we did not find evidence that there is any negative connotation associated with Chinese luxury brands. Instead,

Chinese consumers endorse Chinese luxury brands and relate them to their self-identity and social identity as Chinese. A perspective of self (Kleine et al., 1993) was little used by scholars in their understanding of luxury brand consumption. Consumer choices are often identity-based (Oyserman, 2009) and consumers are more likely to choose products that are congruent with their self-identity (Ahuvia, 2005; Catalin & Andreea, 2014; White & Argo, 2009). Compared to global luxury brands, Chinese consumers may perceive a greater self-brand image congruity with Chinese luxury brands. And this is in fact we what found through the interviews. Interviewees commented that not only do they accept Chinese (luxury) brands (BY, Male, 40), but they tend to think that using Chinese luxury brands (i.e., Shanghai Tang (上海灘) reinforces their identity as Chinese (CH, Female, 27). The findings also show that patriotism plays a role when it comes to Chinese consumers purchasing and using national and domestic luxury brands.

9.5.5 Theoretical Implications

This research is the first investigation of Chinese luxury brands from the Chinese consumers' perspective. The findings of this research have contributed to the CCT (Arnould & Thompson, 2005) by viewing luxury consumption as lived consumer experience embedded in Chinese culture. CCT researchers (Askegaard & Linnet, 2011) argue that consumers as "free agent" should not be confined by the closed categories of the scales or the controlled environment of the experimental design. This research has contributed to the CCT research and provides a new perspective to the study of luxury consumption as it naturally occurs in the lives of Chinese consumers. We have explored through three case studies the underpinning social and cultural meanings of Chinese luxury brands Chinese consumers tend to draw upon in both their interpersonal relationships (i.e. Guanxi) and their own sense of self-identity (Askegaard & Linnet, 2011). In contrast to the literature which focuses on luxury consumption as a symbol of wealth and social status, the research findings indicate that the consumption of Chinese luxury brands often involves a public display of celebrations of big life events and traditional Chinese festivals in the context of social gatherings.

9.5.6 Practical Implications

The findings demonstrate that Chinese consumers are equally, if not more, receptive to Chinese luxury brands than they are to global luxury brands. By focusing on exploring the meanings of Chinese luxury brands, this research shows that China is still a country where people follow ancient traditions, and when it comes to special occasions of cultural significance, Chinese consumers continue to prefer purchasing and using Chinese luxury brands. Chinese luxury brands may not have to go global partly due to the fact that they have been tailored to the taste of the Chinese. The research findings correspond to Heine and Gutsatz (2015) who argue that Chinese consumers are living up to their culture and traditions by consuming Chinese luxury brands. From the perspective of marketers, it is important to recognize that there are social and cultural dimensions to Chinese consumers adopting Chinese luxury brands as opposed to global luxury brands. The uniqueness, as pointed out by this research, is related to collectivist culture, Guanxi, self-brand image congruity, and cultural symbols (Figure 9.1). It is possible that Chinese versus global luxury brands, respectively, fulfill different types of needs and different types of goals in terms of purchase intention and consumption.

This research responds to the previously identified call for research on identifying opportunities for developing China-specific luxury brands from the perspective of Chinese consumers (Heine and Gutsatz, 2015). This research suggests that Chinese consumers seem to be critical of whether a global luxury brand operating in China could demonstrate a good understanding of Chinese culture as reflected in product design, aesthetic appeal, and marketing communication. A good example is the Dolce & Gabbana's With Chopsticks advertisement that provoked public outrage in China in 2018; they experienced a massive amount of financial loss that year (BBC News, 2019). This may not be the last time we will see a misinterpretation of the meaning of Chinese culture by global luxury brands. Thus any adaptation to Chinese culture by global luxury brands should be handled with care. The challenge for global luxury brands is to find the balance between maintaining their global appeal and adapting to Chinese culture.

9.6 Conclusion and Future Research Direction

In this research, we used three case studies to demonstrate the importance of Chinese luxury brands for Chinese consumers, and the reasons behind their consumption of Chinese luxury brands may be fundamentally different from the reasons for consuming global luxury brands. The literature has focused on the latter and largely ignored the existence of the former. Chinese consumers' preferences for Chinese luxury brands are based on a collectivist culture where Guanxi is important and Chinese luxury brands may be used as a cultural symbol, which is congruent to their self-identity.

This research is the first in the luxury brand literature to explore local consumer culture in relation to the consumption of Chinese luxury brands, it provides insights into local versus global luxury branding. The findings of this research, however, are only limited to Chinese consumers and cannot be generalized to other nationalities. There are several suggestions for future research directions. Future research is needed to understand luxury branding in developing countries and to examine consumer perceptions of local versus global luxury brands in China and other developing countries.

References

Ahuvia, A. C., 2005. Beyond the extended self: Loved objects and consumers' identity narratives. *J. Consum. Res.* 32(1), 171–184.

Algharabat, R., Rana, N. P., Alalwan, A. A., Baabdullah, A., Gupta, A., 2020. Investigating the antecedents of customer brand engagement and consumer-based brand equity in social media. *J. Retail. Consum. Serv.* 53, 101767.

Arnould, E. J., Thompson, C. J., 2005. Consumer culture theory (CCT): Twenty years of research. *J. Consum. Res.* 31(4), 868–882.

Askegaard, S., Linnet, J. T., 2011. Towards an epistemology of consumer culture theory: Phenomenology and the context of context. *Market. Theo.* 11(4), 381–404.

Baptista, E., 2018. A weekend in Maotai: Inside the bizarre cult of China's most notorious liquor. Available at: https://radiichina.com/a-weekend-in-maotai-inside-the-bizarre-cult-of-chinas-most-notorious-liquor/ (accessed 20 June 2019).

BBC News, 2019. Racist D&G ad: Chinese model says campaign almost ruined career. Available at: https://www.bbc.com/news/world-asia-china-46968750 (accessed 12 August 2020).

Berthon, P., Pitt, L., Parent, M., Berthon, J., 2009. Aesthetics and ephemerality: Observing and preserving the luxury brand. *California Manag. Rev.* 52(1), 45–66.

Boado, C., 2012. Importance of silk. *Art of silk*. Available at: https://www.artofsilk.com/blogs/news/6565365-importance-of-silk#.XRlsLIVOKUk (accessed 20 June 2019).

Butt, R., Roberts, A., 2014. Prada falls most in 17 months as revenue growth slows in Asia. *Bloomberg*. Available at: https://www.bloomberg.com/news/2014-02-12/prade-full-year-sales-climb-9-boosted-by-asia-america-demand.html (accessed 12 August 2020).

Catalin, M. C., Andreea, P., 2014. Brands as a mean of consumer self-expression and desired personal lifestyle. *Pro-Soc. Behav. Sci.* 109, 103–107.

Christies, 2018. Collecting guide: Moutai, China's 'national liquor'. Available at: https://www.christies.com/features/Maotai-collecting-guide-Chinas-national-liquor-9335-1.aspx (accessed 21 June 2019).

Christodoulides, G., Michaelidou, N., Li, C. H., 2009. Measuring perceived brand luxury: An evaluation of the BLI scale. *J. Brand. Manag.* 16(5–6), 395–405.

CNBC, 2022. China's consumers spent $73.6 billion on luxury goods at home last year, up 36% from 2020. Available at: https://www.cnbc.com/2022/01/24/chinas-consumers-spent-73point6-billion-on-luxury-goods-at-home-in-2021.html (accessed 11 June 2022).

Danziger, P. N., 2020. Largest luxury market by 2025, but American brands may miss out. Available at: https://www.forbes.com/sites/pamdanziger/2020/11/22/china-is-headed-to-be-the-worlds-largest-luxury-market-by-2025-but-american-brands-may-miss-out/?sh=6b08fae96a3b (accessed 12 June 2021).

De Barnier, V., Rodina, I., & Valette-Florence, P., 2006. Which luxury perceptions affect most consumer purchase behavior? A cross-cultural exploratory study in France, the United Kingdom and Russia. *Proceedings des Congrés Paris-Venise des Tendences Marketing, Paris,* 2(3), 8–17.

Deloitte Consulting, 2021. Global power of luxury goods 2021. *Deloitte Consulting.* Available at: https://www2.deloitte.com/content/dam/Deloitte/at/Documents/consumer-business/at-global-powers-luxury-goods-2020.pdf (accessed 11 June 2022).

Eckhardt, G. M., Belk, R. W., Wilson, J. A., 2015. The rise of inconspicuous consumption. *J. Mark. Manag.* 31(7–8), 807–826.

Farquhar, J. D., 2012. *Case study research for business.* New York: Sage.

Fogel, J. A., 2010. The recent boom in Shanghai studies. *J. His. Ideas.* 71(2), 313–333.

Hamelin, N., Thaichon, P., 2016. Consumer motives and impact of western media on the Moroccan luxury buyer. *J. Retail. Consum. Serv.* 32, 164–170.

Han, Y. J., Nunes, J. C., & Drèze, X., 2010. Signaling status with luxury goods: The role of brand prominence. *J. Mark.* 74(4), 15–30.

Heine, K., Gutsatz, M., 2015. Luxury brand building in China: Eight case studies and eight lessons learned. *J. Brand Manag.* 22(3), 229–245.

Hofstede, G., 2001. *Culture's consequences: Comparing values, behaviours, institutions and organizations across nations* (2nd ed.). Thousand Oaks, CA: Sage.

Hsu, T., Lucas, A., Qiu, Z., Li, M., Yu, Q., 2014. Exploring the Chinese gem and jewellery industry. *Gems. Gemo.* 50(1), 1–29.

Hyun, H., Thavisay, T., Lee, S. H., 2021. Enhancing the role of flow experience in social media usage and its impact on shopping. *J. Retail. Consum. Serv.* 65(3), 102492.

Jinkins, D., 2016. Conspicuous consumption in the United States and China. *J. Econ. Behav & Organ.* 127, 115–132.

Kajornboon, A. B., 2005. Using interviews as research instruments. *Edu. J. Res. Teachers.* 2(1), 1–9.

Kleine III, R. E., Kleine, S. S., Kernan, J. B., 1993. Mundane consumption and the self: A social identity perspective. *J. Consum. Psycho.* 2(3), 209–235.

Ko, E., Costello, J. P., Taylor, C. R., 2019. What is a luxury brand? A new definition and review of the literature. *J. Bus. Res.* 99, 405–413.

Kuang-peng, H., Annie, H. C., Peng, N., Hackley, C., Rungpaka, A. T., Chun-lun, C., 2011. Antecedents of luxury brand purchase intention. *The. J. Product. Brand Manag.* 20(6), 457–467.

Lao Feng Xiang, 2017. China's oldest jewellery company: Lao Feng Xiang. Available at: http://lfxjewelry.ca/2017/06/chinas-oldest-jewellery-company-lao-feng-xiang/ (accessed 20 June 2019).

Li, G., Li, G., Kambele, Z., 2012. Luxury fashion brand consumers in China: Perceived value, fashion lifestyle, and willingness to pay. *J. Bus. Res. Special Iss. Fash. Mark. Luxury Brands.* 65(10), 1516–1522.

Li, N., Robson, A., Coates, N., 2014. Luxury brand commitment: A study of Chinese consumers. *Mark. Intell & Planning.* 32(7), 769–793.

Liang, Y., Ghosh, S., Oe, H., 2017. Chinese consumers' luxury value perceptions - A conceptual model. *Qualitative. Mark. Res.* 20(2), 247–262.

Lin, Y. C. J., 2011. *Fake stuff: China and the rise of counterfeit goods.* London: Routledge.

Oyserman, D., 2009. Identity-based motivation and consumer behavior. *J. Consum. Psycho.* 19(3), 276–279.

Pino, G., Amatulli, C., Peluso, A. M., Nataraajan, R., Guido, G., 2019. Brand prominence and social status in luxury consumption: A comparison of emerging and mature markets. *J. Retail. Consum. Serv.* 46, 163–172.

Reed, M., 2016. The mogao caves as cultural embassies. Available at: https://bulletin.hds. harvard.edu/the-mogao-caves-as-cultural-embassies/ (accessed 20 June 2019).

Rovai, S., 2016. *Chinese luxury brands: The new creative phase and identity in the local market in luxury the Chinese way* (pp. 134–144). London: Palgrave Macmillan.

Schmitt, B., 2012. The consumer psychology of brands. *J. Consum. Psychol.* 22(1), 7–17.

Schroeder, J., Borgerson, J., Wu, Z., 2017. *A brand culture approach to Chinese cultural heritage brands.* London: Palgrave Macmillan.

Schuiling, I., Kapferer, J. N., 2004. Executive insights: real differences between local and international brands: Strategic implications for international marketers. *J. Int. Mark.* 12(4), 97–112.

Seo, Y., Buchanan-Oliver, M., & Cruz, A. G. B., 2015. Luxury brand markets as confluences of multiple cultural beliefs. *Int. Mark. Rev.* 32(2), 141–159.

Steenkamp, J. B. E., 2019. Global versus local consumer culture: Theory, measurement, and future research directions. *J. Int. Mark.* 27(1), 1–19.

Steenkamp, J. B. E., Batra, R., Alden, D. L., 2003. How perceived brand globalness creates brand value. *J. Int. Bus. Studies.* 34(1), 53–65.

Sun, Z. J., Hsing, I. T., Liu, C. Y., Lu, P., Tseng, L. L. Y., Hong, Y., Zhang, Z. Y., 2017. *Age of empires: Art of the Qin and Han dynasties.* New York: Metropolitan Museum of Art.

Thaichon, P., Quach, S., 2016. Dark motives-counterfeit purchase framework: Internal and external motives behind counterfeit purchase via digital platforms. *J. Retail. Consum. Serv.* 33, 82–91.

Vogel, C., 2014. Phoenixes rise in China and float in New York. Available at: https://www.nytimes.com/2014/02/15/arts/design/xu-bing-installs-his-sculptures-at-st-john-the-divine.html (accessed 21 June 2019).

Vogue, C., 2022. Shang Xia. Available at: https://www.vogue.com/fashion-shows/fall-2022-ready-to-wear/shang-xia (accessed 11 June 2022).

Waltersdorfer, G., Gericke, K., Blessing, L., 2015. Designing meaning to change consumer behaviour: An exploration. In: Chakrabarti, A. (ed.). *ICoRD'15-research into design across boundaries volume 1* (pp. 341–351). New Delhi: Springer.

Walley, K., Li, C., 2015. The market for luxury brands in China: Insight based on a study of consumer's perceptions in Beijing. *J. Brand Manag.* 22(3), 246–260.

Wang, Y., 2017. How China's Kweichow Moutai is intoxicating liquor market. Available at: https://www.forbes.com/sites/ywang/2017/04/13/how-chinas-kweichow-moutai-is-intoxicating-liquor-market/?sh=93d529626e44 (accessed 12 June 2019).

Wang, C. L., Lin, X., 2009. Migration of Chinese consumption values: Traditions, modernization, and cultural renaissance. *J. Bus. Ethics.* 88(3), 399–409.

Wang, Y., Sun, S., Song, Y., 2011. Chinese luxury consumers: Motivation, attitude and behavior. *J. Promo. Manag.* 17(3), 345–359.

White, K., Argo, J. J., 2009. Social identity threat and consumer preferences. *J. Consum. Psycho.* 19(3), 313–325.

Wiedmann K. P., Hennigs, N., Siebels, A., 2007. Measuring consumers' luxury value perception: A cross-cultural framework. *Acad. Mark. Sci. Rev.* 11, 1–21.

Wong, N. Y., Ahuvia, A. C., 1998. Personal taste and family face: Luxury consumption in Confucian and Western societies. *Psycho & Mark.* 15(5), 423–441.

Wu, Z., Luo, J., Schroeder, J. E., Borgerson, J. L., 2017. Forms of inconspicuous consumption: What drives inconspicuous luxury consumption in China? *Mark. Theory.* 17(4), 491–516.

Yiu, E., 2017. Chinese Valentine's Day boosts gold sales by 13pc in third quarter. *South China Morning Post.* Available at: https://www.scmp.com/business/commodities/

article/ 211917 4/chinese-valentines-day-boosts-gold-sales-13pc-third-quarter (accessed 22 June 2019).

Yin, R. K., 2003. Designing case studies. *Qual. Res. Methods.* 5, 359–386.

Yu, S., 2016. Luxury consumption motivations of the younger generation in Wuhan, China. Available at: https://core.ac.uk/download/pdf/80992456.pdf (accessed 10 September 2020).

Yu, S., Hu, Y., 2020. When luxury brands meet China: The effect of localized celebrity endorsements in social media marketing. *J. Retail. Consum. Serv.* 54, 102010.

Zaidah, Z., 2007. Case study as a research method. *Jurnal Kemanusiaan*, 9, 1–6.

Zhan, L., He, Y., 2012. Understanding luxury consumption in China: Consumer perceptions of best-known brands. *J. Bus. Res.* 65(10), 1452–1460.

Zhang, B., & Kim, J. H., 2013. Luxury fashion consumption in China: Factors affecting attitude and purchase intent. *J. Retail. Consum. Serv.* 20(1), 68–79.

Zhou, L., Hui, M. K., 2003. Symbolic value of foreign products in the People's Republic of China. *J. Int. Mark.* 11(2), 36–58.

10 Luxury Marketing within a Chinese Consumers' Perspective

Local versus Global Luxury Brand Consumption

Ting Jin, Wei Shao and Park Thaichon

10.1 Introduction

Industry experts predict that China will become the world's largest luxury market by 2025 (Danziger, 2020). Chinese consumers purchasing global luxury brands, such as LV, Channel, Gucci, Dior, and Hermes, contribute to the recognition of individual social standing and position (Li et al., 2012; Walley and Li, 2015; Wu et al., 2017; Zhan and He, 2012). The symbolic value of status and prestige is important for Chinese consumers, which explains why Chinese consumers hold preferences for well-known foreign luxury brands with popular logos (Wang et al., 2011). Global brands are strategically appealing to a growing segment of consumers around the world with similar preferences, thus they do not design their products in a way to attract consumers with a particular nationality (Roy and Chau, 2011), whereas Chinese luxury brands have been created to strategically appeal to the tastes and preferences of Chinese consumers (Heine and Gutsatz, 2015).

However, understanding luxury consumption in China should not be limited to and considered to be equivalent to Chinese consumers simply purchasing global luxury brands. More recently, market research studies show that Chinese consumers are showing increasing preferences for Chinese luxury brands due to a rise in national loyalty (Danziger, 2020). In recent years, there has been renewed interest in domestic (Chinese) luxury brands and a number of the most successful luxury brands turn out to be Chinese. One good example is the domestic luxury brand from mainland China, Lao Feng Xiang 老鳳祥, ranked number 15 on the Global Powers of Luxury Goods Top 100, FY 2020 (Deloitte Consulting, 2021). Another jewelry brand Chow Tai Fook 周大福 (Hong Kong and mainland) was ranked number 10 on the list. This significant market potential is contrasted by a dearth of knowledge of Chinese luxury brands. How Chinese consumers purchase Chinese luxury brands is largely unknown by managers and academic researchers.

Phau and Leng (2008) argued that the nationality and originality of the luxury brand matter to consumers. They found that status-seeking becomes

DOI: 10.4324/9781003321378-10

less important when young consumers in Australia buy "Made in Australia" (domestic) products compared to foreign (i.e. Italy, Japan) luxury brands. In the same way, we may argue that status-seeking may not be important for Chinese consumers when purchasing Chinese luxury brands as opposed to global luxury brands. Wang et al. (2011) argue that Chinese consumers are similar to luxury consumers in other countries/cultures using luxury brands as a symbol of wealth and social status. However, in their conclusion, the authors did not take into account the originality of the luxury brand or the uniqueness of local or domestic luxury brands. Rather than seeking social status, Chinese consumers may be seeking Chinese luxury brands that "revitalize the artful roots of China" (Kapferer, 2015, p. 718). For Chinese consumers, there are in fact many local luxury brands that tend to have deep historical roots (Schroeder et al., 2017) that combine distinct aspects of Chinese aesthetics, culture, and values with the notion of luxury (Eckhardt et al., 2015). For example, high-end consumer goods majorly in clothing are Shang Xia (上下) and Shanghai Tang (上海滩).

The overarching aim of the research is to investigate how Chinese consumers view Chinese (versus) global luxury brands. We examined the differences between Chinese and global luxury brands in terms of customer value perceptions, brand experience, and purchase intention using a survey approach. This research draws on the Theory of Consumption Values (Sheth et al., 1991) based on previous research that has developed various customer value frameworks for luxury goods (e.g. Tynan et al., 2010; Vigneron and Johnson, 2004). Specifically, the purpose of this research is to measure the overall luxury value proposition and to examine how these perceived values associated with Chinese versus global luxury brands affect brand experiences and purchase intention among Chinese consumers. While China is the most lucrative market for luxury goods, it is also the top counterfeiting country of luxury products (Herman, 2022; Lin, 2011; Phau and Teah, 2009). Therefore, as part of our research into counterfeiting, we also aim to investigate as part of the research whether counterfeit ownership will influence consumers' perceived values, brand experiences, and purchase intentions for both Chinese and global luxury brands. This research provides significant practical implications regarding how Chinese consumers view global luxury brands as compared to Chinese luxury brands as they coexist and both are trying to target the lucrative Chinese market.

10.2 Literature Review

10.2.1 Value Perceptions and Purchase Intention

Consumers' perceived value has been considered the most important indicator of the purchase of luxury brands (Cheah et al., 2020; Park et al., 2021; Shankar and Jain, 2021). Based on the Theory of Consumption Values (Sheth et al., 1991), previous research shows that luxury value perception has a positive influence on purchase intention and consumer choice (Cheah et al., 2020; Kim and Park, 2016; Tynan et al., 2010; Wiedmann et al., 2009) and repurchase intentions (Parasuraman and Grewal, 2000).

The luxury brand value consists of several dimensions as indicated by multiple frameworks (Berthon et al., 2009; Burmann et al., 2009; Shukla and Purani, 2012; Vigneron and Johnson, 1999, 2004; Wiedmann et al., 2007, 2009). Vigneron and Johnson (1999, 2004) developed a theoretical framework of luxury brand value focusing on both non-personal (i.e. conspicuousness, uniqueness, and social values) and personal-oriented value perceptions (i.e. hedonism and extended self). Wiedmann et al. (2007, 2009) extended Vigneron and Johnson's (1999, 2004) luxury value framework by adding a financial value dimension to consumer perceived value. More recently researchers have argued that luxury brand value can be co-created by brand owners, consumers, employees, and other stakeholders (Burmann et al., 2009; Tynan et al., 2010). Luxury brand purchases may be influenced by a combination of different value perceptions (Jin et al., 2021). In this study, we predict that luxury value perceptions will positively influence Chinese consumers' purchase of luxury brands.

H1A: Luxury brand value perceptions will positively influence Chinese consumers' purchase of *Chinese* luxury brands.

H1B: Luxury brand value perceptions will positively influence Chinese consumers' purchase of the *global* luxury brands.

10.2.2 Value Perceptions and Luxury Brand Experience

Ryan and Deci (2000) argue that there are intrinsic versus extrinsic motivations toward consumer behavior. For individuals, intrinsic motivation reflects the satisfaction and pleasure derived from engaging in or understanding activity for its own sake (Walker et al., 2006) and is associated with high levels of self-determination (Fairchild et al., 2005). Alternatively, extrinsic motivation reflects behavior viewed more as a means to an end (Walker et al., 2006) and is more reliant on external rewards or demands (Ryan and Deci, 2000). In the context of luxury brand consumption, consumer preferences could be underpinned by their willingness to seek a public display of wealth and use conspicuous consumption to enhance one's prestige in society (Shao et al., 2019a, 2019b). By contrast, we have seen a shift toward inconspicuous consumption of luxury brands where more sophisticated consumers are moving away from social class and status-seeking and toward satisfying their inner desire to live a certain luxurious lifestyle through creating brand-related experiences (Atwal and Williams, 2009). In a postmodern society, consumers will acquire luxury brands for both conspicuous and inconspicuous reasons as influenced by personal goals and aspirations (Eckhardt et al., 2015; Thaichon and Quach, 2016). Thus, we argue that luxury value perceptions, whether intrinsically or extrinsically oriented, will have a positive influence on brand-related experiences for different types of consumers.

H2A: Luxury brand value perceptions will positively influence Chinese consumers' brand-related experiences for *Chinese* luxury brands.

H2B: Luxury brand value perceptions will positively influence Chinese consumers' brand-related experiences for *global* luxury brands.

10.2.3 Luxury Brand Experience and Purchase Intention

Consumers can develop or construct personalised product meanings through consumption experiences (Desmet and Hekkert, 2007; Rochberg-Halton, 1979). Researchers argue that luxury brand experiences are linked to the individual in a meaningful way (Hemetsberger et al., 2012) and no luxury brand can simply rely on their logo and hope to be able to survive in the long term without creating value or meaning to consumers through creating or co-creating luxury brand experiences (Kapferer and Bastien, 2009; Tynan et al., 2010). Furthermore, empirical research shows that consumer brand-related experiences are indicators of brand purchases and repeat purchases (Kim and Sullivan, 1998; Ramaseshan and Stein, 2014; Shao et al., 2019a; Thaichon and Quach, 2016). Accordingly, we argue that brand-related luxury experiences will have a positive influence on Chinese consumers' purchase of luxury brands. Thus, the following hypotheses:

H3A: Luxury brand experiences will positively influence Chinese consumers' purchase of *Chinese* luxury brands.

H3B: Luxury brand experiences will positively influence Chinese consumers' purchase of the *global* luxury brands.

10.2.4 The Moderating Role of Counterfeit Brand Purchase

An important issue facing luxury brand marketers would be the threat of counterfeit (Ngo et al., 2020). Previous research shows that consumer preferences for counterfeit luxury brands are influenced by their need to impress others in order to fulfill important social goals (Wilcox et al., 2009). Whereas consumers who tend to view luxury brands as an extension of the self (Ahuvia, 2005; Mittal, 2006) are less likely to purchase counterfeit luxury brands (Sharma and Chan, 2017; Wilcox et al., 2009). Nia and Zaikowsky (2000) examined consumers who are fully aware that they are purchasing a nongenuine product, a concept known as "non-deceptive" counterfeit brand purchase (Bian and Veloutsou, 2017). Counterfeiting is regarded as a serious economic, social, and political problem (Bian and Veloutsou, 2017). However, Nia and Zaikowsky (2000) found that access to counterfeits does not reduce the image of the luxury brand, nor does it negatively impact the desire to own the genuine product. Rather, it is the image of the luxury brand and the original product that influence the perceived equity of the luxury brand.

Unlike previous research, we do not focus on counterfeit luxury brand purchases, but on counterfeit luxury brand ownership. This is because consumers may have purchased the counterfeit but have owned it and/or experienced it. For example, it could be a gift that's given to the consumer by others and the consumer could have used it since then. Therefore, we focus on whether or not the consumer has ever owned or experienced any counterfeit luxury brand regardless of how he or she has acquired it or whether or not he or she has purchased it. Secondly, we consider the concept of counterfeit ownership as a moderator, rather than an independent variable to influence luxury brand experience and purchase intention. This is because previous research (Nia and Zaikowsky, 2000) failed to find a direct link between counterfeit luxury brand purchases and luxury brand equity. Specially, we argue that counterfeit luxury brand ownership will reduce the impact of luxury brand value perceptions on luxury brand experience and purchase intention for Chinese consumers.

H4A: Counterfeit ownership will reduce the impact of luxury brand value perceptions on the consumer experience of *Chinese* luxury brands.

H4B: Counterfeit ownership will reduce the impact of luxury brand value perceptions on the consumer experience of the *global* luxury brands.

H5A: Counterfeit ownership will reduce the impact of luxury brand value perceptions on the purchase intention of *Chinese* luxury brands.

H5B: Counterfeit ownership will reduce the impact of luxury brand value perceptions on the purchase intention of the *global* luxury brand.

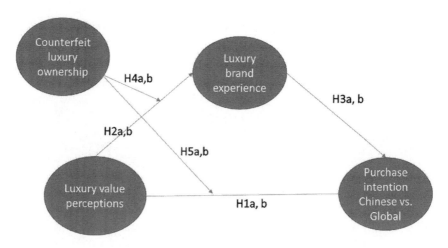

Figure 10.1 Conceptual model.

The hypotheses are summarised in the conceptual framework in Figure 10.1, demonstrating the relationships between the key constructs and illustrating the influence of luxury value perceptions on purchase intention, mediated by luxury brand experience, and the moderating role of counterfeit luxury ownership.

10.3 Methodology

10.3.1 Overview

The purpose of the research is to test the hypotheses and the conceptual model (see Figure 10.1) regarding Chinese and global luxury brands using existing luxury value-driven theories and frameworks. An online survey was conducted in Shanghai due to its high economic status and large market share for consuming luxury brands (Pope et al., 2020).

All questionnaires were distributed and collected via a web-based market research list service in China named "WenJuanXing" (问卷星) from May to June 2021, resulting in a total of 400 completed surveys, including a group of 200 respondents who completed surveys based on purchasing Chinese luxury brands, and another group of 200 respondents who completed surveys based on purchasing global (foreign, non-Chinese) luxury brands. Between the Chinese and the global brand, the respondents are different. The demographic profile of the 400 respondents is summarised in Table 10.1.

At the beginning of the survey, respondents were asked to name three Chinese (global) luxury brands based on their previous experiences. Next, they were asked to select their favorite brand, for example, Gucci (global brand) or Maotai (茅台Chinese liquor). The following questions measuring luxury value perceptions, luxury brand experiences, and consumption behavior were based on the favorite brand the participants have selected. Respondents were asked to indicate whether they have purchased or owned any counterfeit luxury brand, and counterfeit luxury ownership was coded as a categorical 1 = Yes and 0 = No variable. Finally, demographic questions were completed.

The scale items used to measure the variables of interest in this study were sourced from the literature. All of the items relating to luxury value perceptions, luxury brand experience, and purchase intention were measured on a five-point Likert scale (1 = strongly disagree, 5 = strongly agree). All construct items appear in Table 10.2.

The original survey questionnaire was translated into Chinese by the research team who were proficient in both Chinese and English. The Chinese questionnaire was then back-translated into English by an independent, NAATI Certified translator to ensure the accuracy of the meanings was not lost during the translation process. NAATI stands for National Accreditation Authority for Translators and Interpreters in Australia.

Table 10.1 Demographics of respondents

Age	Chinese Luxury Brands (n = 200)		International Luxury Brands (n = 200)	
	Frequency	*Percentage (%)*	*Frequency*	*Percentage (%)*
18 to 24	30	15	43	21.5
25 to 34	123	61.5	111	55.5
35 to 44	47	23.5	46	23
Gender				
Male	100	50	100	50
Female	100	50	100	50
Marital Status				
Single	49	24.5	62	31
Married or De facto	151	75.5	135	67.5
Divorced or separated	0	0	3	1.5
Widowed	0	0	0	0
Level of Education				
High school or below	4	2	2	1
College	15	7.5	10	5
Bachelor	155	77.5	161	80.5
Master or above	26	13	27	13.5
Occupation				
Full-time	173	86.5	166	83
Part-time	4	2	1	0.5
Unemployment	1	0.5	0	0
Student	15	7.5	23	11.5
Retired	0	0	0	0
Self-employed	6	3	9	4.5
Others	1	0.5	1	0.5
Yearly Income				
0–20,000RMB	16	8	16	8
20,001RMB– 50,000RMB	17	8.5	21	10.5
50,001RMB– 100,000RMB	54	27	30	15
100,001RMB– 150,000RMB	56	28	55	27.5
Over 150,000RMB	54	27	71	35.5
Prefer not to say	3	1.5	7	3.5

[a] Note: The 400 participants in the sample were split into two groups, one group (n = 200) completed the survey for Chinese luxury brand, another group (n = 200) completed the survey for global luxury brand.

10.4 Results

Estimation of the model (Figure 10.1) was conducted using the PROCESS method (Hayes, 2018), which is a conditional process analysis that examines the combination of mediation and moderation in the same model. The research model (Figure 10.1) corresponds to PROCESS model 8 (see Appendices in Hayes, 2018) which can be installed and executed in SPSS. The research estimates the effect of luxury value perceptions on purchase

Table 10.2 Constructs and measurement

Constructs	Measurement Items	Cronbach's Alpha
Luxury value perceptions		0.85
Functional value	• The products of this Chinese/global luxury brand provide the best quality-to-money ratio. • The products of this Chinese/global luxury brand are characterised by high-class craftsmanship/design. • The products of this Chinese/global luxury brand are of superior quality. • The products of this Chinese/global luxury brand have superior functional features. • The products of this Chinese/global luxury brand are the symbol of elegance. • The products of this Chinese/global luxury brand are the symbol of top design.	0.58
Financial value	• This Chinese/global luxury brand is reasonably priced. • This Chinese/global luxury brand offers value for money. • This Chinese/global luxury brand is a good product for the price. • This Chinese/global luxury brand is economical. • It is worth of economic investment to buy the products of this Chinese/global brand.	0.70
Individual value	• I derive self-satisfaction from purchasing this Chinese/global luxury brand. • Purchasing this Chinese/global luxury brand makes me feel good. • Using this Chinese/global luxury brand gives me a lot of pleasure. • When I am in a bad mood, I may purchase the products of this Chinese/global luxury brand to please myself. • I view the products of this Chinese/global luxury brand as gifts for myself to celebrate something that I do and feel excited about. • As a whole, I may regard the products of this Chinese/global luxury brand as gifts that I purchase to treat myself.	0.69
Social value	• Owning this Chinese/global luxury brand indicates a symbol of achievement. • Owning this Chinese/global luxury brand indicates a symbol of wealth. • Owning this Chinese/global luxury brand indicates a symbol of prestige. • Owning this Chinese/global luxury brand attracts attention from others.	0.85

(Continued)

Table 10.2 (Continued)

Constructs	Measurement Items	Cronbach's Alpha
	• I purchase this Chinese/global luxury brand just because it has status. • This Chinese/global luxury brand is very important to me because it makes me feel that acceptable in my work circle. • This Chinese/global luxury brand is very important to me because it makes me feel that acceptable in my social circle. • I purchase this Chinese/global luxury brand to gain/increase social status.	0.72
Luxury brand experience	• This Chinese/global luxury brand makes a strong impression on my senses. • This Chinese/global luxury brand is interesting in a sensory way. • This Chinese/global luxury brand appeal to my senses. • This Chinese/global luxury brand influences how I feel about myself. • This Chinese/global luxury brand is emotional. • I have personal feelings toward this Chinese/global luxury brand. • The products of this Chinese/global luxury brand satisfy my needs.	
Purchase intention	• I would like to continue purchasing the products of this Chinese/global luxury brand. • I intend to increase the number of the products of this Chinese/global luxury brand that I purchase. • The probability that I would purchase this Chinese/global luxury brand within the next six months is high.	0.62
Counterfeit luxury ownership	• Have you ever purchased or used any counterfeit Chinese/global luxury goods? (1 = yes; 0 = no)	Categorical variable

intention directly as well as indirectly through luxury brand experiences, with the direct and indirect effects moderated by counterfeit luxury brand ownership. Ownership of counterfeit luxury, as a moderator, is a categorical variable (yes, no). The PROCESS model was conducted for Chinese luxury brands (relating to H1a–H5a see Figure 10.1) based on 200 respondents, and for global luxury brands (relating to H1b–H5b see Figure 10.1) based on another 200 respondents. Altogether there were 400 respondents in the survey (see Table 10.1).

Table 10.3 Regression coefficient for the model (Figure 2) and testing of hypotheses (Study 2)

	Coefficient	t	P	R(R²)	Hypotheses	Supported
Chinese Luxury Brand						
Outcome variable: *purchase intention*				0.6196 (0.3839)		
Luxury value perceptions	0.6196	2.5105	0.0129		H1a	Yes
Luxury brand experience	0.2712	2.9656	0.0024		H3a	Yes
Counterfeit luxury ownership	−0.0273	−0.0414	0.9670		H5a	No
Luxury value perceptions × counterfeit luxury ownership	0.0061	0.0361	0.9712			
Outcome variable: *brand experience*				0.6676 (0.4457)		
Luxury value perceptions	0.6934	3.7036	0.0003		H2a	Yes
Counterfeit luxury ownership	−0.2528	−0.4888	0.6256		H4a	No
Luxury value perceptions × counterfeit luxury ownership	0.0638	0.4822	0.6302			
Global Luxury Brand						
Outcome variable: *purchase intention*				0.5680 (0.3226)		
Luxury value perceptions	−0.1833	−0.6128	0.5407		H1b	No
Luxury brand experience	0.5020	5.0187	0.0000		H3b	Yes
Counterfeit luxury ownership	−1.2137	−1.7122	0.0885			
Luxury value perceptions × counterfeit luxury ownership	0.3229	1.7566	0.0806		H5b	No
Outcome variable: *brand experience*				0.7101 (0.5042)		
Luxury value perceptions	1.2612	6.4438	0.0000		H2b	Yes
Counterfeit luxury ownership	0.9832	1.9412	0.0537			
Luxury value perceptions × counterfeit luxury ownership	−0.2625	−1.9992	0.0470		H4b	Yes

The results indicate that 130 respondents had not purchased nor owned products of Chinese luxury brands as compared to 108 respondents who have never purchased nor owned counterfeit products of the global luxury brands. Estimation generates 95% percentile bootstrap confidence intervals based on 5,000 bootstrap samples for the conditional indirect effect of luxury value perceptions on purchase intention through luxury brand experience. The results of the regression analyses are summarised in Table 10.3.

10.4.1 Chinese Luxury Brand

As shown in Table 10.3, the effect of luxury value perceptions on purchase intention was significant (t = 2.5105, p = 0.0129), supporting H1a. In addition, luxury brand experience moderates this relationship, with luxury value perceptions having a positive influence on luxury brand experience (t = 3.7036, p = 0.0003), which then positively influenced purchase intention (t = 5.0187, p = 0.0000). These results support H2a and H3a. The results did not support a moderating effect, as the interaction of the independent luxury value perceptions and the counterfeit luxury brand ownership (moderator) was insignificant for luxury brand experience (t = 0.0638, p = 0.6302) and insignificant for purchase intention (t = 0.0061, p = 0.9712), thus not supporting H4a and H5a.

10.4.2 Global Luxury Brand

For global luxury brands, the relationship between luxury value perceptions and purchase intention was not significant (t = −0.6128, p = 0.5407), not supporting H1b. Instead, the mediating effect was significant, with luxury value perceptions having a positive influence on luxury brand experience (t = 6.4438, p = 0.0000), which in turn influenced purchase intention (t = 5.0178, p = 0.0000). These results support H2b and H3b. Counterfeit luxury brand ownership, as a moderator, was found to be significant, negatively impacting the relationship between luxury value perceptions and brand experience (t = −1.9992, p = 0.0470), supporting H4b, but it was not a significant moderator for the relationship between luxury value perceptions and purchase intention (t = 1.7566, p = 0.0806), thus not supporting H5b.

10.5 Discussion

10.5.1 General Discussion

The extant literature has placed a great deal of emphasis on how Chinese consumers purchase global luxury brands (Zhan and He, 2012), and has largely ignored that there is a significant market for Chinese luxury brands. This research applies the established scale measurements of luxury value perceptions to Chinese luxury brands. The findings of the research show some key differences regarding how Chinese consumers view Chinese versus global luxury brands. Previous research has mainly focused on global luxury brands appealing to consumers with similar tastes and preferences (Roy and Chau, 2011). However, as China has been leading in the global luxury market, Chinese consumers have started to show a greater preference for Chinese luxury brands (Heine and Gutsatz, 2015; Kapferer, 2014). This research fills a gap in the literature by examining differences and similarities in Chinese consumers' luxury value perceptions, brand experiences, and purchase intention of Chinese versus global luxury brands.

For global luxury brands, luxury value perceptions influence purchase intention indirectly through luxury brand experience, whereas for Chinese luxury brands, luxury value perceptions influence purchase intention both directly and indirectly via luxury brand experience. These findings confirm the previous research regarding the importance of luxury brand experience in creating personalised meanings (e.g., Hemetsberger et al., 2012) and driving consumer purchase (e.g. Kapferer and Bastien, 2009; Tynan et al., 2010). For marketers, these results seem to suggest that the glamorous and high-end appeal of a global luxury brand that appeals to consumers' senses and contributes to their personal experience could be the main reason for making a purchase. By contrast, Chinese consumers tend to consider both luxury brand values, including functional, financial, individual, and social as well as luxury brand experience to be the main reasons for purchasing Chinese luxury brands.

The second key difference is that counterfeit luxury brand ownership was a significant moderator, reducing the impact of value perceptions on brand experience for the global luxury brand. By contrast, the moderator was insignificant for Chinese luxury brands. Previous research focused on why consumers purchase counterfeit luxury brands (e.g. Wilcox et al., 2009) and how consumers construct identity through the consumption of counterfeit luxury brands (Perez et al., 2010). However, previously researchers could not find a direct link between counterfeit purchases and luxury brand equity (Nia and Zaichkowsky, 2000). In this research, counterfeit luxury ownership, as a moderator, was shown to have a negative impact on Chinese consumers purchasing global luxury brands. The moderator seems to have no effect on Chinese luxury brands. It's also important to note that there were more respondents who owned counterfeit global luxury brands than those who owned counterfeit Chinese luxury brands.

This research also shows that there are similarities between Chinese and global luxury brands as indicated by the findings. First, luxury brand experience is a significant mediator between luxury value perceptions on purchase intention, whether it is fully (in the case of the global luxury brand) or partially (in the case of Chinese luxury brand) mediating the main effect. Second, the regression results (Table 10.3) show that counterfeit luxury brand ownership has no direct impact on luxury brand experience or purchase intention. This finding seems to suggest that it is difficult to establish a direct link between counterfeit luxury brand purchases and purchases of the genuine brand (Nia and Zaichkowsky, 2000). Rather we might need to start thinking about counterfeit luxury ownership as a moderator, interacting with various forces that help predict luxury brand consumption. From a marketer's point of view, counterfeit luxury purchases and ownership seem to be a bigger and more serious issue for global luxury brands than for Chinese luxury brands. The findings also suggest that the most appealing aspect of a global luxury brand, which is luxury brand experience, could be jeopardised and threatened the most by the presence of the counterfeit.

10.5.2 Theoretical Implications

The research draws upon and contributes to the Theory of Consumption Values (Sheth et al., 1991). Researchers have developed customer value frameworks for luxury goods (e.g. Tynan et al., 2010; Vigneron and Johnson, 2004) based on the theory, and have mainly focused on how global luxury brands are purchased by Chinese consumers (e.g. Walley and Li, 2015; Zhan and He, 2012). This research shows that Chinese consumers' value perceptions differ between Chinese and global luxury brands. More importantly, this study demonstrates that, depending on whether they purchase a Chinese or global luxury brand, luxury value perceptions have direct and indirect effects on purchase intention through luxury brand experience. The conceptual model (Figure 10.1) incorporates mediation (luxury brand experience) and moderation (counterfeit luxury ownership) effects. The results show that counterfeit luxury ownership has a negative effect on global luxury brand experience, but has no significant effect on Chinese luxury brand experience. Overall, this research shows that Chinese consumers have differential preferences for Chinese luxury brands versus global luxury brands.

10.5.3 Practical Implications

This research shows that luxury value perceptions have differential effects on purchase intention for Chinese luxury brands versus global luxury brands. For global luxury brands, luxury brand experience fully mediates the relationship between luxury value perceptions and purchase intention. From the perspective of marketers, they need to highlight, through marketing communications, global luxury brand experiences, such as the glamorousness or globalness of the brand, the media exposure, and the high-end appeal of the brand through luxury retailing. Current marketing strategies used by global luxury brands in China have been successful. However, for Chinese luxury brands, luxury brand experience only partially mediates the relationship between luxury value perceptions and purchase intention. Thus Chinese luxury brands will appeal to Chinese consumers when they consider the functional, financial, individual, and social values of Chinese luxury brands as well as the luxury brand experience. For marketing managers, Chinese luxury brands can be highlighted in terms of providing greater luxury value, and Chinese luxury brands' marketing strategies may need to emulate global luxury brand marketing techniques to enhance luxury brand experiences. Marketers need to be aware that Chinese versus global luxury brands, respectively, fulfill different types of needs and different types of goals in terms of purchase intention and consumption. Compared to global luxury brands, Chinese luxury brands have a better understanding of Chinese culture, which is reflected in product design and aesthetic appeal. As a result, Chinese luxury brands can be seen to offer more premium value.

Furthermore, this research shows that counterfeit luxury ownership has a negative influence on global luxury brand experience. For marketers, counterfeiting in China is indeed a threat that undermines the luxury image or experience of global luxury brands in the Chinese market. It is possible that Chinese consumers may switch to alternative Chinese luxury brands where counterfeiting does not influence consumer brand experience or purchase intention. For global luxury brands, China represents significant opportunities as well as challenges as competition arises from Chinese luxury brands, and counterfeit luxury ownership can dilute the image or experiences of global luxury brands.

10.6 Conclusion

This research compares and demonstrates the differences between Chinese and global luxury brands. The literature has focused on the latter and largely ignored the existence of the former. This research shows that Chinese consumers' preferences for Chinese luxury brands are based on luxury value perceptions and luxury brand experiences. By contrast, Chinese consumers' preferences for global luxury brands are mainly focused on the luxury brand experience. These goals always coexist and shape consumer behavior toward domestic (Chinese) and international (global) local luxury brands. This research fills a gap in the luxury brand literature to explore local consumer culture in relation to the consumption of Chinese luxury brands. This research has significant practical implications about the marketing of the global luxury brand in China and/or advertising to Chinese consumers. Finally, the research sample was recruited from Shanghai, one of the wealthiest cities in China. This sample section may not represent the Chinese population. Thus, the findings from this sample cohort are cautioned for researchers and practitioners. Future research shall include a mixed sample of Chinese from different regions and cities.

References

Ahuvia, A. C., 2005. Beyond the extended self: Loved objects and consumers' identity narratives. *J. Consum. Res.* 32(1), 171–184.

Atwal, G., Williams, A., 2009. Luxury brand marketing – The experience is everything! *J. Brand. Manag.* 16(5–6), 338–346.

Berthon, P., Pitt, L., Parent, M., Berthon, J., 2009. Aesthetics and ephemerality: Observing and preserving the luxury brand. *California Manag. Rev.* 52(1), 45–66.

Bian, X., Veloutsou, C., 2017. Consumers' attitudes regarding non-deceptive counterfeit brands in the UK and China. In Balmer, J. M.T. & Chen, W. (eds.), *Advances in Chinese brand management* (pp. 331–350). Palgrave Macmillan, London.

Burmann, C., Jost-Benz, M., Riley, N., 2009. Towards an identity-based brand equity model. *J. Bus. Res.* 62, 390–397.

Cheah, J. H., Waller, D., Thaichon, P., Ting, H., Lim, X. J., 2020. Price image and the sugrophobia effect on luxury retail purchase intention. *J. Retail. Consum. Serv.* 57, 102188.

Danziger, P. N., 2020. Largest luxury market by 2025, but American brands may miss out. Available at: https://www.forbes.com/sites/pamdanziger/2020/11/22/china-is-headed-to-be-the-worlds-largest-luxury-market-by-2025-but-american-brands-may-miss-out/?sh=6b08fae96a3b (accessed 12 June 2021).

Deloitte Consulting, 2021. Global power of luxury goods 2021. *Deloitte Consulting.* Available at: https://www2.deloitte.com/content/dam/Deloitte/at/Documents/consumer-business/at-global-powers-luxury-goods-2020.pdf (accessed 11 June 2022).

Desmet, P. M., Hekkert, P., 2007. Framework of product experience. *Inter. J. Des.* 1(1), 57–66.

Eckhardt, G. M., Belk, R. W., Wilson, J. A., 2015. The rise of inconspicuous consumption. *J. Mark. Manag.* 31(7–8), 807–826.

Fairchild, A. J., Horst, S. J., Finney, S. J., Barron, K. E., 2005. Evaluating existing and new validity evidence for the Academic Motivation Scale. *Contem. Edu. Psycho.* 30(3), 331–358.

Hayes, A. F. 2018. Partial, conditional, and moderated moderated mediation: Quantification, inference, and interpretation. *Comm. Monographs.* 85(1), 4–40.

Heine, K., Gutsatz, M., 2015. Luxury brand building in China: Eight case studies and eight lessons learned. *J. Brand Manag.* 22(3), 229–245.

Hemetsberger, A., Von Wallpach, S., Bauer, M., 2012. Because I'm worth it-luxury and the construction of consumers' selves. *ACR. North. Am. Adv.* 40, 483–489.

Herman, S., 2022. US says China remains global top source of counterfeit goods. Available at: https://www.voanews.com/a/us-says-china-remains-global-top-source-of-counterfeit-goods/6446528.html (accessed 11 June 2022).

Jin, T., Prentice, C., Shao, W., 2021. Identifying antecedent conditions for luxury brand purchase. *J. Rtl. Consum. Serv.* 60, 102466.

Kapferer, J. N., 2014. The future of luxury: Challenges and opportunities. *J. Brand Manag.* 21(9), 716–726.

Kapferer, J. N., 2015. *Kapferer on luxury: How luxury brands can grow yet remain rare.* Kogan Page Publishers, London.

Kapferer, J. N., Bastien, V., 2009. The specificity of luxury management: Turning marketing upside down. *J. Brand. Manag.* 16(5/6), 311–322.

Kim, B. D., Sullivan, M. W., 1998. The effect of parent brand experience online extension trial and repeat purchase. *Mark. Letters.* 9(2), 181–193.

Kim, K.-H., Park, D. B., 2016. Relationships among perceived value, satisfaction, and loyalty: Community-based ecotourism in Korea. *J. Travel & Tourism Mark.* 34(2), 171–191.

Li, G., Li, G., Kambele, Z., 2012. Luxury fashion brand consumers in China: Perceived value, fashion lifestyle, and willingness to pay. *J. Bus. Res. Special Iss. Fash. Mark. Luxury Brands.* 65(10), 1516–1522.

Lin, Y. C. J., 2011. *Fake stuff: China and the rise of counterfeit goods.* Routledge, London.

Mittal, B., 2006. I, me, and mine—How products become consumers' extended selves. *J. Consum. Behav: An Inter. Res. Rev.* 5(6), 550–562.

Ngo, L. V., Northey, G., Tran, Q., Septianto, F., 2020. The Devil might wear Prada, but Narcissus wears counterfeit Gucci! How social adjustive functions influence counterfeit luxury purchases. *J. Retail. Consum. Serv.* 52, 1–7.

Nia, A., Zaichkowsky, J. L., 2000. Do counterfeits devalue the ownership of luxury brands? *J. Product. Brand Manag.* 9(7), 485–497.

Parasuraman, A., Grewal, D., 2000. The impact of technology on the quality-value loyalty Chain: A research agenda. *J. Acad. Mark. Sci.* 28(1), 168–74.

Park, J., Hyun, H., Thavisay, T., 2021. A study of antecedents and outcomes of social media WOM towards luxury brand purchase intention. *J. Retail. Consum. Serv.* 58, 102272.

Perez, M. E., Castaño, R., Quintanilla, C. (2010). Constructing identity through the consumption of counterfeit luxury goods. *Qual. Mark. Res.: An Int. J.* 12(3), 219–253.

Phau, I., Leng, Y. S., 2008. Attitudes toward domestic and foreign luxury brand apparel: A comparison between status and non status seeking teenagers. *J. Fash. Market. Manag: An Inter. J.* 12(1), 68–89.

Phau, I., Teah, M., 2009. Devil wears (counterfeit) Prada: A study of antecedents and outcomes of attitudes towards counterfeits of luxury brands. *J. Consum. Market.* 26(1), 15–27.

Pope, J. A., Koch, B. J., Tremain Koch, P., 2020. Choosing between genuine luxury products and counterfeits in China. *J. Asia. Pacific. Bus.* 21(4), 246–270.

Ramaseshan, B., Stein, A., 2014. Connecting the dots between brand experience and brand loyalty: The mediating role of brand personality and brand relationships. *J. Brand Mang.* 21(7), 664–683.

Rochberg-Halton, E., 1979. The meaning of personal art objects. In Zuzanek, J. (ed.), *Social research and cultural policy* (pp. 155–181). Otium Publications, Waterloo, ON.

Roy, R., Chau, R., 2011. Consumer-based brand equity and status-seeking motivation for a global versus local brand. *Asia. Pac. J. Market. Log.* 23(3), 270–284.

Ryan, R. M., Deci, E. L., 2000. Intrinsic and extrinsic motivations: Classic definitions and new directions. *Contem. Edu. Psycho.* 25(1), 54–67.

Schroeder, J., Borgerson, J., Wu, Z., 2017. *A brand culture approach to Chinese cultural heritage brands.* Palgrave Macmillan, London.

Shankar, A., Jain, S., 2021. Factors affecting luxury consumers' webrooming intention: A moderated-mediation approach. *J. Retail. Consum. Serv.* 58, 102306.

Shao, W., Grace, D., Ross, M., 2019a. Consumer motivation and luxury consumption: Testing moderating effects. *J. Retail. Consum. Serv.* 46, 33–44.

Shao, W., Grace, D., Ross, M., 2019b. Investigating brand visibility in luxury consumption. *J. Retail. Consum. Serv.* 49, 357–370.

Sharma, P., Chan, R. Y. K., 2017. Exploring the role of attitudinal functions in counterfeit purchase behavior via an extended conceptual framework. *Psycho & Mark.* 34(3), 294–308.

Sheth, J. N., Newman, B. I., Gross, B. L., 1991. Why we buy what we buy: A theory of consumption values. *J. Bus. Res.* 22(2), 159–170.

Shukla, P., Purani, K., 2012. Comparing the importance of luxury value perceptions in cross national contexts. *J. Bus. Res. Special. Iss. Fash. Mark. Luxury Brands.* 65(10), 1417–1424.

Thaichon, P., Quach, S., 2016. Dark motives-counterfeit purchase framework: Internal and external motives behind counterfeit purchase via digital platforms. *J. Retail. Consum. Serv.* 33, 82–91.

Tynan, C., McKechnie, S., Chhuon, C., 2010. Co-creating value for luxury brands. *J. Bus. Res.* 63(11), 1156–1163.

Vigneron, F., Johnson, L. W., 1999. A review and a conceptual framework of prestige-seeking consumer behavior. *Acad. Mark. Scie. Rev.* 1, 1–14.

Vigneron, F., Johnson, L. W., 2004. Measuring perceptions of brand luxury. *J. Brand Manag.* 11(6), 484–506.

Walker, C. O., Greene, B. A., Mansell, R. A., 2006. Identification with academics, intrinsic/extrinsic motivation, and self-efficacy as predictors of cognitive engagement. *Learn. Indiv Differ.* 16(1), 1–12.

Walley, K., Li, C., 2015. The market for luxury brands in China: Insight based on a study of consumer's perceptions in Beijing. *J. Brand Manag.* 22(3), 246–260.

Wang, Y., Sun, S., Song, Y., 2011. Chinese luxury consumers: Motivation, attitude and behavior. *J. Promo. Manag.* 17(3), 345–359.

Wiedmann, K. P., Hennigs, N., Siebels, A., 2007. Measuring consumers' luxury value perception: A cross-cultural framework. *Acad. Mark. Sci. Rev.* 11, 1–21.

Wiedmann, K. P., Hennigs, N., Siebels, A., 2009. Value-based segmentation of luxury consumption behavior. *Psycho & Mark.* 26(7), 625–651.

Wilcox, K., Kim, H. M., Sen, S., 2009. Why do consumers buy counterfeit luxury brands? *J. Mark. Res.* 46(2), 247–259.

Wu, Z., Luo, J., Schroeder, J. E., Borgerson, J. L., 2017. Forms of inconspicuous consumption: What drives inconspicuous luxury consumption in China? *Mark. Theory.* 17(4), 491–516.

Zhan, L., He, Y., 2012. Understanding luxury consumption in China: Consumer perceptions of best-known brands. *J. Bus. Res.* 65(10), 1452–1460.

Index

Note: **Bold** page numbers refer to tables and *italic* page numbers refer to figures.